GO ABX 188

Nature, Reason, and the Good Life

BJ
37
T445
2011
WEB

Nature, Reason, and the Good Life

Ethics for Human Beings

Roger Teichmann

OXFORD
UNIVERSITY PRESS

OXFORD

UNIVERSITY PRESS

Great Clarendon Street, Oxford OX2 6DP

Oxford University Press is a department of the University of Oxford.
It furthers the University's objective of excellence in research, scholarship,
and education by publishing worldwide in

Oxford New York

Auckland Cape Town Dar es Salaam Hong Kong Karachi
Kuala Lumpur Madrid Melbourne Mexico City Nairobi
New Delhi Shanghai Taipei Toronto

With offices in

Argentina Austria Brazil Chile Czech Republic France Greece
Guatemala Hungary Italy Japan Poland Portugal Singapore
South Korea Switzerland Thailand Turkey Ukraine Vietnam

Oxford is a registered trade mark of Oxford University Press
in the UK and in certain other countries

Published in the United States
by Oxford University Press Inc., New York

© Roger Teichmann 2011

The moral rights of the author have been asserted
Database right Oxford University Press (maker)

First published 2011

All rights reserved. No part of this publication may be reproduced,
stored in a retrieval system, or transmitted, in any form or by any means,
without the prior permission in writing of Oxford University Press,
or as expressly permitted by law, or under terms agreed with the appropriate
reprographics rights organization. Enquiries concerning reproduction
outside the scope of the above should be sent to the Rights Department,
Oxford University Press, at the address above

You must not circulate this book in any other binding or cover
and you must impose the same condition on any acquirer

British Library Cataloguing in Publication Data

Data available

Library of Congress Cataloging in Publication Data

Data available

Typeset by SPI Publisher Services, Pondicherry, India
Printed in Great Britain
on acid-free paper by
MPG Books Group, Bodmin and King's Lynn

ISBN 978-0-19-960617-7

1 3 5 7 9 10 8 6 4 2

For my daughter
Emma

Contents

Introduction

Man is a rational animal. This simple truth provides a sort of foundation for ethics, and much of the history of moral philosophy involves attempts to do justice to both aspects of the human: rationality on the one hand, animal nature on the other.

In more than one sense, human beings are animals first and rational beings second. Perhaps, in the mists of prehistoric time, there was some gradual process that could be called 'the dawning of rationality' in our primitive ancestors (already members of a definite animal species); but it is another sort of primacy of the animal over the rational that is of more fundamental importance for ethics. Rationality cannot in the end be regarded as a feature of something called 'pure thought', a sort of self-sufficient process going on *in* human beings and possibly *in* other creatures or entities. Rationality relates to the having of reasons, in particular reasons for believing things and for doing things; and having a reason is something essentially tied up with the phenomenon of *enquiry*. This shows up in the distinction between good and bad reasons, a distinction which rests upon norms that are shaped and constrained by facts to do with contexts of actual enquiry, contexts in which a person is asked, 'Why do you think that?', 'Why are you doing that?', and related questions. These facts include facts about what we, as human beings, need or want or get up to. Thus our empirical nature helps to shape and determine the norms constitutive of our rationality. And empirical nature means animal nature, since we are animals.

In Aristotle we find the notion that human beings have a first nature and a second nature.[1] Second nature is acquired, through training or learning; it is a second *nature* because its manifestations are as spontaneous and 'natural' as the manifestations of our first nature, the nature we are born with. The manifestations of our first nature include eating, sleeping, laughing—those of our second nature include writing, playing, blaming.

---

[1] For example, *Nicomachean Ethics* 7, x, 4–5. The terminology does not occur explicitly in Aristotle, I believe, though *consuetudo est secunda natura* ('habit [or custom] is a second nature') was a saying well-known in the ancient world. Augustine quotes it in *The City of God* (12.3).

In each case, it is a set of capacities we are talking about, and one can of course say that it is in our nature—it is part of our first nature—to be able to acquire certain capacities. We are born with the capacity to acquire various capacities. This fact indicates the primacy of first over second nature.

For Aristotle, ethics is about virtues or excellences of character. These, as he says, are settled dispositions acquired through training, typically in childhood. Ethical virtues are thus part of our second nature—or rather, part of the second nature of those of us who are virtuous, who have been trained to be virtuous. (Though you needn't be *especially* good to count as having absorbed such training.) The term 'training' should not conjure up a man at the circus holding a whip, nor yet some gentler character with a supply of carrots and sticks. Training is just the teaching of how to do something. The teacher will typically be another human being or human beings, but we should probably leave room for the notion of self-training, as something that can build upon the training received from outside. *What* you can be trained to do, or indeed to feel or to think, depends upon what sort of creature you are. The excellences available to a human being are different from those available to a lion or to an alien. What does a person learn who learns ethical goodness? Such a person learns how to be good, but also (and relatedly) how to justify, criticize, and assess the actions of himself and of others. In that sense, intelligent action and practical rationality come together in a single package.

I have sketched some considerations that would support the idea that our human, pre-rational nature underlies our rationality, i.e. our notions of good and bad reasons, and our notions as to what thoughts, feelings, and actions count as rational or reasonable or justifiable. This idea will be more fully defended in what follows. The role of first nature, especially as embodied in pre-rational impulses and attitudes to one another, is set forth in Chapter 1, and the subsequent chapters elaborate and build on that starting-point. As the investigation proceeds, the aspects of second nature with which ethics is concerned—or some of the main ones—come into view; and by Chapter 4, we will have ascended to the level of Aristotelian contemplation, or something like it, and hence to a point at which we are most distant from our animal brethren.

Possibly the most significant thing separating human beings from other animals is their use of language. Language is learnt; it is part of our second nature. It is also that by which and in which our reasons and our reasoning primarily have their being. If this fact is lost sight of, our account of reasons for action will be in danger of suffering from either of two related defects: that of over-abstraction, and that of subjectivism or, as one might put it, first-personalism. 'Why should I do that?' asks for a reason; but what standard supplies the criteria for a reason's being a good reason, i.e. a good answer to the 'Why?' question? I shall be arguing that the standard is supplied above all by the nature of the language-game in which such a question gets asked, and that the empirical and social nature of that language-game explains such facts as: that not anything goes when it comes to giving reasons for your actions—that giving a reason is not the same as reporting facts about your own psychology—and that the good-ness of many reasons for action is closely connected with facts about human nature (since the language-game only has a point or purpose in so far as it relates to human needs or wants).

The name of John McDowell will be associated by many philosophers with the distinction I have mentioned between first nature and second nature. McDowell, however, thinks that reason, or *logos*, subjects first nature, and the natural needs and goods arising out of first nature, to a sort of 'scrutiny'. Thus he writes:

In imparting *logos*, moral education enables one to step back from any motivational impulse one finds oneself subject to, and question its rational credentials. Thus it effects a kind of distancing of the agent from the practical tendencies that are part of what we might call 'his first nature'.[2]

McDowell imagines a wolf acquiring reason, and states: 'Having acquired reason, he can contemplate alternatives; he can step back from the natural impulse and direct critical scrutiny at it' (p. 153). It seems that for McDowell the crucial point is whether an animal has the mere ability to contemplate alternatives, such as that of following some impulse and that of not following it—for this alone will be enough to give good sense to the animal's question, 'Why should I go along with that impulse?'

The scenario is of course fantastical. But we may allow it as a sort of heuristic device. The question is: what sort of answer is the rational wolf looking for when he asks 'Why should I . . . ?' It can't just be that he is simply looking for someone to persuade him—why should he look for

[2] John McDowell, 'Two Sorts of Naturalism', in *Virtues and Reasons*, eds R. Hursthouse, G. Lawrence, and W. Quinn (Oxford: Oxford University Press, 1995), p. 170.

that, unless he already suspects his thinking might not be up to scratch? McDowell seems to imagine the rational wolf's question as a sort of *challenge*: 'Give me a reason why I should, and then I'll see whether I think it a good one.' But thinking a reason good (or bad) no more makes it good (or bad) than thinking that you are using a word correctly makes your use of it correct. The picture of reason we get from McDowell is strangely abstract, and the question 'Why?', being abstracted from any actual practices of enquiry, justification, or criticism, looks a very hard one to answer. Which can *seem* to make the sceptical wolf's position unassailable. And McDowell does indeed think it unassailable. Thus, another rational wolf might reflect on what its species needs, for example, and be led to see 'real reasons for acting', but for all that, such reflection

would not weigh with a wolf who has never acquired such a mode of evaluation of conduct, or who has come unstuck from it. And there would be no irrationality in thus failing to be convinced. (pp. 172–3)

The sceptical wolf's challenge, it seems to me, may well in fact be unreasonable, even irrational. The illusion that his position is unassailable comes from a picture of contextless enquiry that I criticize in Chapter 1, and the cure for the illusion is to remind oneself of the actual role, or roles, which the question 'Why?' has in human life. There is indeed *one* way in which 'Why should I go along with that natural impulse?' might be impossible to answer, in certain situations—namely, where the sort of natural impulse in question belongs to the very basis or framework of the language-game of asking for and giving reasons. A person in normal circumstances who sincerely asks 'Why should I eat food?' may well be said to have 'come unstuck', and this partly means unstuck from the ways in which reasons for action are assessed as good or bad. His question will, in that sense, be impossible to answer. Moreover, if you respond automatically to cries for help from the wounded, it would perhaps go against the grain to say that you have in mind the *reason* 'Those are human beings'; putting it that way is in danger of treating what is bedrock—'Human beings are important', or something like that—as if it were a rationally debatable proposition. And this means that a question like 'Why should I help those wounded people?' seems as peculiar, and hence as difficult to answer, as 'Why are *you* helping those wounded people?' (Again, these issues are discussed in Chapter 1.) What all this shows is not that the capacity for reason involves any distancing from first nature, but on the contrary that reasoning, if it distances itself too much from nature, ceases to be reasoning at all.

McDowell alludes to the logical peculiarity of statements like 'Human beings have thirty-two teeth', as discussed by Elizabeth Anscombe and later by Michael Thompson,[3] a peculiarity that shows up in the fact that this last statement means neither 'All human beings have thirty-two teeth', nor even 'Most human beings have thirty-two teeth'. Invoking this peculiarity, McDowell writes that 'from "Wolves need such-and-such" and the fact that he is a wolf, our wolf cannot conclude that he needs such-and-such' (p. 153). This is perfectly true, but would only be relevant if the question 'Why should I do that?' necessarily asked for a reason to do with what the agent himself needs (or wants, we may add). The social nature of the language-game of asking for and giving reasons militates against this subjective or first-personalist conception of reasons for action, in ways we shall see.

The reference to Michael Thompson allows me to illustrate further how an account of practical reason, etc., needs to refer to human language use; for in Thompson's work, the account we find of human practices such as promising appears in the end rather mysterious, on account (it seems to me) of its silence about language. Thompson compares statements like 'These creatures make and keep promises' with ones like 'These creatures are spiders'; for him, the concepts of a practice and of a life form belong to the same categorical framework: 'One turn of the categorical framework gives us the concept of a life form or a living nature; the other gives us the concept of "form of life" or a "second nature".'[4] The comparison is extremely interesting. And yet the normativity embodied in 'You are meant to keep your promises' and that embodied in 'A spider is meant to have eight legs' surely have quite different sources. Thompson's account, in stressing the *sui generis* nature of natural-historical propositions such as the one about the spider, discourages us from looking for any source of normativity external to the propositions themselves (in this he is rather like McDowell). A thorough examination of systems of natural-historical propositions should, he thinks, enlighten us as to the kind of

---

[3] See Anscombe, 'Modern Moral Philosophy', in *Ethics, Religion and Politics: Collected Papers Vol. III* (Oxford: Blackwell, 1981), pp. 26–42, and Thompson, 'The Representation of Life', in *Virtues and Reasons*, p. 281.

[4] M. Thompson, *Life and Action* (Cambridge, MA: Harvard University Press, 2008), p. 208.

normativity we are talking about. This may indeed be so, and it is borne out by Thompson's attempts in that direction. But then if our interest is in the normativity associated with practices like promising, it will not be enough to discern structural or formal similarities between systems of natural-historical judgements and systems of judgements within a practice, as Thompson does. We will need to indulge in a thorough examination of (systems of) practice-based propositions, such as 'You are meant to keep your promises' and 'I did such-and-such because I promised to'; for the normativity involved in such propositions is no less *sui generis*, no less internal to the system, than is the normativity of natural-historical propositions. But to carry out such an examination of practice-based propositions will in fact mean looking at language use. A pertinent example would be Anscombe's examination of the nature of those bits of language she called stopping and forcing modals (e.g. 'You can't move that piece', 'You have to give that back', etc.).[5] As it is, a reader of *Life and Action* may feel it to be a rather strange sort of brute fact that human practices have the logical or categorical similarities to life forms which Thompson points out for us.[6]

These two examples from recent philosophy, McDowell and Thompson, instantiate the approach in ethics which may broadly be called 'Aristotelian'. It is an approach I believe to be essentially the right one to adopt; but—as the above remarks very briefly indicate—such an approach, if it is to be convincing, requires one to give due prominence to language, and to its social and empirical nature. I said above that language is that by which and in which our reasons and our reasoning primarily have their being. The Greeks had a single term for 'word', 'speech', 'account', or 'reason', a term of considerable importance in ancient thought—the term *logos*. This word nicely embodies the truth that reason and language are intertwined. And language, as Wittgenstein saw, is not to be conceived of as a sort of conduit or vehicle for inner processes of thought, but rather as a human product, whose nature derives from its place in human life. The tree of *logos* has its roots in the soil of that life.

The relevance to ethics of the fact that human beings have language is obvious, having many different aspects. In this book, the importance of

[5] See Anscombe, 'Rules, Rights and Promises', in *Ethics, Religion and Politics*, pp. 97–103.
[6] None of which is to deny that Thompson's book contains much that is important and true.

language is acknowledged, and moral philosophy is taken to be continuous with philosophy of language, as also of course with philosophy of psychology. For this reason, some readers will be inclined to label the book a work of 'linguistic philosophy'. Given a certain reading, I am happy with this description, and in Chapter 5 I hope to indicate not only how 'linguistic philosophy' (thus understood) is superior to the philosophy of its most vocal attackers, but how an appreciation of the importance of language for philosophy actually helps one to see the relevance of philosophy to real life. Thinking about life and thinking philosophically turn out to be related activities, involving related traits of mind. This is an important fact, and one in danger of being obscured by prevalent ideas about the nature of philosophy.

A denial of the importance of language for philosophy is often associated with a distrust of, or hostility to, the later philosophy of Wittgenstein. Much could be said about this phenomenon. The kindest diagnosis will often be that of ignorance: people who have only a shallow acquaintance with Wittgenstein's thought don't usually have a good grasp of what he was on about, and this is as true of some of those who blithely quote him as it is of most of those who attack or sneer at him. Other diagnoses (than ignorance) of present-day hostility to Wittgenstein are touched upon in Chapter 5. I mention all this mainly because Wittgenstein's ideas do inform some of the arguments in this book, and although I hope that those arguments make sense on their own, their full force—such as it is—may well be more apparent to those who have some acquaintance with those ideas. That said, there is no compulsory reading attached to this course.

Wittgenstein did hardly any moral philosophy himself, though his thoughts on ethics and on the human condition can be found scattered among his writings.[7] In this he differs from his pupil, friend, and translator (not to mention literary executor), Elizabeth Anscombe, whose work in moral philosophy is of great importance. Anscombe realized the close connection between ethics and the philosophy of psychology, and her contribution to the former is embodied as much in works like *Intention* and 'Practical Inference' as it is in the more overtly 'ethical' pieces, such as 'Modern Moral Philosophy'. She can be seen as a sort of bridge between Aristotle and Wittgenstein, in so far as she applies to the concepts and

---

[7] See e.g. 'A Lecture on Ethics', *The Philosophical Review* 74 (1965): 3–12; *Culture and Value*, ed. G. H. von Wright, trans. P. Winch (Oxford: Blackwell, 1980).

claims of Aristotelian ethics insights and methods associated with Wittgenstein's philosophy. This description is not meant to indicate any lack of originality on Anscombe's part, for she was one of the most original and bold thinkers of the twentieth century. My debt to Anscombe is great, and a number of her ideas feature in this book, as also one of her aims. Like Socrates, Anscombe viewed the role of philosopher as being that of gadfly, at least on certain sorts of issue—the gadfly being a person who voices a critique of what appear to be current confusions or mistakes, not only among professional philosophers but in the culture at large. This sort of critical activity will usually be more useful than the providing of 'theoretical foundations' for prevalent nostrums, an essentially sleepy pastime. At any rate, an ethical theory or approach will have little value if it gives us no clue how it bears upon the world around us, and for that reason I have made use of a number of examples of recent or prevalent trends, within and without philosophy. The discussions of these examples are intended to be part and parcel of the philosophical argumentation: whether or not they are swipes, I hope they are not sideswipes.

Some of the material of this book originated in papers read at two conferences. Part of Chapter 2 began life as 'Practical and Theoretical Reasoning', a contribution to *Anscombe's "Intention" and the Renewal of Moral Psychology*, held at the Pontifical University of the Holy Cross, Rome, in February 2008; while part of Chapter 3 began life as 'Is Pleasure a Good?', a contribution to *Elizabeth Anscombe and Contemporary Philosophy*, held at the Université Paris-1 Panthéon-Sorbonne, Paris, in May 2009. I am grateful to the organizers of those conferences for giving me the opportunity to develop my thoughts on the issues in question, as well as for the feedback I received and the hospitality I enjoyed.

Three people have kindly read and commented on parts or all of Chapters 1 and 2: Cora Diamond, Edward Harcourt, and Katharina Nieswandt. I am very grateful to them. Finally, I would like especially to thank Anselm Müller, who read a draft of the whole book. His characteristically detailed and useful comments assisted me greatly.

1

Reasons and Reactions

Ethical thought concerns itself with a range of things. Birth, death, war, lying, government, sex, work, punishment—these are all ethical topics. Not so volcanoes, addition, Persian rugs, football. At any rate, volcanoes, etc., do not as such give subject-matter for ethical thought—though anything, or almost anything, can *assume* ethical significance within a particular human context. (The Persian rug might have been produced with child labour.) This last-mentioned fact may partly explain why some philosophers have suggested that ethics is not characterized by or restricted to a special subject-matter, but relates rather to a way of looking at things, or to a mode of practical reasoning, or to . . . But ethics does have a subject-matter, in a loose and broad sense of that term. Its subject-matter is human life and what is humanly important. Its *range* is thus vague, flexible, and open-ended. But for all that, it is limited, and at its centre stands the human being.

But what about animals?—or God?—or other intelligent life forms? Aren't these non-human beings of ethical significance?—Of course they are, those that exist; and those that don't exist would be if they did. But why do we want to mention *these* non-human items, and not, say, paintings or factories? The latter, it is natural to say, enjoy ethical significance only in relation to human beings and human affairs, whereas God, animals, and aliens have, or would have, 'intrinsic value'—so it might be claimed. As elsewhere in philosophy, this phrase, 'in relation to', can be taken in many different ways. 'Ethical value is relative to human beings', as an unexplained slogan, so far says nothing at all. Nevertheless, in ethics, I shall be arguing, man is indeed the measure of all things, despite what needs to be said about animals and others. In fact the ethical standing of animals will turn out to confirm, rather than undermine, an anthropocentric approach, as we shall see.

The centrality to ethics of the human has two aspects. The first has to do with what I have been calling the subject-matter of ethics, namely human life and what is humanly important. The second is more general, and finds expression in such truisms as 'Our concepts are *our* concepts' and 'Our thought is *our* thought'. These statements don't belong in the same stable as old warhorses like 'Only *I* can feel *my* pain', for they do real work, for example in helping us to see why certain of our concepts and modes of thinking have the features that they do have. For we are not merely, or essentially, or even primarily, thinkers (*pace* Descartes), nor pleasure-seekers (*pace* Bentham), nor self-reproducing robots (*pace* Dawkins). We are a certain sort of animal (*Homo sapiens*), and our modes of perception, action, reaction, thought, and feeling are all determined in large part by our animal constitution—by human nature, that is.

These remarks will perhaps appear obvious. But as we shall see, the implications of such anthropocentrism as has been here sketched are far-reaching, and put paid to much ethical theorizing.

I.

A judge finds the accused standing before him guilty. We object that the previous week he acquitted another person charged with the same offence, on the basis of identical evidence. The judge's reason (confided, perhaps, to close friends) is that the person who appeared before him this week was black. His judgement is unreasonable, arbitrary, and unjust. We might say that the judge is guilty of 'discrimination'.

'Not the only one', a philosopher tells us; 'for many a judge will send one person to gaol, and let another walk free, simply and solely on the basis that the first person and not the second robbed a bank—though in all other respects the two people are identical'. Why is the philosopher's argument absurd? Not because it's always okay to discriminate on the basis of criminality: a doctor who refuses to treat a heart attack victim because he has robbed a bank acts unjustly. (If he has *just* robbed a bank, the doctor might also call the police, of course.) Nor, conversely, is it never okay to discriminate on the basis of skin colour: you might well interview only white applicants for the job of being a film double for Sean Penn.

The corrupt judge's reasons for conviction count as arbitrary because of the context in which he makes his judgement. The point of the legal proceedings in which the judge plays a part is to ascertain, if possible, whether the accused committed a crime, and to deal with him or her accordingly. These facts go to determine what reasons count as good or bad reasons, e.g. for sending someone to gaol.[1]

Consider now an analogous case. Two patients are wheeled into casualty, each with a head wound. The surgeon immediately attends to the one who is white, and does so *because* he is white. Note, by the way, that it's possible for the surgeon to attend to the white person first without acting unjustly, so long as her reason is not such a reason as 'Because he is white'. After all, she has to attend to *somebody* first. But as things are in this imaginary scenario, the surgeon's reason is 'Because he is white', and is consequently arbitrary and unjust. Our friendly philosopher intervenes: 'Similar things happen all the time. If the patient had been a dolphin with a head wound, you can be sure it would have been ignored in favour of a human being with one. Favouring patients just because they're white is racist; favouring patients just because they're human is speciesist.'[2]

If the argument rests on nothing more than a structural similarity of cases—'A and B were treated differently because A and not B had feature F'—then it is clearly as bad as the argument about the judge who convicts on the basis of criminality. But maybe the philosopher wants to indicate that 'It's a human being' cannot, in the medical context, function as a proper reason for action? One might respond that, just as the judge's brief related to dealing with criminals, so the surgeon's brief relates to treating human beings; that's what she's paid for. But this reply wouldn't get to the heart of the matter. After all, most of us would come to the aid of a wounded person rather than to the aid of a wounded dolphin, and our reason for doing so—'It was a human being!'—would be adequate regardless of our job, or of anything along those lines.

It won't do to try to explain all this by saying that we value human beings more highly than dolphins, or impute more value to them than to dolphins.

[1] In a full account of the matter, we would probably want to add that the institution itself (the law, or the particular legal system in question) is a good institution; i.e. good for a society of human beings to have.

[2] This now popular term seems to have been coined by Richard Ryder, who uses it in more than one place; e.g. in 'Experiments on Animals', in *Animals, Men and Morals*, eds S. and R. Godlovitch and J. Harris (London: Gollancz,1971), p. 81.

Whatever such phrases mean—and they generally mean very little—they do not help us; for it is not as if there can *never* be good reason for preferring a dolphin to a human being—e.g. if choosing a creature to train to carry coded messages under water. Everything depends on context: on what is at stake, on the goal of an enterprise, and so on. If humans are more 'valuable' than dolphins, that presumably means: more valuable, full stop. But since we sometimes prefer human beings, sometimes dolphins, such 'value' cannot be the whole story, if indeed it is any part of the story.

'Preferring' is itself an odd term to use here. If you appeared on the scene of a bomb blast, and were confronted with wounded people and animals, let's assume that you would go to the help of some person or persons—but would that be a case of *preferring* them to the animals (or to particular animals)? To choose to do X need not be to choose to do X rather than Y, even if you know that you could instead have done Y.[3] Maybe as you enter the bombed building you notice a picture on the wall hanging crookedly, which in normal circumstances you would have straightened. You do not choose to help the wounded *rather than* straighten the picture; though you do of course choose to help the wounded rather than choose to straighten the picture. (A scope distinction.) Someone who insists that you 'must' be choosing to help-rather-than-straighten is operating with a pre-cooked model of choice, one that is very likely set up so as to be immune to counter-examples. Such immunity is typically effected by postulating unconscious or subconscious mechanisms: you weren't aware of any deliberations about human beings versus pictures on walls, so those deliberations (since they 'must' have been happening) were going on subconsciously.

If in the case in question you did in fact choose to help the human beings *rather than* the animals, perhaps later on explaining yourself by saying, 'I decided to help the human beings rather than help the dogs', that would suggest that your aim was something like: to reduce overall suffering here. And maybe you calculated that this aim could be best achieved by reducing human, rather than animal, suffering. With normal human beings, however, the impulse to help other human beings in dire need is typically more instinctive, and less calculative. This is not to say that

[3] Cf. G. E. M. Anscombe, 'Who is Wronged? Philippa Foot on Double Effect', in *Human Life, Action and Ethics: Essays by G. E. M. Anscombe*, eds M. Geach and L. Gormally (Exeter: Imprint Academic, 2005), pp. 249–51.

the actions that come from this impulse are not rational, for of course they are. If asked why you rushed into the building you can give a reason: 'To help those people', or 'There are people in there', or 'Those screams are human screams', etc.

The anti-speciesist may reply that such reasons can only count as good reasons in the circumstances if they outweigh such reasons as 'Those are dogs over there'. After all, someone who chooses to help the dogs might also be a person who chooses to do X, not one who chooses to do X rather than Y; he's not against people, he's *for* dogs! His 'impulses' are just different from ours, or from those of most of us.

If 'These are human beings' does outweigh 'Those are dogs' as a reason for helping the wounded, in virtue of what does it do so? The question is evidently not as simple as the corresponding question about 'He robbed the bank' and 'He is black', as possible reasons for sentencing a man. Nevertheless, in both sorts of case our task is to look to the background, to a set of empirical facts which provide a framework within which certain statements get to count as reasons for or against courses of action. In one case, the framework is a set of customary (judicial) proceedings. In the other case, we may also discern custom at work, but not convention: any 'customs' here will have been taught and maintained by encouraging some, and discouraging other, already-existing natural impulses. The impulse to help other human beings to which I have alluded is one such impulse.

II.

Demanding, giving, accepting and rejecting reasons—whether for thinking something or for doing something—are moves that take place within a human language-game (or language-games).[4]

This claim involves a number of ideas: (i) that there are (sufficiently) objective criteria for what count as good or bad reasons; (ii) that learning those criteria primarily consists in learning how to use the relevant bits of language; (iii) that the use of these bits of language is paradigmatically within the context of real enquiry; (iv) that the rules governing the uses of these bits of language are not arbitrary, but have their source in the needs and proclivities of the creatures whose language it is, i.e. of us human beings.

---

[4] This semi-technical term is Wittgenstein's, and I trust that the idea it embodies will be best grasped by watching that idea in operation in what follows. (That's to say, an attempted 'definition' would probably be otiose.)

Some comments by way of explication. The giving of reasons, for a belief or for an action, is something done in response to a 'Why?' question—as, 'Why do you [or why should I] believe that?', and 'Why are you doing [or why should I do] that?' Reasons can be given why a third party believes something, or is doing something; but the first- and second-person cases have a certain priority, arising from the point or function of these 'Why?' questions. If I allege that Smith's reason for going to that shop is so he can talk to the check-out girl, then if Smith denies this and gives some quite other reason, I can only defend my allegation by making out that Smith is not being honest, or alternatively is self-deceived. Dishonest and self-deceived accounts of what one is doing are necessarily secondary to normal, honest accounts. This shows up in the fact that a child must first learn the sense of these 'Why?' questions in connection with normal, honest replies; she could not begin by learning about self-deceived or dishonest replies, any more than she could begin her learning of colour-words on moonlit nights or wearing rose-tinted spectacles. Thus Smith's own first-person account of what he is doing has a default weight, one lacking in his accounts, e.g. of what blood group he belongs to. We may well assume that the latter is something he ought to know about if anyone does, but if I allege a mistake on his part, I can be proven right simply by appeal to the normal and standard tests for blood groups—the same tests which Smith himself must ultimately rest his case on. I do not have to allege that *this* case of a person's belonging to a particular blood group is in some sense a secondary or abnormal such case.

The priority of the first- and second-person cases (of giving and receiving reasons for actions) over the third-person case is connected with another feature of reasons for actions—namely, that reasons for actions should not be confused with the efficient causes of actions.[5] If giving a reason for your action were a case of alleging a cause of it (some brain-state, perhaps), then your authority as to your reasons would seem to be of the same kind as your authority about your blood group, and in principle as straightforwardly defeasible by others—e.g. by means of a brain-scan.

---

[5] Of numerous texts that argue this, a good instance is R. Hursthouse, 'Intention', in *Logic, Cause and Action*, ed. R. Teichmann (Cambridge: Cambridge University Press, 2000), pp. 83–105. For a brief history of the confusion in question, see Stewart Candlish and Nic Damnjanovic, 'Reason, Action and the Will: the Fall and Rise of Causalism' (www.philpapers.org).

However, I say only 'would seem to be' since there are in fact cases where a person does have a special authority as to the causes of his actions, namely cases such as that in which he says, 'The martial music excites me, that is why I march up and down'. The example is Anscombe's,[6] and the name she gives to this sort of causation is 'mental causation'. Could knowledge of the reasons for one's actions be a case of knowledge of mental causes? The difficulty in alleging this has to do with the identification of the cause. For you to know that A caused B, you have to be aware of A and of B: that is to say, you have to be aware of them under certain descriptions, such as 'They are playing martial music' and 'I am marching up and down'.[7] If reasons are causes (as it is put), they must be states or processes of the agent—that is certainly how they are conceived of by the adherents of the view that reasons are causes. So if you know that your present action is caused by such and such a reason, where a reason (to follow orthodoxy) is a belief–desire pair, then you must be aware of this complex state or process under some description. A statement like 'I am aware of it under the description *a desire to make tea plus a belief that doing this produces tea*' leaves us with the question, 'But what is a desire to make tea?' And the answer 'It is what you're aware of as part of the cause of your tea-making' is hopelessly inadequate; the resulting position will be akin to that of the person who says, 'I know something that helped cause the patient's death: a contributory cause of his death did'. However, any other description under which you might be alleged to know the cause of your intentional action will be such that it seems impossible that you could *know* about it, with any special authority, under that description—e.g. any description of the form *such and such a brain-state*.

Moreover, a reason for an action is—roughly speaking—something that shows why it was, is, or would be a good idea (*pro tanto*) to perform that action, and this explains why one gives a reason when asked 'Why should I do that?', just as much as when asked 'Why are you doing that?' But if I ask you 'Why should I do X?', I am certainly not asking what will (or might) cause me to do X, or anything of the sort. I don't want information

---

[6] G. E. M. Anscombe, *Intention*, 2nd edn (Oxford: Blackwell, 1963), p. 16.

[7] This is not to imply that I am aware that I am marching because I *perceive* that I am. If Anscombe is right, knowledge of what one is doing (practical knowledge) is to be sharply distinguished from knowledge of facts that are independent of the knowledge of them (contemplative knowledge)—in a certain sense of 'independent'. See *Intention*, pp. 49–57.

about myself at all, but about how the proposed action is meant to help matters, be of use, etc.—or it may be that I want to know why I, instead of another, should be given the task of doing X. That a reason for an action is something that shows why it was, is, or would be a good idea to perform that action also explains why a group of people can have reason to do something, *qua* group, and so can want, plan, or intend to do that thing. 'We want (plan, intend) to give the Elgin Marbles back to Greece' cannot be translated into several concomitant individual wants, expressible as 'I want to . . . ', since giving the Elgin Marbles back to Greece is necessarily something done by a group *qua* group. The question 'Why are you doing that?' still enjoys a sort of primacy in such a case, it is just that the second person is the second person plural. A conflation of reasons with causes is especially perverse when the alleged causes would have to lie in a number of different people (or their brains), even assuming that the list of people can always be determinately specified.[8]

These are just some of the problems that ensue from a conflation of reasons and causes, problems that are in fact very well documented. It is now fashionable to belittle all such difficulties, often by not much more than an appeal to authority (especially as personified by Donald Davidson, the philosopher most associated with the 'Reasons as causes' view). Here we really do have cause for wondering whether there can be such a thing as progress in philosophy: for although in philosophy there are real achievements, real breakthroughs in understanding and in method, even knock-down arguments, it remains forever possible for philosophers to ignore, reject, or bury these achievements, breakthroughs, and arguments, for sociological reasons or just through a lack of comprehension. That this is not a large-scale possibility in the natural sciences is a significant fact, and this difference between philosophy and science is something I will be coming back to in Chapter 5. For now, I would merely beg leave to move on from the old reasons/causes confusion—though it will crop up again in the course of this book—and return to our theme.

---

[8] It is in fact a matter of some ethical importance that there should exist genuine and irreducibly plural action-descriptions and reasons for action. The claim 'We owe it to asylum-seekers to let them into our country' employs such an action-description, namely 'let the asylum-seekers into our country'—the 'we' who owe this are a group of people. Such cases are discussed below in Chapter 2, Section VIII.

Giving and receiving reasons, I have said, is connected with learning to use and respond to the question 'Why?', in its reason-giving sense.[9] There is more to the concept of a reason, to be sure, but these facts—linguistic facts—are central to the concept. That is the purport of (ii), above. But language and life are interwoven; otherwise, the former would be little more than the production of sounds or marks on paper. Words have a function for us—myriad functions, rather—on account of the human activities, behaviours, and interactions with which the use of language is tied up. What you do and what you say are connected. Thus to have mastered the 'game' of reason-giving, your actions must connect appropriately with what you have said, enough of the time. If you give as your reason for laying out plates and cakes in the living room that your aunt is visiting that afternoon, then your statement comes into conflict with your subsequent actions if, when she arrives, you promptly return all the items to the kitchen. In an adult, such behaviour would not on its own lead us to doubt the person's mastery of the concept of a reason for action—it would rather lead us to posit such things as a change of mind, or a hidden aim, or some such. But if, when asked why you have behaved thus, you simply repeat that your aunt was visiting, your answer will not be intelligible. And for you to give such answers habitually would indeed cast doubt on your mastery of the concept of a reason for action. The importance of *intelligibility* in such matters is something we will be returning to in the next chapter. For present purposes, what we need to note is that there are constraints on what can pass for reason-giving, practical or theoretical; this is part of what lies behind (i), above. A parrot that is trained to answer 'Why are you cawing?' by saying 'For fun' does not give a reason; nor does the nephew in the example of the cakes; nor does the harassed parent whose answer to 'Why is the sky blue?' is 'Because it isn't green!' But there are more constraints than are exemplified by these obvious cases.

What is the source of the constraints on what may count as giving a reason? Perhaps there are a number of sources. But one thing that must evidently help determine what counts as giving a reason is the *purpose* (or purposes) of the language-game within which reason-giving takes place. Since giving a reason is paradigmatically done in response to the question

---

[9] As it stands, this sounds circular. But the phrase 'its reason-giving sense' is just shorthand for a fuller explanation of the relevant sense—e.g. as given by Anscombe in *Intention* (secs 5–18).

'Why?', this language-game is a species of the more general one of enquiry. What then is the purpose of enquiry? And more specifically, what is the purpose of the particular form of enquiry that is embodied in the reason-demanding questions, 'Why do you think so?', and 'Why are you doing that?'

In answer to the general question, about the purpose of enquiry as such, it is tempting to give an entirely empty answer: 'The aim is to find out the truth'. But again there are constraints of intelligibility here, and on what counts as genuine enquiry. Hence the possible counter-question, 'Why do you want to know?', a riposte which, when used with cooperative intent, asks for guidance: the person seeks to satisfy a need or a desire of the enquirer, and what that is may well not be conveyed by the form of the enquiry itself. It is a matter of context. 'I just want to know' does not necessarily show a need, or even a real desire, to know something, e.g. if the 'something' is the distance in centimetres between Oscar Wilde's grave and the nearest elm tree. If a person really did feel a desire to find out lots of facts of that sort, there would be something wrong with him, and his answers to 'Why do you want to know?' would be classified as irrational—i.e. as not supplying proper *reasons* for his enquiries.

In philosophy, there is a strong inclination to believe in the pure and unqualified desire for truth, for truth as such. But what is right about this picture of philosophical enquiry is not to be expressed by the claim that 'I just want to know' is always intelligible. It is rather that the things that philosophy *does* aim to find out or understand are, in some sense, worth knowing for their own sakes. The knowledge of philosophical answers is not of merely instrumental value. (These remarks go equally for other disciplines than philosophy.) This does mean that a philosopher may on occasion answer 'Why do you want to know that?' by saying simply, 'I just do want to know it'; though it should be noted that there is another sort of answer that can often be given, namely the sort that aims to *make sense* of one's curiosity, without thereby conferring merely instrumental value upon the knowledge that one seeks—something that is done by describing the subject-matter of one's curiosity in the sort of way and in the sort of detail that may enable a fellow human being to see the point of it.[10] For example, if asked why you are cogitating so much upon the relationship

[10] This mode of explanation will be more fully discussed in Chapter 3, Section V, being there described as 'giving a rationale'.

of the mind to the body, you might in reply mention such things as the possibility of an incorporeal mind's surviving the death of the body. The human interest of such a topic is obvious.

However, the fact that 'I just do want to know it' *is* a possible statement for one engaged in philosophical enquiry to make has arguably had certain consequences within philosophy itself. Consider Descartes' 'project of pure enquiry'. In the *Meditations*, we find the hapless philosopher pitted against his sceptical alter ego, in a game whose rules very much favour the alter ego: for whereas the philosopher may not claim any belief as knowledge unless he can give reasons for believing it, or unless he cannot be wrong about it, the alter ego is released from any equivalent obligation— he is not required to justify his doubts by supplying reasons for *them*. Or rather, the alter ego has an easy time giving reasons for his doubts, since (according to Descartes) a sufficient reason for doubting a given belief is that no adequate reason was given for it. The onus of proof, in other words, is always upon the philosopher, upon the one who professes a belief or who claims it as knowledge. That one's beliefs must, in Descartes' system, be infallible if they are to count as knowledge goes hand in hand with this. The mere logical possibility of error is enough to make problems, and this is because such comments as 'You might be dreaming, or hallucinating (etc.)' cannot, by the rules of the game, be met with 'No I mightn't—what reason is there to think such a thing?' The rules of the game require you to give reasons for thinking that you are *not* dreaming or hallucinating. The onus of proof is on you. Hence the evidence of your senses is never enough, and can never confer 'genuine' certainty.

Why did Descartes stack the odds so much in favour of his sceptical alter ego? No doubt there are a number of reasons. But one of them, it seems to me, is that he thought that the alter ego's enquiry, 'Why do you believe that?' can itself be backed up with 'I just want to know', the respectability of which statement is apparently vouched for by philosophy itself. '*Why* do you want to know?' is not a possible counter-question to the sceptic's badgering; and that is not so much a consequence of any arbitrary Cartesian rules as of the fact that what we have is an imaginary and contextless dialogue. There is no real-life enquiry going on in the pages of the First Meditation, and no enquirer with any real need or desire for knowledge— only a sort of *ersatz* Universal Enquirer. Such a being cannot be assisted in the way that a person can who wants to know the road to Marseilles. It is in this sense that scepticism is unanswerable.

III.

The above considerations have an obvious application to the particular kind of enquiry which is our main concern, namely that which asks after the reasons for an action: 'Why are you doing that?'—'Why did you do that?'—'Why should I do that?', etc.

Roughly speaking, a reason for an action is meant to show why the action was, is, or would be a good idea; and the content of 'good' is provided by the context, by what is at stake, and, in an important class of cases, by what is normal and natural for human beings. It is not surprising that a human being should be able to make sense of activities that are normal and natural for human beings. So it is also not surprising that a human being should be able to make sense of, be satisfied with, a *description* of an actual or proposed action that brings it under the heading of an activity normal and natural for human beings, such as going to get food, or taking a nap, or listening to music. Such a description will enable an enquirer to locate the action within a familiar, or at any rate a known, human pattern. And this 'locating' is not merely a bit of intellectual jigsaw-solving—it is among other things a matter of the enquirer's becoming able, on the basis of what he has been told, to anticipate and extrapolate, in thought or in action.

To give a reason for an action is very often to do nothing more than give such a description of it. 'Why are you going into that building?'—'There are wounded people there—I'm going in to help.' Nothing more needs to be said, for it is part of human nature to look after each other in this sort of way. It is also a part of human nature to fight and kill one another, but as far as reason-giving goes, there is one very obvious thing that distinguishes helping others from harming them. Reasons, as I have said, are paradigmatically given in response to such questions as 'Why are you doing that?', and questions like that can, in principle, be asked *by the person upon whom you are acting*—the person you are helping or harming, that is. Of course what that means is that the phenomenon of human violence is often attended by a breakdown in, or suspension of, or perversion of, the language-game of giving and receiving reasons for action. For human beings would not have developed a concept of a reason for action such that 'I am doing this to harm you' may count all by itself as a good reason, i.e. as one to be recognized and accepted as such by a normal enquirer—hence it is *not* (as such) a good reason for an action, and wouldn't be proffered to a victim by a sane assailant, except by way of mockery.[11] In some contexts, such as where the speaker is acting in revenge, 'I am doing this to harm you' may indeed count as an intelligible reason, as we shall see in a moment; but this does not affect the distinction here at issue, between the statuses of 'I am doing this to help you' and 'I am doing this to harm you'.

A Kantian philosopher approaches this matter rather differently, and often in a way that manifests one of the tendencies I mentioned in the Introduction (p. ix), that of over-abstraction. Christine Korsgaard asserts: '... if I am to think I have a reason to shoot you, I must be able to *will* that you should shoot me. Since presumably I can't will that, I can't think I have a reason to shoot you.'[12] Korsgaard is considering a case where two people 'are competing for some object we both want'; and she says that, on the view of reasons for action she is attacking, each person must indeed think the other has a genuine reason to shoot him (her). She goes on: 'I simply acknowledge that fact, and conclude that the two of us are at war.' And this result, she thinks, is a damning one. But the obvious riposte would seem to be, 'What if we *are* at war?' We could be two soldiers on opposing sides attempting to take the same strategically situated house. Surely each of us *can* rationally acknowledge that the other person has a reason to shoot him (her)? Korsgaard's approach is in danger of ruling out the rationality of warfare *a priori*. If there is a plausible form of pacifism, it will surely not achieve its conclusion so easily.

Now it is true that the reason (for shooting) *I mean to harm or kill you* would, in the imagined case, embody a means to a further end—taking the house, for instance. And perhaps Korsgaard would have done better to restrict her argument to the putative reason *I mean to harm or kill you*, as that is meant to embody an end, not a means. Doesn't her mode of argument succeed in ruling out *such* reasons for action? The problem now is with the general claim that I must be able to will that you should harm me, if I am to be able rationally to intend to harm you. That claim, it seems, is just false, even if restricted to harming as an end in itself, and this is something that can be seen from the case of revenge. An act of revenge is

[11] The sadist or psychopath who in a serious tone explains himself by saying 'I am doing this to hurt you' may indeed be said to explain *himself*, rather than explain (justify) his actions: we are here moving away from the practice of giving an account of yourself and of your deeds, towards the different practice of describing your own psychology.
[12] C. Korsgaard, *Self-Constitution: Agency, Identity, and Integrity* (Oxford: Oxford University Press, 2009), p. 192.

accompanied by the thought 'I am harming you, because you have harmed me (or mine)', in which the 'because'-clause cannot be regarded as implicitly alluding to a further end or goal of the agent[13]; and this thought will, in many cases, supply an intelligible, perhaps even a *good*, reason for action. In such a case there is no need to postulate the ability to will harm upon oneself, despite the subsequent availability to the other person of the thought 'You have harmed me, so I now intend to harm you!' (A cycle of revenge.) Where 'In order to harm you' *fails* to give a good reason, as it very frequently does, the source of this fact has nothing to do with any Kantian manoeuvre of hypothetical self-application. It has to do with the social contexts in which the practice of asking for and giving reasons goes on. As I put it above, human beings would not have developed a concept of a reason for action such that 'I am doing this to harm you' may count all by itself as a good reason.

The qualification 'all by itself' is of course a necessary one, especially because of those cases in which another's harm is rationally aimed at, but only as a means, such as the case of soldiers on opposite sides. As I said, a soldier may well see that his opposite number has good reason to shoot him, and part of what this means is that if the other does shoot him, he will have no cause for complaint. This way of putting it coheres with what we need to say about licit and illicit military actions, for whereas a soldier has the right to shoot an enemy soldier, he has no right to shoot civilians, or his own commanding officers; and to say that he has a *right* to shoot an enemy soldier is to say, roughly, that if he does, he can't be held to account for it, by the other soldier or by anyone else (even though the other soldier may shoot him back). The Kantian thought that I must be able to will that X be done to me if I am to be able rationally to intend to do X to another might be taken as misstating something that is true, namely that if I can't be held to account for doing X to another person (e.g. shooting him), then if ever I am in the same position as that other person and have X done to me, I likewise cannot hold the doer of it to account—I can't *complain* if it's done to me, and in that rather minimal sense ought to accept its being done to me.

---

[13] The putative goal, *So as to have my revenge*, relies on the idea of revenge—which, however, can only be understood by reference back to a reason like 'Because you harmed me' (and not, say, to some special feeling of satisfaction). Hence, the basic reason here will be the backward-looking one, 'Because you harmed me', which does not state any goal or end. See Anscombe, *Intention*, p. 13.

Kantians are right to say that there is something 'universalizable' about a good reason for action, i.e. that what's sauce for the goose is sauce for the gander. But the explanation for this does not lie in the nature of the individual self-legislating Will, or anything like that. It lies in the social nature of linguistic intercourse. Language is rule-governed and rules are general[14]—hence similarly-situated participants in a given language-game (such as that of asking for and giving reasons) are necessarily 'in the same boat'.

It is within our language that statements like 'I am doing this to help (or harm) you' are made, and it is within our language that they play the role or roles that they do. Statements, like words, are tools, and their function or purpose, like those of any tools, must relate in some way to general human needs and proclivities. These facts enable us to see why 'In order to help you' and 'In order to harm you' function quite differently as reasons for action; but they also enable us to see why such a position as anti-speciesism is mistaken. The anti-speciesist will be inclined to protest, 'SHOULD the statement that N is a human being count all on its own as a reason for helping N?' He may even go on: 'Actually, there is a higher level of rationality, one divorced from any facts about human gregariousness and conspecific impulses, which dictates that "N is a human being" cannot on its own count as a reason for action—or at any rate, for *ethical* action.' But there is no such higher level of rationality, just as there is no higher language which we should be aspiring to master (a sort of cosmic Esperanto). And the felt need for the addendum, 'ethical action', is significant. It appears to be necessary lest we start calling irrational those who e.g. choose as sexual mates only fellow human beings. Presumably a person's reason for making sexual advances only to human beings and not to horses might simply be, 'These are people—those are horses'. So 'N is a human being' is granted reason-giving force by our anti-speciesist, but not in connection with 'ethical action'. But the idea that action is neatly divisible into the ethical and the non-ethical is a pipe dream, as is the idea that reasons for action can be thus divided. And in any case, isn't the forming of sexual relationships a matter of ethical significance? Kant would

---

[14] It is true that this statement is quasi-tautologous, amounting as it does to 'A rule applies to all its various instances'. But 'Reasons are universalizable', in so far as it is a *true* (or valid, or okay) principle, seems also to have the status of a tautology—something that thus speaks in favour of drawing a connection between it and 'Rules are general' in the way here suggested.

reply, 'Only in so far as the other person is a rational being like yourself'; but this gets things the wrong way round. Rationality is important because of the role it plays in human interactions—those interactions don't get to count as important because of their embodiment of rationality.[15]

In an extremely incisive article, 'The Human Prejudice', Bernard Williams diagnoses the anti-speciesist's illusions as stemming from an imaginary 'viewpoint of the universe', from which viewpoint it makes sense to ask, e.g., what sorts and quantities of mental states should exist. This cosmic point of view performs the same sort of function as the 'higher rationality' I mentioned in the previous paragraph. Philosophers have sometimes hoped to indicate what they take to be standards of pure, perspectiveless rationality by ascribing those standards to an imaginary Ideal or Impartial Observer; and where the actual agenda is a utilitarian one, such an Ideal Observer will, as Williams notes, have to be credited with benevolence, rather than indifference.

> With his omniscience and impartiality he, so to speak, *takes on* all suffering, however exactly we are to conceive of that, and takes it all on equally [thus he isn't liable to the sympathy fatigue that besets us human beings]. He does look, of course, a lot like a slimmed-down surrogate of the Christian God, and this may well suggest that he represents yet another re-enactment of the cosmic point of view: suffering or its absence is what has absolute importance.[16]

Williams suggests that the anti-speciesist's way of thinking has religious roots, referring to the notion of absolute importance as a 'survivor from the enchanted world' (p. 144). It makes sense within a religious framework to ask what temporal things have most ultimate value, for this is the same as asking what temporal things are most valued by God. And since it is a central part of religious, especially Judaeo-Christian, thought to ascribe to God a special concern for human beings above other animals and objects,

---

[15] There is a connected point to do with how a person's moral goals might be 'arrived at'; as Anselm Müller writes: 'The idea of measuring morality by an independent standard of rationality has an air of absentmindedness about it. I mean to say that a man in his senses will not forget that he is a human being; he will not try to reconstruct (from what premises?) a deliberation that results in the choice of a good life. He may indeed choose to lead a good life—in the sense of *giving prominence* to goals like justice; but he will not *arrive at these goals* as a result of deliberation.' ('Has Moral Education a Rational Basis?', in *Moral Truth and Moral Tradition: Essays in Honour of Peter Geach and Elizabeth Anscombe*, ed. L. Gormally (Blackrock, Ireland: Four Courts Press, 1994), p. 219.)

[16] Bernard Williams, 'The Human Prejudice', in *Philosophy as a Humanistic Discipline*, ed. A. W. Moore, (Princeton: Princeton University Press, 2006), p. 145.

a concern made manifest in His plans for us, the answer to the question as to what things are of most value is: 'Human beings'. But the secularized, cosmic version of the idea of *concern*, lacking as it does any person or intelligent being who might feel such concern, thereby lacks requisite conditions of meaningfulness. This explains the temptation to insert that notional subject, the Ideal Observer.

Though Williams doesn't put it like this, concepts such as importance, value, and to-be-minimizedness are surely as much dependent for their meaningful application on the obtaining of certain background facts as are concepts like price and illegality. And his diagnosis of the anti-speciesist illusion has an obvious parallel in Elizabeth Anscombe's diagnosis of the idea of 'moral obligation' as deriving from an earlier, religious viewpoint, according to which certain things were actually prescribed or forbidden— by God, as opposed to 'by the universe'.[17] Anscombe's critique did in fact extend to casting doubt on the meaningfulness of certain statements, such as 'There is a moral obligation to be honest'; and similar doubt can surely be cast on the meaningfulness of statements about absolute importance. The illusion that it always makes sense simply to ask, 'Is X important?', or 'Is X of ultimate value?', is also a typically *philosophical* illusion, akin to (though not in quite the same boat as) the illusion which we have already encountered, that it makes sense to ask, 'Why do you believe that?' even in the absence of contextually-provided standards of justification. It is not as if we can always say, 'if we like', that X is of *no* importance, thus covering all eventualities. 'Is the tie you're wearing important?' will likely provoke the reply, 'Important for what?', or 'Important to whom?'—a reply expecting such answers as, 'For making the right impression at work', or 'Important to *you*, since I was wondering if I could use it to wipe some grease off these trousers'. To say, 'No, I just mean *important*' will produce only bafflement or irritation—and not, by the way, the rejoinder, 'Well, it's of no importance, since you ask'.—We might wonder whether the tie is of ultimate importance, in the grand scheme of things. But if that means anything, it means something like, 'Does this tie, do ties in general, matter much in life, really? What are clothes, after all? Aren't all those frantic Saturday shoppers acting foolishly? Happiness lies elsewhere . . . etc. etc.'

---

[17] See G. E. M. Anscombe, 'Modern Moral Philosophy', in *Ethics, Religion and Politics: Collected Papers Vol. III* (Oxford: Blackwell, 1981), pp. 26–42.

'The Human Prejudice' does not only offer diagnosis. It ends with some prognosis:

> When the hope is to improve humanity to the point at which every aspect of its hold on the world can be justified before a higher court, the result is likely to be either self-deception, if you think you have succeeded, or self-hatred and self-contempt when you recognize that you will always fail. The self-hatred, in this case, is a hatred of humanity. Personally I think that there are many things to loathe about human beings, but their sense of their ethical identity as a species is not one of them. (p. 152)

There is in fact a third possibility, over and above the self-deception and self-hatred described by Williams, and that is deluded optimism: maybe a utilitarian Utopia *can* be established on earth, with equal consideration accorded to all sentient beings. Not quite all, of course—exceptions tend to be made, as Williams reminds us, notably of such non-persons as 'the infants, the Alzheimer's patients, and some others' (p. 144). But you can't make an omelette without breaking eggs. The Utopia project is certainly underway in various universities and research centres, and moreover seems to attract funding. Such is human nature; and although, as I have been arguing, human nature is the necessary keystone of ethical thought, not everything that flows from it can be defended.

IV.

I began by putting forward the claim that ethical thought is, in a certain sense, anthropocentric. This led us to examine the status of 'This is a human being' as a reason for action, one that in certain contexts (such as scenes of carnage) has greater weight than, say, 'That is a chimpanzee'. Our discussion consequently turned to the nature of reasons in general, and I argued that the requirement of contextual standards in the language-game of reason-giving already points us towards the human dimension: for the concept of a good reason is *our* concept, and it has a function (or functions) for *us*. What we are liable to accept as a good reason, and therefore what can count as a good reason, must in large part be determined by what sort of creature we are.

These reflections are more bolstered than undermined by the observation that when it comes to such things as helping those in dire need, talk of our having a *reason* for what we do ('They're human') can seem to over-intellectualize matters. I spoke above of the 'impulse' to help other human beings; and in so far as one who sincerely asked, 'Why are you helping those wounded people?' would appear himself to lack or be deficient in such an impulse, his very question might have to count as just stupid. If genuine reasons are such as could only ever be given in response to a genuine or proper demanding of reasons, then 'They're human' doesn't count as a genuine reason for action in such contexts. The very human-centredness of the concept of a reason for action excludes it. If this is right, then our earlier discussion of helping human beings instead of animals (pp. 3–5) would need some careful re-stating: in situations where 'Those are human beings' gives genuine information (e.g. where screams that could be human or animal are heard), the statement can indeed supply a reason for your rushing in a certain direction, say—but where it's clear that these are human beings and those are dogs, you have already reached bedrock, and to say 'Those are human beings', while it might have *some* point (e.g. to shame your inert neighbour), is not really to give your reason for acting.

'One has good reason to help the wounded or dying' could in fact be called a hinge proposition of ethics, in Wittgenstein's sense: 'the *questions* that we raise and our *doubts* depend on the fact that some propositions are exempt from doubt, are as it were like hinges on which those turn'.[18] But what exactly is involved in this notion of a hinge proposition?

Here is a parallel case. 'Human beings can see' is a hinge proposition in relation to all our colour-judgements—'Grass is green', 'Sarah has a brown scarf', and so on. There would be no such thing as colour-judgements, no such thing as colour-concepts, if the makers of judgements and havers of concepts did not see; which is not to say that grass wouldn't be green if they (= we) didn't see, for the statement 'Grass would still be green if human beings couldn't see' is itself meaningful—and true—courtesy of our actual ability to see, since it amounts to (though it is not synonymous with) 'Grass would still be the colour we actually call "green" if, etc.'[19] Doubts or questions about what colour a thing is presuppose both that human beings see and that this proposition is not up for grabs—for if it were, the content of those same doubts and questions would be up for

[18] Ludwig Wittgenstein, *On Certainty*, eds G. E. M. Anscombe and G. H. von Wright (Oxford: Blackwell, 1969), para. 341.

[19] See G. E. M. Anscombe, 'The Question of Linguistic Idealism', in *From Parmenides to Wittgenstein: Collected Papers, Vol. I* (Oxford: Blackwell, 1981), pp. 113–14.

grabs as well. But the status of 'Human beings can see' as a hinge proposition militates against our imputing to Emma, as one of her background
reasons for thinking that Sarah has a brown scarf, the belief that human
beings can see. (A desire to posit the belief as a 'subconscious' reason for
Emma's judgement about the scarf would only betoken the sort of rigid
model of the mental we have already encountered; see p. 4, above.) Emma
might well answer 'Yes' to the question 'Can human beings see?', and we
can, if we like, take that as a criterion of belief, thus fixing a pretty minimal
sense for 'believe'; but by that criterion she also believes that she is not an
extinct dinosaur, that 307 is smaller than 523, and infinitely many other
propositions—and in general such 'beliefs' are not suited to serve as the
reasons behind one's assertions and judgements.

Doubts and questions as to what to do at the scene of a bomb blast
likewise presuppose (in the sense I have indicated) that one has good
reason to help the wounded or dying. It's conceivable that this reason
could be overridden, e.g. if there were a possibility of another bomb going
off. But its status as a weighty reason is not in question for human beings
on the spot. Even one of the terrorists responsible for the blast would hear
it as a reason; hence the fact that (unless unbalanced or drugged or similar)
he would not be surprised at people's going in to help, getting others to
help, etc., and this despite his knowing nothing of the beliefs, desires,
ideology, or characters of those people. He might think something along
the lines of: 'I'd do the same in their position'.

My point could be put this way: it isn't the *opinion* of the person who
rushes in to help the wounded that there's reason to help them. And here
we may link the instinctive character of our impulses towards one another
with the instinctive character of our ascriptions to them of psychological
states. Here is Wittgenstein:

'I believe that he is suffering.'—Do I also believe that he isn't an automaton?
It would go against the grain to use the word in both connexions.
(Or is it like this: I believe that he is suffering, but am certain that he is not an
automaton? Nonsense!) [...]
My attitude towards him is an attitude towards a soul. I am not of the *opinion* that
he has a soul.[20]

[20] L. Wittgenstein, *Philosophical Investigations*, 2nd edn, trans. G. E. M. Anscombe (Oxford: Blackwell, 1958), p. 178.

Wittgenstein's use of 'attitude' (*Einstellung*) and 'opinion' (*Meinung*) in this passage is intended to effect a contrast: between judgements like 'He has a mind (has mental states, etc.)' and ones like 'He is suffering'. It can be your *opinion* that someone is suffering, namely in those cases where there is room for real doubt, as where the person might in fact be shamming. But as Wittgenstein emphasizes elsewhere, there are many cases in which there is no room for doubt that someone is suffering, e.g. if they have just been dragged screaming from a burning car. So we might use the distinction between attitude and opinion in order to effect another sort of contrast: between judgements like 'She is suffering', made in what might be called paradigm circumstances, and ones like 'She is 58 years old'. The latter is rationally debatable, it is open to question (except perhaps in extraordinary circumstances), while the former, given that it is made in paradigm circumstances, is not. And this difference between the two judgements corresponds to a difference concerning the grounds on which such judgements are made. My very ability to come out with judgements like the first depends upon my having certain natural human reactive capacities, capacities which will be activated e.g. if I see and hear someone wincing and groaning in a certain way. If asked *why* I think the person is suffering, I may say, 'She is wincing and groaning', thus giving grounds for my assertion; but to see something as a wince (as opposed e.g. to a moue of disdain) and to hear something as a groan (as opposed e.g. to a sigh of regret) are not things that I need, or typically can, justify, by further description of the sights and sounds—say, in terms of the distances between the corners of the person's mouth and her nostrils. Rather, these sights and sounds simply *strike* me a certain way. And concepts like pain and suffering are taught, learnt, and used by creatures with natural reactive capacities that are like this; moreover, the usefulness of these concepts is bound up, not with scientific enquiry (though such enquiry can be brought to bear upon pain and suffering), but with human interaction.

The distinction between attitude and opinion is correlative with the distinction mentioned earlier, between hinge proposition and non-hinge proposition. 'People have minds', or 'He has a mind', have the status of hinge propositions for the reason that 'has a mind' is a sort of portmanteau for all those judgements like 'He is bored', 'She is suffering', 'They are angry', judgements one's very ability to make which presupposes that one sometimes makes them (a) instinctively and spontaneously, and (b) warrantedly, i.e. correctly. (The truth of (b) derives from the truth of (a).) So if you are able to make the judgement 'People have minds', you cannot doubt it. But something very similar goes for 'One has good reason to help the wounded or dying'. For this judgement can only be understood by someone with sufficiently normal human impulses—you need these if you are to have an adequate understanding of 'has good reason to'—and central among normal human impulses is the impulse to help those who are wounded or dying. The term 'central' is not meant to imply that every normal human being *will* feel such impulses in the relevant situations. Rather, the social character of the language-game of asking for and giving reasons, and indeed the social character of human life, guarantee a central position for such impulses. At the same time, these impulses are pre-rational and instinctive in just the way that the capacity to respond to others as angry or amused is; and it is on the back of these impulses that certain concepts involved in ethical reasoning get introduced, just as it is on the back of our reactive capacities that many, if not most, psychological concepts get introduced.

One's natural reactions to others are reactions to what they do, how they appear, what they say—in short, to their behaviour, in a suitably extended sense of that term.[21] In order to understand what is going on here, it is essential we recognize the following fact: that human behaviours and capacities, like other human features, very often come in syndromes. That is to say, several of them will often, or even usually, come together, as a bunch—e.g. crying, wincing, nursing a body part, rocking. Of course to see such a bunch *as* a bunch is itself a characteristic sort of human capacity, one that is important in the context of our philosophical enquiries, since it is part of what enables us to invent words for psychological states (modes, manifestations, etc.). As to syndromes, there is a natural analogy: that of diseases. The analogy is useful, but it has perhaps misled philosophers. A syndrome of symptoms—spots, sore throat, and fever, say—is of concern to us especially because of the need to prevent, cure, or alleviate those symptoms, and so it is natural for us to shape our concepts with an eye to

---

[21] The word 'behaviour' will ring alarm bells for those who think of 'behaviourism' as an antiquated theory, long since refuted. But the term 'behaviourism' is fatally vague, and for that reason (if for no other) behaviourism cannot usefully be said to have been refuted—nor successfully argued for. The case is similar to that of verificationism, which 'we all know' was thoroughly refuted decades ago. Each term now typically functions as a mere boo-word.

I discuss some of the reasons why '-isms' in philosophy are necessarily liable to be unhelpful in Chapter 5.

the cause(s) of the symptoms, often the hidden cause(s). The primary meaning of 'aetiology' relates to the causes of diseases, and is derived from the Greek word *aitia*, which means both cause and what is to *blame*, and which thus illustrates the impulse I have in mind—the impulse to hunt out the causes of disease, malfunction, etc. In the light of this impulse, it is understandable why a name for a condition often begins life as a sort of shorthand for the group of symptoms, but, as soon as investigations allow it, becomes a word applicable on the basis of the presence of a particular germ or virus, the entity which is to blame for the symptoms, and which we will endeavour to attack or neutralize. But it is different with concepts like pain, joy, nervousness, sleepiness, anger, ecstasy, concentration, and so on. In so far as we are interested in causes here, the kinds of causes we look for are extremely diffuse and varied, and typically not 'hidden'. And an interest in causes is just one strand in our interest in the feelings, doings, and sayings of other human beings. (Once again, a word—'interest'—can itself seem to over-intellectualize matters.)

The way philosophers have been misled is this: impressed by the scientific model, they have proposed an account of psychological expressions according to which those expressions are 'about' inner causes of outward behaviours, in the sort of way in which many medical terms are 'about' inner causes of outward symptoms. The obvious candidate here is functionalism, according to which a given psychological state of a creature is identified as whatever state of the creature it happens to be that is causally responsible for certain outputs (e.g. given certain inputs). But, for the reasons I have sketched, such theories are misguided. To speak of psychological expressions being 'about' this or that is already to risk confusion, but if we are to speak that way, then evidently many of these expressions are about outward behaviours, at any rate in the following sense: mastery of the relevant concepts is derived from an instinctive capacity (in the sense in which the capacity to learn language is instinctive) to react to other human beings in certain ways, and, correlatively, to perceive them in certain ways.

And this brings us to a kind of 'syndrome' that is of great importance for ethics, namely the sort of collection of reactions and behaviours that may be said to involve both judgement and action. We already have grounds for regarding these two categories as not wholly distinct, for the purposes of language are interwoven with the activities of life, and learning to use words must very often involve *action*, in addition to assertion, questioning, and the other speech-acts. To learn the meaning of 'apple' paradigmatically involves learning to do such things as pick out, collect, distribute, hunt for, and (very often) eat, apples.[22] Judgement and action are intertwined. When it comes to ethics, there are a number of concepts where thought, judgement, perception, and action are all crucially involved, notably concepts to do with human psychology, broadly construed. Those who hear the moans of the wounded and rush to their aid perceive things a certain way, judge (can assert) certain things, feel the impulse to do certain things, have reason to act in this way not that, experience a certain kind of anguish or alarm . . . They thus manifest what is a humanly normal syndrome of responses, and the reasons they give and the concepts they use will typically derive their force and their identity from the whole syndrome, not from some element or elements within it.

The main error of Humean moral philosophy can arguably be diagnosed as the pulling apart of strands that hold ethical concepts together, strands of judgement and of action. Hume drove a wedge between Reason and Passion, calling the former impotent when it came to producing (or justifying) action. Only passion could, he thought, produce action; and since morality evidently has to do with action, morality must derive from our passions (sentiments, desires, feelings), and not from our reason (judgements, beliefs, opinions). Hume's position can be attacked from two directions: either by showing how judgement and feeling cannot be hived off from one another in the case of ethics, or by showing that non-ethical judgement is itself ultimately to do with action, and not just with thought (conceived of as a sort of interior monologue). Various philosophers have successfully adopted the first tactic, of which I have already been making some use. But the second tactic is quite as effective, and it can be pursued in the following way.

There is a strong inclination to regard concepts (square, red, cow, normal, future, nothing . . .) as having their primary residence in the basically passive activities of thinking and perceiving, mental activities which are conceived of as independent of, and prior to, action. Language is then taken to be the 'vehicle' of thought, and actions are taken to be effects, typically bodily, of these mental states. (So far, so dualist—but the picture is not essentially altered if the mental states get identified with

---

[22] That precisely *this* is not true of concepts like 'atom' and 'prince-bishop' does not detract from the point.

brain-states.) But could the thought or judgement 'That is red' be thus independent of action? We might think that the way with this question is to attempt to picture to ourselves a paralysed deaf-mute entertaining the proposition 'That is red'. We might even decide that our 'intuition' yields the conclusion: 'Yes, he could entertain that proposition'. But let us leave the deaf-mute aside, as also the issue of whether philosophical enquiry is a sort of ping-pong of intuitions, and ask instead: When a child learns to use colour-words, calling tomatoes red, fetching yellow books when asked, and all the rest, is there room for the hypothesis that his outwardly expressed colour-judgements are in fact systematically mistaken? The hypothesis needs to be considered because the role of the interior colour-judgements would appear to be that of 'giving meaning' to the outward utterances, etc.—and *what* the interior colour-judgements are (their content, that is) is meant to be something prior to, and independent of, any outward behaviour. So it would seem that the child's overt colour-judgements could be all awry. But any such 'systematic error' would be of no consequence: the child would get along fine, succeed in communicating, pass its driving test, and so on. In other words, there would be no reason to call any of this 'error' (about colours). If, on the other hand, the correctness of the outward judgements is admitted to be independent of any interior processes, then (a) it is worth noting that any concepts discussed (in language) between philosophers will have outer and not inner standards of application, and (b) it is doubtful whether the interior 'concepts', having their own standards of application, can properly be called concepts at all. Why call certain interior goings-on colour-judgements? Why, that is, put them in the same category as outwardly expressed colour-judgements?—for to put them in the same category would be to posit shared standards of application, which hypothesis we have seen to be empty, at any rate if the interior 'judgements' are themselves conceived of as independent of outward action and behaviour. But if the mental goings-on are so independent of colour-words, and of the actual live use of those words, as to belong properly speaking to a distinct and unrelated category, then their relevance to our enquiries appears doubtful (cf. the beetle in the box of Wittgenstein's *Philosophical Investigations*, para. 293). Indeed, it looks as if the very identity and existence of these mental whatsits has become a nebulous matter, in so far as they were posited in the first place to perform what turns out to be a non-job.

Anyone who has read Wittgenstein will be familiar with the tenor of these remarks; indeed, to such a person I will probably seem to have been labouring the point. Applied to Hume's, and Humean, moral philosophy, our considerations yield the objection that *no* products of what Hume calls Reason—beliefs, judgements, knowledge, etc.—can possibly be inert and impotent in the way that Hume needs in order to set up his contrast—a contrast that has come down to us as the 'fact/value distinction'. They cannot be thus impotent because they cannot be independent of the outward expression of concepts, in language and in action.

If there is a special connection between ethical thought and action, it is not to be explained as the ethical subjectivist would explain it, by reference to an impassable mental fence separating the cognitive from the conative. There is no such fence.

V.

Hume did see the importance for ethics of natural and instinctive inter-active responses between human beings. The terms he especially tended to use in this connection were 'sympathy' and 'benevolence'. The list of ethically relevant interactive responses is a long one, and includes what Hume would call 'painful', as well as 'pleasant', responses (e.g. righteous anger). But the Humean conception of such responses or feelings, as akin to sensations, is mistaken in a way that is liable to distort moral philosophy and ethical thought in general.

The reason for this is that the ethical significance of a particular feeling or response typically derives, at least in large part, from the thoughts and/ or reasons that lie behind it; it does *not* derive from any putative 'qualitative feel', nor in any straightforward way from whether the feeling or response is pleasant or painful. For Hume, since pleasure and pain are the ultimate springs of human action,[23] one or both of them must be crucially involved in all the various moral sentiments, since (being *moral*) such sentiments are responsible for much action. He also thought that the pleasantness or painfulness of a sentiment was down to the particular 'way it felt'. One result of all this was that he ended up regarding approbation and disappro-bation as themselves quasi-sensations. Approbation, being pleasant, leads

---

[23] For example, David Hume, *Enquiry Concerning the Principle of Morals*, Appendix I, sec. 5.

us to encourage the performance of (more and more of?) those actions which produce this feeling in us, while disapprobation, being painful, leads us to discourage the performance of those actions which produce *that* feeling in us. The psychological mechanism is much the same as the one that explains people's pursuit of cigarettes or avoidance of rotten meat.

I said a moment ago that the ethical significance of a particular feeling or response typically derives from the thoughts and/or reasons that lie behind it. The truth of the matter goes further; for the *identity* of a particular feeling or response typically derives from such thoughts and/or reasons. Hence it is no surprise that ethical significance is in the same boat. Philippa Foot pinpointed this aspect of the problem in 'Moral Beliefs', writing:

Consider, for instance, the suggestion that someone might be proud of the sky or the sea: he looks at them and what he feels is *pride*, or he puffs out his chest and gestures with *pride* in their direction. This makes sense only if a special assumption is made about his beliefs, for instance that he is under some crazy delusion and believes that he has saved the sky from falling, or the seas from drying up. The characteristic object of pride is something seen (a) as in some way a man's own, and (b) as some sort of achievement or advantage; without this object pride cannot be described.[24]

Sensations, like pain or dizziness, do not have *objects* in the sense in which emotions like pride do,[25] though they do have *causes*. If Jack looks at the sea and feels dizzy, he might tell us, 'Looking at the sea makes me feel dizzy', or even just, 'The sea makes me feel dizzy'; and although this may be odd, it makes perfectly good sense, as 'I am proud of the sea' does not (without the sort of crazy background belief Foot alludes to). To be proud e.g. of a bookcase one has made is not simply to have a certain experience upon looking at or contemplating the bookcase—for if it were, then it *would* be possible to find that one was proud of the sea or sky. Here we encounter that difference, already mentioned, between reasons and causes (see pp. 6–8, above). But we must be careful not to expunge causation completely from our account of the emotions. For sensations, experiences, current contents of consciousness—whatever we call them—are evidently an *element* in those psychological syndromes that count as emotions, and as

---

[24] Philippa Foot, 'Moral Beliefs', in *Virtues and Vices* (Oxford: Blackwell, 1978), pp. 113–14.

[25] Unless perhaps one is to call the place where a pain is felt the (intentional) object of the pain; cf. Anscombe, 'The Intentionality of Sensation' (in *Metaphysics and the Philosophy of Mind: Collected Papers, Vol. II* (Oxford: Blackwell, 1981), p. 20.

such are often to be spoken of as having causes. Recall the people we imagined running into a bomb-blasted building; these people, I said, 'perceive things a certain way, judge (can assert) certain things, feel the impulse to do certain things, have reason to act in this way not that, experience a certain kind of anguish or alarm . . . ' If nothing else, we would expect the effects of adrenaline on such occasions to include various characteristic sensations, and 'anguish and alarm' can be thought of as frequently involving these and other sensations.

One of the main sources of the idea that emotions, and mental states generally, are current experiences must be that the philosopher who wants to discover the nature of (e.g.) thinking, or remembering, or being proud, tries to do so by the simple method of seeing what's going on when he's thinking or whatever. What he actually finds is thus restricted to being a process in time: it can only be something of which it makes sense to say, 'Such-and-such is happening now'. And this will be, if anything, a current experience, or perhaps a current physical process—such as the slight movements of the larynx which J.B. Watson identified as thinking.[26] If the philosopher is prone to look into his consciousness rather than into his throat, he will quite often find *something* there, and it may well be something characteristic of the state in question; so that he is liable to conclude that alarm *just is* a particular adrenaline rush, or remembering *just is* the having of certain images. But the method is no better than that of trying to find out what makes a ten pound note a ten pound note by examining one very closely. What you find—paper of a particular shape and appearance—will give you a good way of identifying ten pound notes, for the institution of money requires such easy identification; but the shape and appearance are non-essential, as can be seen from the fact that the design of ten pound notes periodically changes. With both mental states and money, it is the bigger picture that determines the identity of the thing in question: a background of banks, transactions, rules, etc., in the case of money, and a background of other and various human phenomena (both personal and social) in the case of mental states.

The issues here are not of merely academic interest. A false picture of mental states of the sort I am describing will be especially seductive in a

---

[26] In Watson, 'Psychology as the Behaviorist Views it' (*Psychological Review* 20 (1913): 158–77): 'Since, according to my view, thought processes are really motor habits in the larynx . . . '.

culture like ours which prizes scientific investigation, conceived of rather simplistically as homing in on a phenomenon in order to understand it. It will be salutary to spend a moment or two considering some of the recent manifestations of this false picture, if only because of its capacity to skew ethical thinking, which is after all our main theme. I shall return to the topic of the emotions and what they *really* are in the next section.

The research programme devoted to examining current processes in the hope of discovering the nature of mental states is one that has received impetus in recent years from advances in the technology of brain-imaging. J. B. Watson lacked a brain-scanner, and found himself attending only to his larynx; now we can see what's happening in our hemispheres. In February 2005 it was announced that 'a multidisciplinary research centre at Oxford which will examine [religious] belief and the brain has been launched, with $2 million funding'. Among other questions to be addressed by those working at the Centre would be 'whether there is a detectable difference in the brain between religious and secular faith'. The Deputy Director of the Centre was quoted as saying that 'what we believe in makes us who we are, and yet our beliefs can change from moment to moment', while the Director, Baroness Susan Greenfield, explained that 'it is now possible to explore mental processes by experimental means, on time and space scales commensurate with real physico-chemical events within the brain and body'.[27]

There is a buried dualist assumption lurking in the undergrowth of all this cutting-edge physicalism, which comes out when we ask, 'How are we to know whether someone is religious, or that she is thinking about God, or whatever?' For we need to know these things *before* we can point to the brain-scan and say 'Look! These neurons fire during religious experience!'—or whatever we end up saying. The brain-scan only tells us about the neurons; what has told us that here we have a religious person or experience? The answer, of course, has to be: 'Well, she herself told us she was religious/was having a religious experience.' In other words, the person herself has a special authority about her mental states. If asked how a person can have such authority if a religious experience is 'really' a brain process (after all, I don't generally know what's going on in my brain), what can the physicalist say? Not much. The assumption here of first-

---

[27] From 'Belief and the Brain', *Blueprint* 5(6) (Feb. 3, 2005).

person authority surely has its source in mind–body dualism; for although there exist alternative explanations of this authority (e.g. Wittgenstein's), the dualist explanation goes with a picture of the mind as 'inner', and of psychological verbs as referring to 'inner states/processes', which is shared by physicalism—the difference being that the physicalist intends 'inner' in a more literal sense than the dualist.

The strange picture of religious belief conjured up by the Director and Deputy Director of OXCSOM is one in which belief can change 'from moment to moment', possibly on time scales 'commensurate with real physico-chemical events within the brain and body'. (Note the use of the word 'real': if it's detectable by a scientist, then rest assured, it's real.) What would a person with such a belief look like? 'There's a God . . . no, there isn't . . . yes, there is . . . no, there isn't . . . ' Does a person who says or thinks such things have a belief at all? To be sure, I can change my beliefs back and forth if the subject is whether the horse I bet on is in the lead, since things are changing fast out there on the race-track. And in some circumstances I can change what I *say* back and forth if I'm undecided, in particular about something where a decision is demanded; as, 'I'll have the bouillabaisse . . . no, the crêpe . . . no, the bouillabaisse . . . ' But one's belief in whether there is an omnipotent and omniscient personal creator of the Universe? Not to mention one's love and worship of such a being?

The main danger of such 'research' is that a spurious scientific stamp is put upon conclusions which simply express the already established non-scientific viewpoints of the researchers. It is a point familiar to philosophers of science that the interpretation of data is not a neutral thing, but is typically determined by what can be called theory, in a broad sense. Where a theory has in reality come into being independently of any facts of the kind that are now being adduced as data, and where it simultaneously serves to shape the interpretation of the data and is alleged to receive confirmation from the same data, the result will probably be not science, but pseudo-science. Sometimes the 'theory' is even an ethical one, such as utilitarianism. Here is a report from the Oxford Centre for Neuroethics:

Employing neuroimaging and psychological experiments, Haidt (2001), Hauser (2006) and others have documented unconscious influences on moral judgement with little input from consciousness. In one influential study, Greene et al. (2001) used fMRI to study the neural correlates of responses to moral dilemmas, showing that subjects who responded in a non-utilitarian manner exhibited strong activation in brain areas associated with emotion. These claims have been supported by studies of patients with frontal damage (Koeings et al. 2007; but see Kahane & Shackel 2008). Others studies show that the reasons people adduce to justify moral judgements are often merely post-hoc rationalizations (Haidt 2007). Finally, surveys of the intuitions of lay persons have shown moral judgements vary across cultures and classes (Haidt 2001). Such research has been claimed to support far-reaching conclusions such as the denial of the viability of virtue ethics (Harman, 1999; Doris 2002) and of common views about killing (Greene 2003), risk, punishment, and reproduction (Sunstein 2005). Utilitarians such as Peter Singer (2005) claim that it shows that opposition to utilitarianism is due to irrational emotions.[28]

It is interesting to be told that researchers have managed to identify 'brain areas associated with emotion'. (Which emotions? *All* of them? Or just the irrational ones? And which ones are those?) Presumably the methods used were similar to those that will eventually show us which brain areas are associated with religious belief. But I have said enough about the bank-ruptcy of the methods. What of the conclusions? Utilitarianism receives confirmation, while virtue ethics and common views about killing and reproduction appear dodgy. It is sociologically unsurprising that such conclusions are reached by such investigators, and one can even imagine a piece of psychological research that set out to examine why it is so unsurprising; it would perhaps include the statement: 'A number of studies indicate that subjects who respond to moral dilemmas in a utilitarian manner have a marked preference for tasks which involve measurement, with the minimum number of parameters'.

As an antidote to the views of human psychology expressed by such as Baroness Greenfield and Professor Singer, here is a passage in which is conveyed something of the breadth of context which in reality informs a person's beliefs, emotions, and actions. With breadth can also go depth; and to psychological depth there surely corresponds moral depth, some-thing believed by the author of the passage to have a mystical aspect:

When Pierre, struck sometimes by the force of his remarks, asked him to repeat what he had said, Platon could never recall what he had said the minute before, just as he could never repeat to Pierre the words of his favourite song. There came in, 'My own little birch tree,' and 'My heart is sick,' but there was no meaning in the words. He did not understand, and could not grasp the significance of words taken apart from the sentence. Every word and every action of his was the expression of a

---

[28] Source: www.neuroethics.ox.ac.uk/research.htm. The last reference is to P. Singer, 'Ethics and Intuitions', *Journal of Ethics* (2005) 9: 331–52.

force uncomprehended by him, which was his life. But his life, as he looked at it, had no meaning as a separate life. It had meaning only as a part of a whole, of which he was at all times conscious. His words and actions flowed from him as smoothly, as inevitably, and as spontaneously, as the perfume rises from the flower. He could not understand any value or significance in an act or a word taken separately.[29]

VI.

Let us return to the topic of emotions, and of what might be called their cognitive aspect. The fact that emotions, feelings, and responses are connected with a person's judgements and reasons, in the way outlined earlier on, has two important consequences. The first is this: there are limits on the possible objects of emotions, etc. You cannot feel proud of the sky; you cannot feel sympathy towards a toenail; you cannot disapprove of death. Sometimes, as has been noted, we need to add: 'Unless you crazily believe that . . . ' But since there are also limits on what can count as really believing something, it won't always be possible to concoct even such 'unless'-clauses. The second consequence is this: since reasons can be good or bad, and since they can be missing when required, an emotion will very often be assessable as rational or irrational.

An extreme case is that of phobias. With many phobias it is probably unclear whether fear, or rather something like extreme revulsion, is at issue, but let us assume for the sake of argument that it is fear. The judgement that is paradigmatically relevant to the state of fear is: 'Such-and-such is dangerous'; and so either the person who has, say, a phobia of mice wrongly (and probably irrationally) believes mice to be dangerous to human beings, or he knows they are not dangerous, but can't help himself from going on as if they are—screaming, jumping on chairs, pleading for somebody to remove the mouse, and so on. The irrationality of the fear here is the irrationality of the behaviour, as comes across if we ask the person a question like, 'Why are you standing on that chair screaming?' The question, as it were, expects an answer of the form, 'There is an F present', where Fs are dangerous; but no such answer, nor any other rationalizing answer, is available.[30]

---

[29] L. Tolstoy, *War and Peace*, trans. Constance Garnett (Oxford: Oxford University Press, 1904), part 11, ch. 13.

[30] Here in fact we have a grey area, in which there can be as good grounds for talking of a cause as of a reason. 'She jumped on the chair because a mouse appeared' has an affinity with

A phobia is often known to be such by the one who suffers from it; i.e. he or she often knows that there is no good reason to fear the thing in question, or to go on as if it is dangerous. Of more interest, for our purposes, are those cases where someone manifests or expresses some emotion for which there is no good reason, or for which there is insufficient reason, but where he is unaware of this state of affairs. Such cases come in at least three different varieties: (a) the person denies feeling (manifesting, etc.) the emotion; (b) he presents certain reasons as his reasons which are not in fact his true reasons, his actions being properly describable as having a non-rational explanation; (c) his reasons are simply bad or insufficient reasons. (a) and (b) are of particular interest to students of the unconscious or subconscious. They are not without interest for the ethicist; but it is especially (c) that presents itself as a problem in the context of ethical debate and discussion, for rather obvious reasons.

While driving, Mike flies into a rage. When later on he is asked by the police why he did so, he splutters, 'Cos of that bastard in the BMW who overtook me on the roundabout.' Mike's reason for getting angry—that he was overtaken on a roundabout by a BMW—is not unintelligible; it is not as if he got angry at the colour of someone's socks. On the contrary, Mike's reaction is one of the most tediously natural and intelligible of reactions, especially among male drivers. Nevertheless, the reason for his anger is not a good or adequate reason, and this fact is at once a fact about his psychology and an ethical fact: Mike is worthy of criticism for having a short fuse, and also for what he does, if he manifests his childish rage in overt action—e.g. by shaking his fist and honking his horn. (The severity of the criticism is a function both of the silliness of his reasons and of the form his anger takes.) Discussion of the matter with Mike will clearly be hampered if he will not accept that his rage was unjustified; and yet what can we say to him if he is thus stubborn?

In any real-life scenario of this sort, the answer to the last question will depend, to repeat an earlier theme, upon what is actually at stake. If Mike's

'She jumped because a face appeared at the window'. The latter cites what Anscombe calls a mental cause (*Intention*, p. 16). Mental causes can be of voluntary as well as involuntary actions, so the voluntary/involuntary distinction will not on its own differentiate the mouse case from the face case. That there is no hard and fast distinction between reasons and (especially mental) causes in no way detracts from the general importance of the distinction; as, day and night, blue and green, etc. (cf. *Intention*, pp. 23–4—and see also Chapter 3, pp. 120–2).

discussion is with a policeman who has pulled him over for dangerous driving, then the policeman has no cause to try to persuade Mike of his foolishness. He can simply book him, give him a warning, or whatever the case merits. Mike's girlfriend, on the other hand, may well have reason to get Mike to see the error of his ways. What can she say? Various things, obviously; e.g. that last week he cut up another driver in exactly the same way—or that there was nothing dangerous in the BMW driver's man-oeuvre—or that they were having such a nice afternoon until he flew off the handle. But she must rely on Mike's having the sense to accept her reasoning, and it may be a part of the syndrome associated with his bad temper that he rejects criticisms of his angry actions.

What is wrong with Mike is his *character*. He has a bad character trait, i.e. a vice: namely, a bad temper (and possibly also an aggressive streak). His anger was intelligible, but it was excessive, for while nobody would criticize a loud 'Tut!' and no more, shouting and swearing go too far. The model of reasonable behaviour that applies most naturally here is Aristotle's. For an important class of cases, Aristotle saw vice as consisting in an excess or a defect, and virtue in achieving the right amount, e.g. of anger. This is his well-known Doctrine of the Mean. The 'right amount' is not meant to be a calculable quantity, and this is at least in part because (as we have seen) the 'thing measured' will not lie on a single dimension, but will instead be a syndrome—a bunch of deeds, words, expressive behaviours, and the like. We often see a given action as a manifestation of a certain syndrome, and as such, and together with attendant contextual factors, may judge it to be *prima facie* excessive or unreasonable. The latter term has application because of the possibility of asking 'Why did you do that?', and (we assume) getting no adequate answer. Our capacity to see the action in this light will be the sort of natural human reactive capacity discussed above—part of our 'attitude to a soul'—which is at bottom pre-rational.[31] The language-game of giving and demanding reasons rests upon it, not vice versa; and this accounts for one feature of ethical judgement to

---

[31] This term should not be interpreted in too chronological a fashion. The reactive capacities from a certain point develop *alongside* the (primarily linguistic) 'rational capacities', and although the form taken by the former capacities must be influenced by the development of the latter, they are nevertheless independent of them, something that is manifest in such things as a person's inability to say how he knows that another person is frightened or bored or whatever. And after all, many of the reactive capacities in question exist also in non-rational animals.

which Aristotle drew attention, namely that such judgement involves a sort of sensitivity to the particulars of a case that cannot be taught or justified by laying down rules, but which people develop as they acquire an experience of life. They are able to develop such ethical judgement for the same reason that they are able to develop common sense: because they are normal human beings. Ethical judgement and common sense are part of our second nature—but this second nature presupposes a (sufficiently) normal, non-defective first nature.

I said above that Mike's behaviour was not only intelligible, but natural, in the sense of showing a familiar side to human nature. Going to the aid of the wounded and dying is also natural in this sense. But wasn't I defending or justifying the latter by appeal to this very naturalness? So shouldn't I be defending the obnoxious Mike's actions on the same grounds? In answer to this query one can make use of what was pointed out in connection with helping vs. harming (pp. 12–15), *viz.* that the demand for reasons is a demand for reasons that normal human beings will in general be liable to accept. Accepting a reason as a good reason means acquiescing—it means dropping any cause for complaint or dissatisfaction as far as the matter in hand goes. And this is something that shows as much (if not more) in what you do as in what you say. Mike is showing the characteristics of a sort of person who makes himself a nuisance in certain definite ways, and the naturalness of those characteristics will not save them from our strictures, practical as well as verbal. How could it be otherwise?

Nevertheless, there is much more to this issue than these remarks suggest. This has to do, in part, with the complexity and cultural variability of the factors that determine what actions appear to fellow human beings as anti-social, as rocking the boat. Consider revenge. The urge to harm those who have harmed us, or those dear to us, is one of the most deeply ingrained in human nature, and it would be naïve to think that the idea of revenge has not had a crucial part to play in shaping human systems of punishment from ancient times to the present day. Of course one of the standard justifications for the state's taking on the task of punishing malefactors is that, by doing so, she takes that task *out of* the hands of vengeful citizens. The social benefits of this are undeniable, especially that of discouraging vendettas, or cycles of revenge. But this very justification of state punishment appears to trade on the fact that unless people can expect those who have harmed them to suffer for it, they will very often, if they physically can, seek revenge. And a statement like 'I killed him because he killed my daughter' is not only intelligible to us, not only natural-seeming—it undeniably elicits a basic sympathetic response. After all, the tribe, the village, the society, may feel that it is well rid of the person upon whom revenge has been wrought: as far as being anti-social goes, it is often the victim of revenge and not the perpetrator who stands most accused. So human beings have very often found 'Revenge!' to provide an excellent reason for action. Christianity teaches us to love our enemies and to forgive those who have wronged us, not seven times, but seventy times seven times; and this shows just how radical is its message. But this teaching may be like 'Give to the poor all that ye have'—a counsel not a precept.[32] We are surely being presented with an ideal, to achieve which is very fine, but failure to achieve which need not betoken badness of character. And indeed the mother who genuinely forgives her daughter's murderer is out of the ordinary. In so far as there are often only two psychological possibilities for a person, forgiveness and hatred, the one who hates will not necessarily be blamed for it, though she may well be pitied, since unquenchable hatred, like inconsolable grief, is a painful burden. It also has a tendency to poison a person's thoughts and feelings, and to be secretly nurtured: 'And I water'd it in fears, / Night & morning with my tears; / And I sunned it with smiles, / And with soft deceitful wiles.'[33] Which all goes to show why the Christian ideal might well be worth aiming at.

There seems, then, to be no *simple* answer to the question whether the desire for revenge is a good or a bad thing. It is probably both. And there will be other examples of human traits and impulses that pose a similar question. But to admit this is not to say of such traits and impulses that they are utterly divorced from reason. 'Because he killed my daughter' always gives an intelligible *reason* for hurting or harming another person; but sometimes it will be a good reason and sometimes it will not.

VII.

The idea that an emotion, being an emotion, is above rational criticism has various interconnected sources. There is the picture which I have already

---

[32] See Matthew 19:16-26. I am assuming that Jesus' words can be read as being addressed to everybody, and not just to the rich young man he spoke them to—a debatable assumption.
[33] From William Blake, 'A Poison Tree'.

mentioned, of emotions (and mental states generally) as quasi-sensations without cognitive content. There is the tendency to ascribe first-person authority to all psychological statements ('I ought to know what I feel/believe/want/enjoy . . .'). In addition, there is the individualism that is so often looked upon as one of the great achievements of the West, according to which everyone has a right to be what he chooses to be, this being embodied in a person's lifestyle, beliefs, and feelings, where the only constraint is Mill's: that we don't hurt other people. (Individualism will be discussed in Chapter 4.) If emotions are thought of as inner experiences, rather than as intrinsically tied to their manifestations in action, then they will in general be acquitted of the charge of hurting other people even before the case is heard.

There is a related way of thinking, perhaps above all associated with Romanticism, to the effect that the grander passions are a law unto themselves. 'All's fair in love and war' must have been quoted by many a self-serving Don Juan (as well as many a self-serving Machiavelli), and the ideal behind it can produce some curious behaviour—like Hans von Bülow's renunciation of his wife Cosima, a self-sacrifice on the altar of Richard Wagner's genius that achieved its apotheosis when von Bülow conducted the premiere of Wagner's opera about transcendental infidelity, *Tristan und Isolde*. The Romantic conception of the emotions did not go with a denial of their possible baleful effects; rather, it put the importance of life lived according to the passions above that of 'morality'. In these respects, it differs from the modern view of things which I mentioned a moment ago, despite being like it in putting (at least some of) the emotions above rational criticism.

For the Romantics, the emotion whose word was law was Love (or *eros*); for us, or many of us, it is perhaps Offence. There is a characteristic species of confusion associated with this concept. The confusion involves a sort of double-think: there is (a) the recognition that a person really can, in being offended, have just cause for complaint, on account of the *reasons* behind his taking offence—but on top of this there is (b) a denial of the requirement that taking offence itself be justified by reference to any reasons. Given (b), the only thing to point to as the ground of your complaint must simply be the painfulness of the emotion; and so the whole phenomenon is subsumed under a general utilitarian proscription on causing suffering. But even a little reflection leads one to see how taking offence can be unreasonable, and can on that account fail to provide any reason why another should alter his or her behaviour. (I might unreasonably take offence at not being addressed as 'Sir' by my neighbour's children.) Moreover, as with pride, there are conceptual constraints on what can count as offence. Someone who insists that he is *offended* by the actions of the government of a foreign country, e.g. its passing certain laws, is like someone insisting that he is proud of the sea, when what he feels is properly called awe (say). What the first person feels may properly be called anger or disgust, but not offence. Things are not necessarily any better if he calls the foreign government's actions 'offensive', for although he need not in that case claim to feel the offence himself, he must be able to say who could, and he must also justify calling it offence.

Both kinds of error are common, that of putting offence above rational criticism, and that of describing something as offensive when offence is the wrong concept to use. These errors are not mere mistakes, however, for they have a (typically unconscious) motivation: to confer on one's moral stance *both* an immunity from criticism *and* the flavour and seriousness of an accusation. But nothing can combine these two features. The language-game of accusation is one in which reasons and counter-reasons play an essential role. Without such reasons, all that you have is a kind of shout: 'Stop it!'

Alasdair MacIntyre discusses this kind of false consciousness within ethical debate in his book *After Virtue*, where he claims that emotivism—the theory that moral utterances are simply expressions of subjective non-rational preference—is in fact *true*, not of moral utterance as such, but of much if not all of the moral (or perhaps 'moral') discourse of today. More specifically, he writes that

Emotivism . . . turns out to be, as a cogent theory of use rather than a false theory of meaning, connected with one specific stage in moral development or decline, a stage which our own culture entered early in the present [i.e. twentieth] century.[34]

As often as not, the person who says, with that special *moral* emphasis, 'I am offended', or 'That is offensive', is just emoting. For MacIntyre, the really grave danger is that such a person, reflecting on his own and others' use of such utterances, comes to realize the nature of that use, and then concludes, 'It must be thus; I see now that morality is all just a matter of personal opinion, of how you—personally—*feel* . . . etc. etc.' And this has

---

[34] Alasdair MacIntyre, *After Virtue* (London: Duckworth, 1981), p. 17.

in fact come to pass on a grand scale, according to MacIntyre. As he puts it: 'Emotivism has become embodied in our culture.'[35]

Our Victorian ancestors regarded various expressions and various topics as unfit for polite company, and while they may often have gone too far in this, the nature of their reasons was perhaps not always as absurd as we now complacently like to think. And it's likely that whatever absurdity there was rarely approached the level of absurdity to be found in that *fear of words* which is now so often expressed by the term 'offensive'. There is a kind of superstition in the idea that a word should be imbued with an evil atmosphere—a word, which in itself is a mere sound or shape, and whose function is bestowed on it by us human beings, in virtue of our using it in certain ways. To be sure, as dictionaries tell us, it can be intrinsic to a word's (current) use that it is pejorative in force—as, 'git' or 'slimeball'. But when the *Guardian and Observer Style Guide* asserts that both 'cripple' and 'crippled' are 'offensive and outdated', adding the advice, 'do not use',[36] a familiar diagnosis presents itself: that of the ever elusive perfect euphemism.

The perfect euphemism, like the rainbow's end, draws us on in a futile quest, its image constantly retreating before us. For since what a euphemism names is some thing or phenomenon that is in some way unfortunate, or imperfect, or repulsive, or . . . which is why we wanted a euphemism in the first place—since it *is* thus, we keep finding that a euphemism, once lit upon, takes on the negative atmosphere of that which it names. For a settled euphemism quickly becomes an ordinary

---

[35] Ibid., p. 21. MacIntyre makes his point by distinguishing between (a theory of) use and (a theory of) meaning, and this aspect of his account does invite interrogation. For familiar reasons, it can't in general be true of an expression that most competent speakers misuse it. But the sort of 'use' of such terms as 'offensive' which MacIntyre has in mind is arguably not that which determines meaning. For more on this topic, see Teichmann, *The Philosophy of Elizabeth Anscombe* (Oxford: Oxford University Press, 2008), pp. 105–7.

[36] Source: www.guardian.co.uk/styleguide. The full extent of the *Guardian*'s worries is apparent from the Style Guide entry for *disabled people*: 'not "the disabled"/ Use positive language about disability, avoiding outdated terms that stereotype or stigmatise. Terms to avoid, with acceptable alternatives in brackets, include victim of, suffering from, afflicted by, crippled by (prefer person who has, person with); wheelchair-bound, in a wheelchair (uses a wheelchair); invalid (disabled person); mentally handicapped, backward, retarded, slow (person with learning difficulties); the disabled, the handicapped, the blind, the deaf (disabled people, blind people, deaf people); deaf and dumb (deaf and speech-impaired, hearing and speech-impaired).'—For what it is worth, I write as one fairly crippled by rheumatoid arthritis.

word for the thing in question—it no longer veils it with the cloak of another meaning or other associations. And so we set off again in search of a better euphemism. This story has been played out in numerous cases. 'Crippled' was once all right; so later on was 'invalid'; ditto 'handicapped'. Each in its turn becomes offensive, not to mention (significant that this is in itself pejorative) outdated. The human capacity for superstition when it comes to words, together with the special value assigned to *taking offence* which I have mentioned, plus a general impulse to puritanical arbiter-ship—all this goes to produce what might only be a favourite laughing-stock of *Guardian*-haters were it not for the fact that it is symptomatic of wider and deeper currents. None of this is to deny that changes for the better in prevalent attitudes to certain groups have often been attended by, and even assisted by, an increasing eschewal of various common terms for members of those groups; for vulgar prejudices are typically kept alive, among other things, by their characteristic modes of expression, and so weaning people off those modes of expression can help in weaning them off their prejudices. But there is still such a thing as a superstitious attitude to the very words themselves.

Superstitious attitudes to words are of especial interest in philosophy, and we will be coming back to them in Chapter 5. My present concern has been with current thinking on the subject of the emotion of offence, as good an illustration as any of how important it is to give due recognition to the actual place of emotions, feelings, and human responses—namely, within the space of reasons.

VIII.

I hope thus far to have made a case for the claim made at the start of this essay, that ethics is necessarily anthropocentric. This anthropocentrism derives in large part from the complicated interplay between the nature of reasons for action, on the one hand, and our natural conspecific impulses, on the other. In order to clear the ground so as to obtain an adequate view of this interplay it was necessary to dispose of a number of errors and myths, such as the myth of a higher rationality (or cosmic point of view), the conflation of reasons and causes, the picture of emotions and other mental states as experiences or processes, and the related picture of emotions as disconnected from reasons. Against these claims and illusions

I argued that practical rationality is tied to the purpose or purposes of a certain language-game; that the relative weight of reasons for action derives from the needs, proclivities, and impulses of human beings; that important among these impulses are emotions and reactions of a pre-rational nature, especially those which come into play in the interactions between people; that the pre-rational nature of these emotions and reactions does not preclude their connection with rationality, since the language-game of demanding and giving reasons is in large part built *upon* them; that emotions, like many other psychological states, can be seen as a species of syndromes; and that the connection of emotions and reactions with reasons and judgements is crucial both for moral philosophy and for ethical thought in general.

Needless to say, there are number of loose ends and avenues still to explore. One of these is the question of the ethical status of animals. I said earlier on that 'the ethical standing of animals will turn out to confirm, rather than undermine, an anthropocentric approach' (pp. 1–2). How is this possible?

A range of pre-rational and instinctive responses to one another constitute the source, I have argued, of our capacity to learn and use many psychological concepts. For a child to master the concept *anger* it must be able to see others as being angry in all sorts of different situations and in all sorts of different ways. This 'seeing' involves a syndrome of reactions on the part of a normal child, and comes about on the basis of perceptible cues whose variety, subtlety, and sheer range is extraordinary. If we are to talk of the evidence of the senses here, that 'evidence' is something a person can usually only frame in terms that are vague, and which themselves involve the psychological notion in question—as, 'He shouted'; 'But how did he shout?'; 'Well, *angrily*'.

Given that this is the nature of the relevant human responses, it is not surprising that those same responses can be 'triggered' by non-human animals. We often naturally see what an animal is doing as a case of anger, or of fear, or of sleepiness—and this means that we ourselves respond in the way that we respond to angry or fearful or sleepy human beings, or in a similar way. I use 'respond' in a sense that encompasses such things as anticipation (e.g. that the animal will attack), searching for a cause (e.g. looking to see what has made it afraid), and also, of course, the linguistic response of spontaneously *calling* it 'angry', 'fearful', 'sleepy', or whatever. Our capacity to see animals *as* this or that is very useful, for many animals are akin to us in many ways, ways that biology can elaborate upon, and which include syndromes of behaviours. If a savage beast is whimpering, limping, and starts to lick its back leg, we will feel wary of it and we will know not to touch that leg. And we will call this *pain*.

To say that our reactions here are instinctive is not to say that they cannot become more sophisticated with greater experience of animals of that sort. Something similar is true, after all, of the purely human case: for example, a child who sees her mother cry may not be old enough yet to realize that these are tears of joy, not of sorrow. But for her to learn this it isn't necessary for Mummy to *say*, 'It's all right, darling, I'm happy, not sad'—she may simply smile through her tears, give her child a hug, and so on. The child's responses gradually become more sophisticated and nuanced, and we may if we like (so long as we don't mislead ourselves) call this the child's acquiring a deeper knowledge of what joy is.[37] In the same sort of way, experience of the habits of elephants may bring with it a more sophisticated and nuanced set of responses to elephants and to how they behave, something manifested in a person's ability to anticipate, act appropriately, etc.

If these remarks are along the right lines, one would expect that our readiness to ascribe psychological states to animals would be roughly proportionate to how perceptibly similar they were to human beings, especially in those respects that are relevant to our ascription of such states to one another (i.e. in certain respects both of appearance and of behaviour).[38] For if our responses can be triggered by a range of phenomena, with paradigm human instances at the centre, then it would seem that the closer a phenomenon is to that centre, the stronger and more definite will be the response in question. This is an empirical hypothesis—and one that appears to be true. We do not doubt that a dog can feel pain; but a worm? A chimpanzee sharpening a small branch is evidently planning to use it (given what it later does with it); but can the same be said of a bird that makes a nest out of twigs? To say that the bird's actions are 'instinctive' is

---

[37] For an account that stresses the social setting of the child's developing knowledge of psychology, see J. Carpendale and C. Lewis: 'Constructing an Understanding of Mind: The Development of Children's Social Understanding within Social Interaction', *Behavioral and Brain Sciences* 27 (2004): 79–150.

[38] Cf. Wittgenstein, *Philosophical Investigations*, para. 281: 'only of a living human being and what resembles (behaves like) a living human being can one say: it has sensations; it sees; is blind; is deaf; is conscious or unconscious.'

simply to register our inclination to withhold from the bird the title of 'planner'. It does not *justify* that inclination. In some sense, what the chimp does is instinctive too, after all. There are of course differences between the two cases, to do with adaptability of behaviour, imitation of other members of one's species, and so on—but it is precisely these differences that show the chimp as more like us than the bird, and hence as more deserving of such descriptions as 'intelligent' and 'planning'.

People are often tempted to regard the doubt that one can feel in such cases as an epistemic sort of doubt. 'Is the worm feeling pain? There's just too little to go on—one could only really know by BEING the worm, which is impossible.' Thomas Nagel's famous reflections on what it is like to be a such-and-such (e.g. worm) is one product of this way of thinking.[39] It is radically mistaken, and would in fact lead us into a quite general worry about what other people, let alone animals, feel, and indeed whether they feel anything at all. Fortunately, however, the doubt that we do sometimes (not always) feel, as to whether certain sorts of creature can be angry/think/plan/etc., is not an epistemic sort of doubt. It is rather a hesitation as to whether to apply a certain concept, a hesitation *in* applying it. It is thus similar to such doubts as: (looking at a cat) Is that a smile? or (looking at a snail) Is that a face? How much information do you need before you decide whether a snail has a face or not? The question is rhetorical; *information* is clearly not what we lack here.

None of this involves a denial that additional empirical information can affect (i) how we respond to a particular animal's behaviour, and (ii) how we describe it. This was the gist of what I was saying three paragraphs back: responses, and therefore descriptions, can become more sophisticated with experience. Note that such sophistication is not a feature of a response taken all by itself: a response counts as more sophisticated when it is part of a more sophisticated syndrome of actual and possible responses. Now although it may sometimes be misleading to describe what experience brings as 'extra information', it need not be, especially in so far as a reflective person will likely be able to *tell* us more, e.g. about elephants, than she could have before she began living among them.

But there is one species of empirical information about animals whose status needs rather careful consideration, and that is information about

---

[39] See Nagel, 'What Is It Like to Be a Bat?', in *Mortal Questions* (Cambridge: Cambridge University Press, 1979), pp. 165–80.

brains, nervous systems, hormones, and the like. Our interest in just these bits of physiology derives in this context from the fact that it is brains, etc., that are responsible for those observable signs of psychological states which are criteria of those states, and without which no experimental results could exist that might tell us that brains etc., are indeed important.[40] Could it be that, against the background of extensive shared knowledge about neurophysiology, information concerning a type of creature's neurophysiology should come to impress us in a way comparable to the ways in which animal behaviour can impress us? Could our inclination to ascribe to an animal pain, or depression, or fraternal affection, be 'triggered' by beliefs about its brain in the way in which it can be triggered by seeing and hearing the animal itself? I think that on the whole it could not. If many of us do in fact privilege neurophysiological facts in discussions of such things as fox-hunting or trout-fishing, this would seem to be a sign of that scientism in our culture of which we have already had a glimpse in these pages. It is another matter to *bolster* claims about animal behaviour with neurophysiological claims, for although the latter put forward circumstantial evidence only (to use a legal notion), they do still put forward evidence, evidence that might really be useful if, for instance, the habits of the creatures in question weren't very well documented.

As I have said, the approach to psychology I have been adumbrating would encourage us to predict something that is in fact true, namely that our readiness to ascribe psychological states to animals is roughly proportionate to how perceptibly similar they are to human beings. I have also argued that many ethical responses and impulses, of the sort that generate reasons for action, belong among the responses that underpin our psychological concepts. Taken together, these claims would predict what also appears true, that our ethical concern for animals is roughly proportionate to how perceptibly similar they are to human beings. Ask a number of people to put chimps, dogs, dolphins, crows, spiders, and so on in a list, ranked according to ethical significance, and you will get pretty similar results—those variations that there are typically arising from the vagueness that unsurprisingly surrounds the notion of similarity which is here at issue. The phrase 'ethical significance' can be given (some) content by tying it, say, to the question, 'Which would show more cruelty...?', or 'Which

---

[40] A similar point was made above concerning the linguistic expression of mental states (pp. 29–30).

animal would it be best to use in laboratories, *ceteris paribus*?' But there are other dimensions of ethical significance than that of the capacity to suffer. One important question that can be asked is, 'What animals can people have relationships with?—or treat as pets?'

IX.

We can most naturally speak of a kind of action as morally wrong when we have some firm grasp of what *kind* of beings are involved. But there are some actions, like giving people names, that are part of the way we come to understand and indicate our recognition of *what* kind it is with which we are concerned. And "morally wrong" will often not fit our refusals to act in such a way, or in an opposed sort of way, as when Gradgrind calls a child 'Girl number twenty'. Doing her out of a name is not like doing her out of an inheritance to which she has a right and in which she has an interest. . . . Again, it is not 'morally wrong' to eat our pets; people who ate their pets would not have pets in the same sense of that term. . . . A pet is not something to eat, it is given a name, is let into our houses and may be spoken to in ways in which we do not normally speak to cows or squirrels. . . . Treating pets in these ways is not at all a matter of recognizing some *interest* which pets have in being so treated.

This passage comes from Cora Diamond's classic essay, 'Eating Meat and Eating People'.[41] In that essay, she looks among other things at two concepts that we use when talking about animals, that of *pet* and that of *fellow creature*. Each of these concepts requires us to be able to see an animal as akin to a human being, but not in the sorts of respects in which biology teaches us that we are akin to animals. 'Seeing . . . as akin to . . . ' involves the sorts of pre-rational responses which I have been talking about, and for that reason explanations or expressions of that in which a creature's fellowship to us consists will often involve uses of concepts, such as *companion*, or *enemy*, or *fellow mortal*, which can seem not wholly literal, and of which it is thus natural to look to poetry for paradigmatic instances—as Diamond does, citing Walter de la Mare's 'Titmouse', with its reference to a titmouse as a 'tiny son of life' (p. 328). The reason these uses of these concepts can seem non-literal is that their central and defining use is in connection with human beings. But we do not here have mere 'projection', of the sort that arguably occurs when we describe the sun's

---

[41] Cora Diamond, 'Eating Meat and Eating People', in *The Realistic Spirit* (Cambridge, MA: MIT Press, 1991), pp. 323–4.

warmth as beneficent, or the ocean as mighty. For the ways in which we interact with animals are themselves akin to the ways in which we interact with other people: an angry cow is dangerous just as an angry man can be, and our responses will often be very similar—as will our precautions, etc. After all, the cow, like the man, can run at us. Our responses to and precautions respecting the anger of a storm-tossed sea are different in kind, though of course in a *very* general way similarly motivated—in both cases, we usually desire not to be injured or killed.[42]

The fact that we can see other animals as akin to us, in many and varied ways, is what grounds our ethical attitudes towards them. There will be two sorts of objection to this claim: (a) it seems unfair on those unfortunate creatures who happen not to be as like us as, say, primates and higher mammals; (b) it seems to make everything subjective, since surely these 'responses' and 'seeings as' are hardly objective. The reader can probably predict what sort of response I would make to (a), in the light of what has already been argued in these pages. The alleged unfairness is connected with a mistaken picture of things like pain and suffering, such that a flea's pain is just as 'intrinsically bad', unit for unit, as a human being's, pain itself being a single currency. But pain is not a single currency. The idea that it is is connected with the thought that 'pain' is a label for a particular sort of simple inner state, a state that occurs in human beings, dogs, sparrows, probably fleas, and—who knows?—possibly computers. (See the as-yet-unwritten 'What Is It Like to Be a Laptop?')

Part of the answer to (b) will allude to the fact, already mentioned, that there are criteria for goodness and badness of reasons for action that derive from our (pre-rational) attitudes and responses to one another; these same

---

[42] We should not, in the nature of the case, expect a hard and fast line to exist between the extension to animals of a paradigmatically human concept and 'projection' (or 'anthropomorphism'). There will be borderline cases, of which the following may well be an example: 'Birds can sometimes be observed engaged at something that looks like definite 'practice'. The fine vocalist, Ffrangcon Davies (*The Singing of the Future*, 1905), describes an instance of an American robin which he noticed to be so engaged, day after day, in Central Park, New York. The bird gradually acquired the power to utter clearly the notes at which he was striving, and then it was easy for the observer to record his song in musical notation . . . '. (Percy Scholes, *The Oxford Companion to Music*, 10th edn, (Oxford: Oxford University Press, 1970): entry for *Bird Music*.) Here we have a concept, *practice*, that usefully exemplifies the actual breadth of the category I have been simply referring to as 'psychological'.—But *was* the robin practising? Perhaps those 'strivings' really did sound like nothing so much as strivings, and its clear utterance like the confident result of an achievement. In such a case, the experienced observer is in the best position to pass judgement.

attitudes and responses come into play in our dealings with animals, and along with them reasons for and against doing things to animals. Here is the desired objectivity, an objectivity that is qualified, not undermined, by the fact that there will borderline or indeterminate cases—just as it *can* be indeterminate whether a creature has a face.

However, a full answer to worries of the sort that is expressed by (b) will mention more than just this. People can see an animal as a companion, or as noble, or as practising its singing—but people can also see animals as 'stages in the production of a meat product, or as "very delicate pieces of machinery"'.[43] Who is to say which of these 'ways of seeing' is closer to, or further from, the truth? What indeed does truth amount to in this context?

Alternative 'ways of seeing' are connected with what Wittgenstein would have called alternative *pictures*. There is the picture of an animal as a fellow creature, and there is the quite different picture of an animal as a sophisticated machine. Wittgenstein is not *against* pictures; thus he writes:

What am I believing in when I believe that men have souls? What am I believing in, when I believe that this substance contains two carbon rings? In both cases there is a picture in the foreground, but the sense lies far in the background; that is, the application of the picture is not easy to survey . . . The picture is *there*; and I do not dispute its *correctness*. But *what* is its application? Think of the picture of blindness as a darkness in the soul or in the head of the blind man.[44]

At the same time it is one of the most characteristic of Wittgenstein's warnings that we should beware of being captive to a picture. A picture may force itself upon you, to the point where you have eyes only for it—a huge mental effort would be required to look at things in another way. And, as we have in the passage just quoted, the important thing above all for Wittgenstein is how the picture gets *applied*. A picture stands or falls by the application to which it is put, and one who wields a picture may be required to show us how it is applied, what its consequences are.

When Wittgenstein talked in this way, was he doing philosophy or psychology? The quick answer is 'Both'. Wittgenstein was surely right to think that much progress in philosophy is made if we not only detect error or confusion, but diagnose its source. For one thing, this enables those in error, or those tempted by erroneous thought, to cure or secure themselves.

[43] Diamond, 'Eating Meat', p. 330. Diamond is quoting a BBC programme about the use of animals in research.
[44] Ludwig Wittgenstein, *Philosophical Investigations*, paras 422, 424.

Where the source of error or confusion is not so much false premises as what might be called aspects of mindset, the task is certainly a psychological one. In ethics, this is particularly important. Being in the grip of a picture will have consequences that are not just intellectual, if the picture relates to human beings or to animals. Habits of thought whereby one thinks of some or all human beings or animals *as* this or *as* that are very seductive.

Turning back now to the purely human case, we find that history bears all this out. Hostility to a group of people often finds expression in talk of them as vermin, or as germs, as things, or as rubbish. Such pictures assist greatly when it comes to indoctrination and propaganda, but they also arise and spread under their own energy. Jonathan Glover in his book *Humanity* discusses this phenomenon, and quotes, among other things, various Nazi sources (including Hitler himself) assimilating the Jews to viruses, lice, maggots, subhuman monsters, etc. Glover remarks about such ways of thinking:

These stereotypes were images rather than literal beliefs. Hitler did not literally think Jews were viruses or maggots. (The question of whether he was mad would have been easier to answer if he had.) Such images and metaphors create a psychological aura or tone which once again may be at least as important as explicit beliefs which can be criticized as untrue.[45]

The Nazis are an extreme case. And seeing human beings as this or as that need not be connected with hostility or hatred, for it may be that you're inclined to see *all* human beings according to some stereotype, yourself included—not just some particular group of human beings. But if you are too seduced by your stereotypes, this will most likely affect your attitudes and responses to a variety of ethical questions.

Here are three characteristic sayings from Richard Dawkins, each of which I have taken from the website, www.world-of-dawkins.com, a website created and maintained not by Professor Dawkins, but with his blessing:

The argument of this book [*The Selfish Gene*] is that we, and all other animals, are machines created by our genes.

---

[45] Jonathan Glover, *Humanity: A Moral History of the Twentieth Century* (London: Pimlico, 2001), p. 339.

We are survival machines—robot vehicles blindly programmed to preserve the selfish molecules known as genes.

What are all of us but self-reproducing robots? We have been put together by our genes and what we do is roam the world looking for a way to sustain ourselves and ultimately produce another robot—a child.

Behind such thoughts there is a picture—the picture of human beings and other animals as machines or robots. What can be said about such a picture?

Descartes regarded the human body as essentially a machine. What made people special, for Descartes, was their having a mind or soul—and the mind was something of which physical science could tell us nothing. For those of a scientistic bent, but whose intellectual roots are in a world with a dualistic view of human beings of the sort typified by Descartes, the price to be paid is simple: reject the mind or soul. Reject, that is, what might be regarded as rendering human beings special, or unique. Exorcise the ghost in the machine.

Giving up dualism can be a bit like giving up religious belief. Someone may jettison a belief in God while being unable to jettison the feeling that life could only have a meaning, or morality have force, if God *did* exist. That person would then, like a character from Dostoyevsky, be in danger of plunging into nihilism or amoralism. Likewise, a person may jettison—or consciously reject—a belief in a Cartesian soul, while being unable to jettison the feeling that only a Cartesian soul could make human beings special, or could justify the centrality of human beings in almost all ethical outlooks. To compare a human being to a machine, for such a person, is a negative move.[46] It is not to imbue the human being with some quality—resilience, for example, or efficiency; it is to deny something. 'But isn't it simply to deny the truth of Cartesian dualism?' it may be asked. No—for what we have here, to repeat, is not so much a philosophical position as a picture, a picture informed by attitudes, wishes, blindnesses, as much as by explicit beliefs. Moreover, many people of a scientistic bent manifest dualistic presuppositions and inclinations in their claims, as we have already

---

[46] Cf. Wittgenstein, *Philosophical Investigations* para. 420: 'Seeing a living human being as an automaton is analogous to seeing one figure as a limiting case or variant of another; the cross-pieces of a window as a swastika, for example.' Someone might ask, 'What is a sash window but a wooden swastika with some glass panels and wooden inserts?'

had occasion to note (pp. 29–30). Given these no doubt unconscious dualistic urges, the denial of the Cartesian soul which I am talking about is clearly not so much a worked out position as a process in the formation of a picture. What is involved in this picture?

For a scientist, or someone in awe of science, there can be a temptation to think that science has all the answers. But there is another temptation, which exists alongside the first: the temptation to think that we should somehow get science to guide our political and ethical decisions, and that we should be at pains to expunge 'unscientific' ideas from our political and ethical thinking. If we could only treat data about human beings as being just like any other scientific data, think what problems we could solve!— think what progress could be made! To act on the data in the required scientific and impartial manner would, of course, involve treating human beings themselves as manipulable things—for that is how science does *get* applied: through calculation, manipulation, experimentation. And if we are to treat human beings in this way, we will need to be able to see them in a certain way. A tendency naturally evolves, of thinking of human beings as machines. Machines can be improved or tampered with; models can be discontinued.

What sorts of 'manipulations of human beings' are at issue here? Perhaps the question should be put to those in the grip of the picture, for, as Wittgenstein said, what we need to know is how the picture is meant to be applied, and that is really the job of those wielding it. A few have already been indicating what applications they have in mind. The general tendency here is predictable: a utilitarian framework with some rhetoric about not letting our emotions stand in the way of progress.

But we should probably not be too alarmed by all this. It is unlikely that the social Darwinism of today will resemble the social Darwinism of a hundred years ago, for one thing. The latter embraced hierarchical notions of race, a glorification of struggle, and other ideas, all of which found particularly fertile soil in the political atmosphere of the time. Ambitions of conquest and dominion, such as those of Kaiser Bill's Germany, fed eagerly off theories of natural selection through violent struggle. And xenophobic forms of nationalism were naturally drawn to theories of racial superiority and inferiority. By contrast, modern social Darwinists have not been brought up in a society with ambitions of conquest or characterized by xenophobic nationalism. In fact, the culture in which such people have been brought up is on the whole opposed to such things, being by and large liberal, tolerant, officially peaceable, etc. Hence it is no surprise to find that Peter Singer actually regards evolutionary biology as giving a sound basis for left-liberal political views of the kind he grew up with—see his *A Darwinian Left*[47] (with Dawkins' puff on the back).

One feature of the earlier social Darwinism does, however, live on in the modern variety, namely the tendency to put some human beings beyond the moral pale, or at any rate very near its periphery, such as the infants and Alzheimer's patients to which Bernard Williams refers in 'The Human Prejudice' (p. 18, above). There is the overarching question, 'From the point of view of total happiness/pleasure/welfare . . . (delete as applicable), *what kinds of people should there be?*' And if you treat that question as a practical question, you will find yourself naturally drawn to issues of ways and means. Abortion, infanticide, euthanasia, and eugenics (now rebranded 'enhancement') are topics in which modern utilitarians have shown a level of interest that distinguishes them from classical utilitarians like Bentham and Mill, whose projects for social reform related more to such things as education, prisons, and voting. These are sociological remarks; but the sociology of philosophy is not a sideshow only, being for philosophers one way of following the Delphic oracle's ancient advice, 'Know thyself'.

X.

The purpose of the last section was to emphasize the philosophical and ethical importance of the Wittgensteinian notion of a picture. What kind of status we see human beings as having is something inevitably expressed and embodied in a picture, or pictures, of the human being. My own talk of the human being as standing at the centre of our ethical world is to some extent such a picture. What is crucial is that the pictures we operate with be detailed and non-simplistic, in the sort of way that requires a proper use of one's observational and imaginative powers, as distinct from one's theory-building powers. All this goes as well, *mutatis mutandis*, for what we say and think about non-human animals.

---

[47] Peter Singer, *A Darwinian Left: Politics, Evolution and Co-operation* (New Haven: Yale University Press, 1999).

One of the things that most separates human beings from other animals is the human capacity for responsible action. Animals do things—but human beings have free agency. This fact derives especially from our capacity to have reasons, good or bad, for what we do. We have so far been looking at the foundational aspects of this capacity. It is time to turn to the capacity's expression in practical deliberation and the adoption of ends and means.

2

Human Agency

It is possible to lead a life never wondering or questioning what one's ends are, or whether they are worth pursuing. A person can come out of school, get a job, make money, raise a family, pursue various recreations, and never (or hardly ever) ask himself, 'Why am I doing this?' If that question did occur or get put to him, he might simply say something that amounted to, 'Because everyone else does'—or he might, e.g. when it came to his recreations, say, 'I enjoy them'. And why *not* take such an approach to life, after all?

The impulse to be like other people—doing as others do, saying as others say, feeling as others feel—is an impulse with deep roots. One can even see the propensity to imitate others as a prerequisite for learning and for socialization; what, for instance, is coming to master a language if not being trained to be in step with those around you, a process reliant on the child's tendency to fall into step? And with a practice so basic and universal as language-use there is no room for the question, 'Why go in for it?' But that question does have application to many other human practices and ways of going on. Consider the well-known snowball effect that can be seen in such phenomena as the runaway success of a new fashion, or of a new film. People will go to see a film because people are going to see it ('Everybody's talking about it')—not because they know from past experience that if lots of people have enjoyed it they will, but solely because doing what the mass of people do brings inclusion rather than exclusion, normality rather than oddity, society rather than self-reliance.[1] These

---

[1]   Many idioms embody and support the impulse to be like others. A notable instance is the use of the opinion-forming passive, as in 'So-and-so has been described as the most promising

things may sometimes be good things, but they may not, for a group can act stupidly even by its own lights.

The other sort of response I imagined, 'Because I enjoy it', is also worth a moment's consideration. The response would most naturally be given in connection with one's recreations, as I said, rather than in connection with such a thing as raising a family; but reductive philosophizing can notoriously lead to the view that enjoyment, or pleasure, is the ultimate goal of *any* rational activity. A number of ideas are involved in this view. One of these is that pleasure is intrinsically good from the agent's point of view, since 'Why do you want what's pleasant?' is a futile question. There is indeed something futile about such an enquiry, but, as we shall see in Chapter 3, the source of this fact is not any 'intrinsic goodness' (even 'subjective' goodness) in pleasure. Another question, '*How* is this activity pleasant?', lacks the pointlessness of 'Why do you want what's pleasant?'—and an examination of the kinds of answer that can be given to it shows that pleasure and enjoyment lie within the space of reasons, just as emotion does in ways that were discussed in the last chapter. For this reason, 'I enjoy it' cannot be the last word on a subject, any more than can 'Other people do it'.

The temptation to do what other people are doing, and the temptation to be content with doing what is pleasant, are coupled, in a reflective person, with the recognition (probably borne out by experience) that 'Other people do it' and 'I enjoy it' do not as such suffice as reasons for doing what one does. Hence the reflective person will be drawn to wondering what reasons for doing things *do* count as sufficient, or at least as stable and weighty reasons. The examined life is one where not only a person's actual ends are examined by him, but also the criteria for deciding among actual and possible ends—seeing some as well-grounded, others as ill-grounded. The overall enquiry concerns how to live, what sort of life to pursue. This of course is the subject-matter of ethics; and since it is a human being asking the questions, those questions concern how to lead a good *human* life. The range of possible answers will thus be constrained by facts about what it is to be a human being.

young playwright to appear in this country in the last twenty years'. Described by whom? It doesn't matter: the view is out there, it's getting quoted. Enough reason to feel a certain respect for it, if not to adopt it as one's own.

I.

So: what is a human being?

'Human being' can be taken as the name of a species of animal, equivalent to *Homo sapiens*. But our present concerns are surely not those of a biologist; ethics is not biology. Does that mean that we need some quite other concept to do justice to our ethical thought, a concept (say) that involves ideas like rationality, consciousness, and desire? Some philosophers have thought so, and have come forward with a term intended to express such a concept, namely the term 'person'. The alleged moral priority of personhood over humanity has been defended by means of anti-speciesist arguments and appeals of the sort that were criticized in the previous chapter. But although those arguments and appeals fail, there does seem to be a problem in putting a strictly biological notion centre stage.

The solution to this difficulty is to be found in those instinctive pre-rational reactions to one another that I have argued lie at the root of our psychological as well as our ethical concept-schemes. A child learns concepts like anger and amusement because she is capable of responding to, and thus of distinguishing, the relevant syndromes of behaviour. The unit of such behaviour is the fellow human being, and of course the child is capable of responding to, and thus of distinguishing, fellow human beings. She does not 'build up' the concept of a human being from more primitive concepts like arm, leg, face, voice, mobility. Nor does a dog need to build up its concept of a fellow dog, or (if talk of concepts seems out of place) construct its capacity to respond intelligently to other dogs, out of more primitive recognitional capacities: from the day it is born, a dog has a quite special repertoire of attitudes and behaviours towards other dogs. The concept which the human child learns may be called the concept of a 'somebody'. 'Somebody is at the door'; 'I wish somebody would help me'—it is in such statements that we see the ethically central concept in play. The word 'person' does perfectly well here, too, as used and explicated by P. F. Strawson, who correctly argued for the primitiveness of this concept, a primitiveness inimical to any conceptual analysis.[2]

Given this sort of origin for the concept of a person, or of a somebody, it is clear that *person* and *Homo sapiens* are co-extensive concepts. For it is a human child's capacity to respond differentially to other human

---

[2] P. F. Strawson, *Individuals* (London: Anchor, 1959), ch. 3.

beings (members of the species *Homo sapiens*) that enables her to learn and use the concept 'person'. And whatever philosophers would like to think, the ordinary English terms 'person' and 'human being' are in fact interchangeable, at any rate interchangeable *salva veritate*—for, as one would expect, the two terms differ in their connotations. (Moreover, in law, 'person' has a quite different sense, covering corporations as well as people.)

'What sort of life should I lead?' and 'What sort of person should I be?' are thus closely related questions. The obvious preliminary answers to both involve the notion of what's good: 'Lead a good life', 'Be a good person'. A good life here means a good life for a human being, while a good person just *is* a good human being. What does this term 'good' mean? A potted history of twentieth-century philosophical accounts of the term might go as follows.

Good things obviously come in all shapes and sizes. You can have good pens, good footballers, good ways of cleaning a window, good paintings; foodstuffs and exercise can be good for you; someone can be good at lying, good at chess, and good at making a fool of himself. The same goes of course for bad things. It almost seems as if there is nothing in common between all these things, the set of which looks to be open-ended—unless it is just *goodness* that they all share! If there is such a property, it is evidently not perceptible, since there is nothing perceptible common to all the items on our list of good things. A few more steps and we are in the company of G. E. Moore, who concluded that goodness must be a simple, non-natural (roughly, non-perceptible) property, known to us by the mysterious faculty of 'intuition'. Moore's account was rightly regarded as obscurantist by philosophers who came after him; their attempt to solve the problem of the open-ended diversity of good things consisted in turning the gaze away from the things and into one's own mind, where, following Hume, they claimed to find a certain sentiment or emotion, produced by all those various things. To call a pen good was to express, in connection with the pen, a certain sentiment, and perhaps to 'project' that sentiment onto the pen. Which sentiment? Well, pleasure, approbation, something like that. Emotions, however, as was argued in Chapter 1, are not sensations or quasi-sensations, produced in us by perception or contemplation of outer or inner objects—they have a cognitive aspect. What could the cognitive aspect of approval and disapproval be, those sentiments which are apparently central in ethical cases? The answer appears to be that these emotions involve the belief that something is somehow good, or bad. But for an emotivist or subjectivist philosophy, this observation is fatal, since for such a philosophy it implies a vicious circle: something is good because it evokes approbation, while approbation involves the idea that it is good.

This is a potted history, and there is much more that could be said about (and in criticism of) both intuitionism and emotivism/subjectivism. This work has already been carried out with much thoroughness by other philosophers, such as Philippa Foot and Alasdair MacIntyre, to name but two. A potted history of twentieth-century moral philosophy might continue with the work of these and other examples of philosophers who have given prominence to notions like character, virtue, and human nature. Such philosophers situate themselves in a tradition going back to Aristotle, in Book 1 of whose *Nicomachean Ethics* we find the remark that 'good appears to be one thing in one pursuit or art and another in another: it is different in medicine from what it is in strategy, and so on with the rest of the arts'.[3] Here we see the germ of an idea which seems capable of explaining the huge diversity of good things, by reference to the diversity of the things themselves. Peter Geach spells this idea out in the article 'Good and Evil',[4] where he argues that 'good' is what he calls an attributive, as opposed to predicative, adjective. This means we have to take it together with the noun or phrase that follows, or goes with, it—as, 'good *footballer*', 'good *at lying*', etc. (Sometimes the word or phrase will be understood, rather than explicitly stated: this is a matter of context.) A good footballer is someone with those features that enable one to play football well, which are different from those that enable a pen to write well, and different from the features that make Vitamin C requisite for human health. The features *constituting* the goodness of a thing thus vary enormously, according to the description under which a thing is given. Hence one and the same thing or person can be both good and bad, e.g. a good footballer who is a bad cook. A noun following 'good' will typically involve the idea of a function, or role, or job, or purpose; a verbal phrase, such as 'at lying', that follows 'good' will typically involve the idea of some activity which itself has a goal or purpose; while 'good for' conveys conduciveness, either to some goal (as, 'Pep talks are good for troop morale') or to the flourishing or maintenance in good order of an organ, organism, machine, etc.

---

[3] Aristotle, *Nicomachean Ethics*, trans. H. Rackham (Cambridge, MA: Harvard University Press, 1975), I.vii.1.

[4] In *Theories of Ethics*, ed. P. R. Foot (Oxford: Oxford University Press, 1967), pp. 64–73.

This account gives a natural explanation of the open-ended diversity of good things. It also shows why e.g. 'A blunt knife is not a good knife' is straightforwardly and unmysteriously true—not a matter of 'intuition' nor yet a matter of subjective preference, though preference comes into the picture, in so far as you will usually prefer a good knife to a bad one when choosing a knife, since you generally want to use a knife for what knives are for, namely cutting. None of this has been seriously debated. What is debated is whether 'good' can be regarded as an attributive adjective as it occurs in *ethical* contexts, and in particular as it occurs in the phrases 'good person' and 'good human being'. I have argued that for all intents and purposes 'person' and 'human being' are equivalent terms; if correct, this means that 'good person' and 'good human being' are *prima facie* equivalent phrases. I will therefore focus on the second.

An eye has a function: seeing; teeth have functions: chewing and ripping; bodily processes such as pupil-dilation have functions. It is natural to see many or most of the various bodily organs and processes as working towards the health and thriving of the creature—though of course that is not always the case. (The function of sperm-production isn't to do with the condition of the male animal itself.) But for this very reason it can seem mistaken to attribute a function to the animal itself, unless one is using the term 'function' in a different way from how it is used in relation to organs and processes; for an animal does not, on the face of it, stand to some other thing as an organ stands to the animal of which it is a part. But if you cannot properly speak of a human being, *qua* human being, having a function, how can the 'good' in 'good human being' be read as the sort of attributive adjective which is found in 'good pen' or 'good teeth'?

It does sound odd to attribute a function to human beings. But we should not be distracted too much by this particular word, as Anscombe argues in the following passage:

It is a curiosity that Aristotle's 'ergon' in the first book of the *Nicomachean Ethics* is regularly and in each application of it translated 'function'. He enquires how, say, the eye can have a function (here the translation is reasonable) and the man whose eye it is, not.[5] Students regularly reject the idea of a human being *qua* human having a *function*. But Aristotle's argument is a good one: if the whole does not have something, or things, it does (the proper meaning of 'ergon'), how can some integral part of it have a function *in* it? We may or may not arrive at the notion of

---

[5]   Aristotle, *Nicomachean Ethics*, I.vii.11–12.

some end that humans are to reach if possible, but it is beyond dispute that there are things it is human to do, and especially that there are ways of conducting their lives (well or badly) that are specifically human.[6]

Legs are for walking and running, i.e. for moving around, across a variety of terrains and at a variety of speeds. And this requires that moving around in these ways is one of the 'things it is human to do'. The extraordinary range of subtly different noises producible by the human voice, mouth, and tongue and distinguishable by human hearing points towards another thing it is human to do—namely, speak a language. These two activities, moving around and speaking, are good examples of things we 'just do', in the sense that they do not themselves have specific biological goals, unlike eating—another 'thing it is human to do', whose biological goal is nourishment. You could say that walking and talking each has a plethora of goals, which is true if it means a plethora of *possible* goals. There are uncountably many things achievable by means of speech, and the list of them is open-ended. Moreover, the possible goals of speech cannot be simply called 'biological goals', since many will be goals aimed at by the (at once socially embedded and idiosyncratic) human being, such as that of buying a newspaper. This fact will not, however, enable us to delineate some finite subset of the goals of speech, the truly 'biological'—on the contrary, either talk of any biological goals of speech should be dropped, or we should allow the categories of the biological and of the humanly intended to be inextricably entangled.

The open-endedness of the set of things achievable through speech, and their part biological, part non-biological nature, make it unclear whether properly functioning speech organs can be said to contribute to one's good *health*. A normal level of mobility, on the other hand, does perhaps strike us as a matter of health; though it is obvious that the boundary between physical unfitness and disease or disability is not a sharp one. But for our purposes it is another concept that needs attention, one related to, but differing from, that of health—and that is the concept of *flourishing*, or *thriving*. And it is clear that to be lame or dumb is to suffer an obstacle, or

---

[6] G. E. M. Anscombe, 'Sin: The McGivney Lectures', in *Faith in a Hard Ground: Essays on Religion, Philosophy and Ethics*, eds M. Geach and L. Gormally (Exeter: Imprint Academic, 2008), p. 122.

hindrance, to full human flourishing, despite the fact that human beings have the sort of intelligence which enables them to overcome such obstacles, often completely.

What is the relationship between such human activities as walking and talking, on the one hand, and human flourishing, on the other? Obviously, a goal had by someone who is walking need not be a goal conducive to human flourishing, but walking itself constitutes a linchpin of human flourishing, largely because to harm or stunt a person's mobility is to cut off or render difficult of attainment many possible goals for that person, including biologically determined ones. But these various goals do not have a primacy over walking itself. Precisely because walking is one of those 'things it is human to do', and is in this way an integral part of human life—part of what Wittgenstein calls our form of life—precisely because of this, facts about walking feed into our concept of human flourishing. Human flourishing is not *produced* by normal, natural, and other human activities—it is *constituted* by them. The thought is an Aristotelian one; and Aristotle would have added that the 'other human activities' include ethically virtuous ones, like keeping your promises.

The most universal human practices and institutions aim at the maintenance, protection, and enhancement of things required for human flourishing, many of these being, or being defined in terms of, 'things it is human to do'. And many of our classifications of human behaviour show how we take such things as providing *standards* of various sorts. A sentence or two after the previously quoted passage, Anscombe goes on:

Suppose there were 'people seeds' blowing about all the time. Suppose anyone killed would come to life again after a month if kept suitably—but unless they did they became literally rooted in the ground like trees. Suppose everyone changed to the opposite sex at the age of about thirty. There would be different rules of behaviour; moral virtues and vices would involve different actions from what they involve in our lives as they are.

Something brought out by this passage is that the concept of a good human being will be complex in a way in which the concept of a healthy human being is not: for the constraints upon the former concept that derive from human nature do so in part via such 'artificial' notions as that of a rule of behaviour. This is because the concept of a good human being has to do with human action, and specifically human action within society. (But remember that it is part of our *nature* to live together in societies.)

This point is closely related to the point that ethics is concerned with the question, 'How shall I live?' You can't ask, 'What level of blood sugar shall I have?', unless this means 'What shall I *do* to achieve the optimum level of blood sugar?' Whether someone is healthy depends constitutively upon such things as her blood sugar level; it does not depend *constitutively* upon what actions she takes, not even upon those actions that are directed to improving or maintaining her blood sugar level. Facts about health are a *guide* to action. Whether somebody flourishes, on the other hand, does in large part depend constitutively on how she behaves. Hence it is true that the content of 'good human being' is not a simple function of the constituent concept, 'human being', in contrast to what can be said about such pairs as 'good barometer' and 'barometer'; and the reason for this is that to be a good human being is in particular to be good *qua* human agent.

II.

As Anscombe famously argued, intentional actions are 'the actions to which a certain sense of the question "Why?" is given application'.[7] The relevant sense is distinct from that sense of 'Why?' which asks after the efficient cause of an occurrence, as, 'Why is your hand trembling?' (see Chapter 1, pp. 6–8). This is connected with the fact that responsibility is paradigmatically associated with the reasons for one's actions, not with their causes: thus (i) criticism of an action typically amounts to criticism of the reasons for which it was done, or of an inadequate taking into account of reasons for and against it; and (ii) the things a person can say to show that the question 'Why?' doesn't have application are also things they can say by way of (defeasible) exculpation: especially 'I didn't know I was doing that' (e.g. disturbing the neighbours), but also, on occasion, 'I knew I was doing that, but only because I *observed* that I was' (e.g. making a squeaking noise with my shoes).[8]

A good human being, as we have said, is good *qua* human agent. This will evidently involve being the sort of person who can give good reasons for her actions, and who reasons well in the domain of action, i.e. the sort

---

[7] G. E. M. Anscombe, *Intention*, 2nd edn (Oxford: Blackwell, 1963), sec. 5, p. 9.
[8] Cf. *Intention*, pp. 11, 14.

of person who can happily accept responsibility for her actions. But what is it to reason well in the domain of action? Is it the same as, or analogous to, or wholly distinct from, reasoning well in the domain of judgement? What, in short, is the relationship between practical reason and theoretical reason? A comparison of the two species of reasoning casts light on both; and it also shows that there is an important sense in which the justification of one's actions rests as much upon what one believes to be the case as does the justification of one's beliefs. The importance for our enquiry of the notion of *truth* is thus established.

Let us begin with an example of practical reasoning:

Guinness is good for pregnant women.
The Half Moon serves Guinness.
I'm a pregnant woman.

Aristotle thought that the conclusion of a bit of practical reasoning was an action, such as setting off for the Half Moon. I will however insert as conclusion a statement of intention:

(C) So I'll go to the Half Moon.

Does this conclusion follow from the given premises? Well, it all depends on what the person wants—the person doing the reasoning, that is. If she wants to drink what's good for her, she might well draw the conclusion; otherwise not. In fact, even if she wants to drink what's good for her she need not draw the conclusion. For there may be something else available that's as good for her, Adnam's Ale, for example; or it may be that Guinness is also served at the Angel and Greyhound. And she might decide to go there instead.

This last fact doesn't show that 'anything goes' when it comes to practical reasoning, which would mean after all that there was no such thing as practical reasoning. Without additional premises, the conclusion 'So I'll smoke a cigar' doesn't follow, for instance. But it is certainly true that practical arguments may well not *necessitate* their conclusions; roughly speaking, this is because a practical argument is very often the mirror image of a corresponding theoretical argument.[9] With this in mind, we can return to the question whether (C) follows from the premises, meaning

---

[9] Cf. A. Kenny, 'Practical Inference', *Analysis* 26(3) (1966): 65–73; R. Teichmann, *The Philosophy of Elizabeth Anscombe* (Oxford: Oxford University Press, 2008), pp. 55–6.

by that the question whether the premises permit, or justify, one's drawing (C) as a conclusion. They do, but only if the person wants to drink what's good for her. And this might lead us to insert an additional premise, if we want to get the conclusion to follow properly, namely 'I want to drink what's good for me'. But such an additional premise cannot be needed, since (for one thing) it wouldn't produce an argument any more powerful. For the agent may not, as they say, identify with the want mentioned. Let us insert 'I want to drink what's good for me' among the premises of the above argument; still, the woman may now conclude 'So I'll steer clear of the Half Moon'—if, for example, she is a sort of Manichean for whom the desire for physical nourishment counts as a spiritual defect. A premise, after all, expresses a proposition or belief, true or false, and so 'I want to drink what's good for me', if it is to function as a premise, will only express a belief the agent has about herself. And, borrowing from Hume, we might say that a set of beliefs won't yield a practical conclusion without benefit of an active want. If a proposition about what you want figures among your premises—if, that is, one of your reasons for acting in a certain way relates to the fact that you want something—then that shows that, for you, the want in question is just one of the facts of the case. This is the state of affairs that obtains when a person doesn't 'identify with' one of her wants.

So if the active want is not to be found among the premises, where is it?—and how is it operating? That the woman draws (C) as a conclusion *shows* that she wants to drink what's good for her, as Anscombe puts it.[10] Her drawing that conclusion is a criterion of her wanting to drink what's good for her. And her setting off in the direction of the Half Moon, we can add, is a criterion of her having drawn that conclusion. This explains the attractiveness of saying that an action is the conclusion of a practical

[10] G. E. M. Anscombe, 'Practical Inference' in *Human Life, Action and Ethics*, eds M. Geach and L. Gormally (Exeter: Imprint Academic, 2005), pp. 115–16. Throughout the present argument I am taking a premise of an argument to express a proposition, true or false; what if we were to construe 'I want X' as some sort of *avowal* of a want, as opposed to *report* of a want, and were then to characterize a practical syllogism as one that contains some such statement as premise? In so far as the alleged effect of doing so would be that we had a premise with 'conative' rather than 'cognitive' force, the proposal would be similar to Kenny's, of having *fiats* as conative premises (as: 'Let me be in London by 7 p.m.!'). Maybe practical *deliberation* can indeed be represented using *fiats* for premises, in so far as deliberation involves starting with some definite aim or aims. But it remains true that a person's adopting an aim *as* his aim is shown in what he does, on the basis of such-and-such factual premises. See Kenny, 'Practical Inference'.

argument, which would be all right (perhaps) if we could include among actions mere attempts: for trying to get to the Half Moon is as much a criterion of having concluded 'So I'll go to the Half Moon' as is successfully getting there.

These remarks show in what sense it is true that *it all depends what you want* whether you draw some practical conclusion from a given set of beliefs. And this idea has had a crucial role to play in many arguments for ethical subjectivism, and for attacks on ethical naturalism. No mere set of facts about the world, it is declared, can rationally compel, nor even rationally justify, acting one way rather than another. For no set of beliefs can on its own yield a practical conclusion.

Here is another argument:

If there were no weapons of mass destruction, the war in Iraq was unjustified.
There were no weapons of mass destruction.
So the war in Iraq was unjustified.

This, surely, is as watertight as they come. A rational person who accepts the premises just has to accept the conclusion. It doesn't depend on what else he happens to want or believe whether he should accept it.

But doesn't it? Lewis Carroll's tortoise[11] would argue that an additional premise was needed, namely:

(T) IF both (if there were no WMDs, the war in Iraq was unjustified) and (there were no WMDs), THEN the war in Iraq was unjustified.

After all, if (T) weren't true, the conclusion wouldn't follow. But of course adding this premise doesn't in fact make the argument any more powerful, as the hapless Achilles found. For if we have to insert (T), then by the same token we have to insert another (extremely long) premise:

(T*) IF (T) and (if there were no WMDs, the war in Iraq was unjustified) and (there were no WMDs), THEN the war in Iraq was unjustified

—and another, and another. It follows that we don't after all need (T) as a premise. But clearly the conditional in question is operating *somehow*; so where is it, if not among the premises?—and how is it operating?

[11] See Lewis Carroll, 'What the Tortoise Said to Achilles,' *Mind* 4(14) (April 1895), 278–80.

It is operating as a rule of inference—*modus ponens*, to be precise. And just as a want shouldn't be recast as a proposition about a want, so a rule of inference shouldn't be recast as a proposition of logic. Someone who learns the rule of *modus ponens* does not learn the truth of some proposition, but rather learns *to* infer 'Q' from the premises 'P' and 'If P, then Q' (for any 'P' and 'Q'). All this shows in what sense it is true that it all depends on what rules of inference you go by whether you draw any given theoretical conclusion from a set of beliefs. Subjectivism in logic, however, looks a bit of a non-starter. So how is logic different from ethics?

The natural reply is that a person must abide by *modus ponens* and similar rules of inference to count as rational at all, and nothing analogous goes for a person's wants. Now a proposed rule of logical inference needn't as such be above criticism or justification. We see this from the case of Arthur Prior's imaginary connective 'tonk', which has the following introduction and elimination rules[12]:

From P, infer P tonk Q
From P tonk Q, infer Q

Use of 'tonk' allows one to infer anything from anything, so the inference rules by which it is defined must be disallowed. It may even be argued that the so-called definition of 'tonk' doesn't really define anything: incoherent rules aren't really rules. This would allow one to say after all that genuine rules of inference are above criticism or justification, since apparent counter-examples don't even count as rules of inference. Naturally, human beings can argue fallaciously and commit logical blunders, and even do so fairly frequently; but they can't adopt illogical modes of reasoning. (An illogical thought isn't really a thought—cf. Wittgenstein, *Tractatus* 3.03.) If rules of logical inference are compulsory in this sense, then subjectivism about logic appears untenable. In fact, things are not quite so simple, as we shall see later; but let us first consider yet another argument:

---

[12] A. N. Prior, 'The Runabout Inference Ticket', in *Analysis* 21, 1960, 38–9. Introduction and elimination rules are a standard way of defining the logical connectives, 'and', or', 'if... then', and so on. Prior's paper is intended to show that there is more to the meaning of a logical connective than its definition by such rules; but it can as well be taken as showing that there are limits on what can *count* as proper introduction and elimination rules.

These things are remarkably like animal bones, only too big for any known animal.

Nobody's ever manufactured such objects before, as far as we know.

So once upon a time there lived animals huger than any now living.

Just as neither 'I want what's good for me' nor *modus ponens* needs to be inserted into an argument as premise, so this latest argument needn't be eked out by the addition of some such premise as 'Nature is uniform'. Induction, like deduction, consists of modes of inferring conclusions from premises: conclusions about unobserved matters from premises about observed matters. That you draw the above conclusion from the two premises *shows* that you reason inductively in a certain way. The question arises: is there room for a sort of subjectivism about induction? Couldn't it be said that it all depends on what canons of inductive inference you go by whether you draw a given conclusion? What *we* would regard as silly inductive reasoning is still reasoning, after all, and this is so even when the reasoner sticks by his conclusion despite having had his attention fully drawn to what he is saying. (As we have seen, it can be argued that the same doesn't go for deductive reasoning.) There are indeed well-known canons of bad inductive reasoning, such as that embodied in the Gambler's Fallacy, the fallacy of thinking that the more often an A is followed by a B, the less likely it is that the next A will be followed by a B. The 'tonker' may be unreal—the gambler is all too real.

'Well', it may be said, 'there are accepted ways of arguing against a bit of bad inductive reasoning'. Certainly there are. But there seem also to be accepted ways of arguing against bits of bad practical reasoning, specifically by criticizing the person's aims, i.e. what they want—which I have argued plays a similar sort of role in a practical argument as does a rule or mode of inference in a theoretical one (deductive or inductive). 'But who's to say which aims are good and which are bad?' Who's to say which inductive canons are good and which bad? In both cases, the answer is 'The reasonable person'; but of course the credentials for being a reasonable person will include reasoning in *this* way, not *that*. The circularity that notoriously attends attempts to justify induction may in fact be a cousin of the kind that we encounter in Aristotle's account of the right act as the one which the virtuous person would do. It seems at least possible that in neither case is the circularity a vicious one.

Subjectivism about logical inference was tackled above by observing that incoherent rules (like those attaching to 'tonk') aren't rules at all. But this was rather swift—at any rate, if the intention was to provide an easy way of excluding rogue inference-rules generally. Philosophers, after all, have disputed among themselves whether the law of excluded middle can be relied on in logical proofs, and relatedly what meanings should be assigned to such connectives as 'or' and 'not'. And criticisms of what is proposed on these matters, say by intuitionist logicians, rarely consist of straightforward accusations of incoherence or inconsistency. Rather, the issues at stake have to do with deeper disagreements about meaning and truth. Now for these disputes to have any direction at all, it seems necessary that there be some agreement as to the *purpose* (or purposes) of logical argumentation. And it is natural to think that a prime purpose can indeed be specified: that of proceeding from true beliefs to true beliefs. This can surely be agreed, even if disagreement remains as to the nature of truth. 'Tonk' was easily disposed of, since it allowed the deduction of anything whatever, which would necessarily include the deduction of falsehoods.

Characterizing the prime purpose of deductive argumentation as that of getting from true beliefs to true beliefs is not a way of characterizing deduction itself, for inductive argumentation shares this purpose. This is why the two modes of reasoning get classed together, as species of theoretical reasoning. In both cases, an extreme, 'anything goes' subjectivism or relativism can be ruled out by saying: 'Given the purpose of this mode of reasoning, some alleged canons of reasoning can't even count as canons of this kind of reasoning.' The 'can't' here is itself a logical 'can't', for what's being said is, in effect: 'Such-and-such alleged canons of reasoning are inconsistent with the purpose of such reasoning.' And this shows why logical deduction is a special case: illogical thought (unlike inductively silly thought) is in a certain sense impossible.

With inductive reasoning, we can still say that some things simply won't count as canons of that sort of reasoning—for instance, the rather tonkish canon 'If all or most As have been found to be Bs, then the next C will be a D'. But with both induction and deduction, once the *ersatz* canons of reasoning have been excluded, there still appears to be room for disagreement about which canons to adopt. I am not saying that this fact in itself points to subjectivism or relativism—on the contrary. But any case for ethical subjectivism will need to make out some suitable disanalogy between practical reasoning and theoretical reasoning if it is not to land us with subjectivism about the latter. A too easy reliance on the truism that *it all depends what you want* must therefore be suspect, as must the simple observation that there is room for disagreement about practical aims.

The chain of steps that you get in a theoretical argument such as a proof can be regarded as the mirror image of a series of answers to the question 'Why?'—as in: 'Why do you think that?', or again: 'Why should I think that?' The starting-point of this series would be the argument's conclusion, thus:

> 'The butler did it.'
> 'Why do you think so?'
> 'The victim died of cyanide poisoning.'
> 'So what?'
> 'Only the butler knew where the cyanide was kept.'
> 'And why do you think the victim died of cyanide poisoning?'
> 'The coroner said so.'

Such a series of answers may split into branches, and may have no definitive terminus. The shape and length of a series typically depends on the curiosity, doggedness, state of ignorance, etc., of the enquirer. But to say that a series of answers has no definitive terminus is not to say that it can go on forever. As the case of the pestering child illustrates, the activity of asking 'Why?' *ad infinitum* is a pointless one—or rather it may well have a point, such as that of holding a parent's attention, but whatever point it has cannot be the point of genuine enquiry. That the language-game of asking for and giving reasons has a humanly-rooted point or purpose is something that has already been argued—see Section II of Chapter 1 (esp. pp. 9–11). And if, within some discourse, *no* reply to the question 'Why?' counts as supplying a sufficient reason (e.g. for believing something), then there is no such thing as a sufficient reason within that discourse—which is to say, there is no such thing as a reason in that discourse, and the question 'Why?' is a mere noise. So a person who won't accept any answer to 'Why?' as providing a terminus to the enquiry isn't really enquiring.

These remarks are like the earlier ones about theoretical reasoning in having to do with *purpose*: they relate to the purpose of (a species of) enquiry. And they seem to hold of practical reasoning as much as they do of theoretical reasoning. With practical reasoning, the starting-point of the series of questions will likely be a present action, my boiling a kettle, say.

> 'Why are you doing that?'
> 'To make jelly.'
> 'Why are you making jelly?'
> 'The vicar can't eat dairy products.'
> 'So what?'
> 'Everyone else I've invited is getting trifle.'
> 'Why feed them at all?'
> . . . .

Again, the series can branch, can involve sub-series of theoretical reasoning, and will often have no definitive terminus. It all depends on the goals of the particular enquirer. The mode of reasoning implicit in this series of answers is means–end reasoning, and is governed by an end, or aim—or thing *wanted*. The thing wanted may be to hold a party, for example. Now as with enquiry generally, if no statement counts as supplying a sufficient reason when given in response to the question 'Why are you doing that?', or to the question 'Why do you want that?', then there is no such thing as a sufficient reason within this discourse— which is to say, there is no such thing as a *reason* here, in which case the question 'Why?' is a mere noise. It needs to be stressed that 'I just want to' does not give a reason, any more than 'I just believe it' gives a reason in the theoretical case. This connects with what was said earlier, that 'I want X' need not, and should not, appear as a premise in a practical argument.

So we have something like *a priori* grounds for thinking that some answers to 'Why do you want that?' will count as sufficient answers. By the same token, some answers will have to count as in themselves insuffi- cient—though the limited aims of an enquirer may in a given case lead him to accept some such answer as adequate. It seems that wants cannot be the 'original existences' that Hume took them for, above or below rational justification and criticism. But what kinds of answers to 'Why do you want that?' could count as sufficient in themselves?

III.

We can make some progress with this question by reflection on what makes for intelligibility in the expression or ascription of a want. Certain constraints of intelligibility relate to the connection between wanting and *trying to get*, in particular the following constraint: you cannot want that to happen which you believe cannot possibly happen. So you can't want to be Napoleon, since you're stuck with whatever identity you've got; and on the face of it, you can't want not to have failed your driving test, though you can certainly wish you hadn't. Are there any further restrictions on what is wantable? Here is Anscombe:

> But is not anything wantable, or at least any perhaps attainable thing? It will be instructive to anyone who thinks this to approach someone and say: 'I want a saucer of mud' or 'I want a twig of mountain ash'. He is likely to be asked what for; to which let him reply that he does not want it *for* anything, he just wants it. It is likely that the other will then perceive that a philosophical example is all that is in question, and will pursue the matter no further; but supposing that he did not realise this, and yet did not dismiss our man as a dull babbling loon, would he not try to find out in what aspect the object desired is desirable? Does it serve as a symbol? Is there something delightful about it? Does the man want to have something to call his own, and no more? [13]

Anscombe further imagines a man who expresses the want for a pin, is given one, and promptly puts it down and forgets about it.

> It is not at all clear what it meant to say: this man simply wanted a pin. Of course, if he is careful always to carry the pin in his hand thereafter, or at least for a time, we may perhaps say: it seems he really wanted that pin. Then perhaps, the answer to 'What do you want it for?' may be 'to carry it about with me', as a man may want a stick. But here again there is further characterisation: 'I don't feel comfortable without it; it is pleasant to have one' and so on. [14]

The point is not simply that it is very strange or unusual, or even crazy, to want a saucer of mud, or a pin, just for its own sake. As Anscombe says of the man who immediately discards the proffered pin, 'it is not at all clear what it meant to say: this man simply wanted a pin'. Or in other words: why call this *wanting*? A connected point can be made about *getting*. If a creature tries, and maybe succeeds, in getting X, then normally we can say of it that it wanted X. But the notion of getting is not a merely behaviouristic one, any more than are those of having or of receiving. We give the pin to the man who asks for it. He takes it in his hand all right; but does he *receive* the pin—receiving being the complement of giving? Does he at any point have the pin in his possession? We have imagined him using the words, 'I want a pin'; but

---

[13] Anscombe, *Intention*, pp. 70–1.   [14] Ibid., p. 71.

He used these words, the effect of which was that he was given one; but what reason have we to say he wanted a pin rather than: to see if we would take the trouble to give him one?[15]

Without further explanation, the statement that someone just wants a pin for its own sake looks to be unintelligible. The same doesn't go for wanting a swim in the sea, or wanting to be loved, or wanting the person in the next room to stop shouting. For in these other cases, it is in most contexts clear how the thing wanted is desirable. A person who says 'I want...' should in principle be able to give some desirability characterization of the thing wanted, in Anscombe's phrase. The range of possible desirability characterizations is very wide, but for these too there is a requirement of intelligibility. 'Because it's a Tuesday' does not without further explanation show why some proposed action is desirable. And while 'For the fun of it' is something that *can* show why something is wanted, it won't do so (without further explanation) if the something is, say, placing a pencil on top of a computer keyboard. (We shall have more to say about 'For the fun of it' in Chapter 3.)

What makes for desirability? The quick answer is: human nature. A desire for food needs no explanation because of what sort of creatures human beings are. The same goes for swimming in the sea or listening to music. To repeat, the issues here have to do with intelligibility, not only of statements but also of behaviour as such. Understanding some bit of behaviour requires a minimum by way of shared form of life. Human nature is of course enormously malleable and versatile, and we are often opaque to each other, so that one person may find it hard to see what another person finds agreeable about some activity. But it would be silly to think that in such a case the first person is doomed to remain in the dark. If he is genuinely curious, and if the other is sufficiently articulate, then mutual understanding is frequently the result.

Now if anything counts as a desirability characterization, or in other words as a sufficient answer to 'Why?', it is the statement that something is or would be good for one. (*Why* it does so is something we will be looking at in Section IV.) Such a statement is implicit in the practical argument with which we began, the Guinness argument. Guinness is good for pregnant women and the agent is a pregnant woman—so it's good for her. The series of 'Why?' questions with their answers might go as follows:

'Why are you going to the Half Moon?'
'To drink some Guinness.'
'Why do you want to drink Guinness?'
'Because Guinness is good for girls like me.'

And it is at this point that further repetition of 'Why?' becomes silly, unless indeed it means something like 'What sort of girl *are* you that Guinness should be good for you?' (Answer: 'A pregnant one.') If the question is, 'Why drink what's good for you?', the onus falls on the enquirer to make sense of himself.[16]

A last-ditch ethical subjectivist might try alleging that 'good' simply expresses an attitude or sentiment, so that sentences containing it are neither true nor false and do not strictly speaking express beliefs at all. As pointed out earlier (pp. 56–7), a major problem with this view arises from that 'cognitive' side to attitudes, sentiments, and emotions which received attention in Chapter 1. But the implausibility of the view is in any case evident when we encounter sentences like 'Guinness is good for pregnant women', something that could be asserted, and believed, by anyone, including those with no interest in or 'attitude towards' pregnant women. This use of 'good' is evidently one of those attributive uses discussed by Geach.

Assuming, then, that 'Guinness is good for pregnant women', and the derivable 'Guinness is good for me', are both of them indicative sentences expressing beliefs that are (*modulo* some vagueness) true or false—assuming this, what we have is a set of premises that justify the conclusion (C)—'So I'll go to the Half Moon'. They justify it in the sense that, given the agent wants what's good for her, and given the truth of the premises, her conclusion does indeed follow. Moreover, the premise 'It's good for me' supplies a desirability characterization, so that the question 'Why do you want what's good for you?' doesn't need to be addressed. The premises do not *necessitate* the conclusion, as we have seen, but that is a different matter.

[16] Anscombe describes how an enquirer might thus be made sense of: '. . . the question "What do you want suitable food for?" means, if anything, "Do give up thinking about food as suitable or otherwise"—as said e.g. by someone who prefers people merely to enjoy their food or considers the man hypochondriac' (*Intention*, pp. 66–7). In other words, the reason 'In order to eat suitable food' is not being rejected *as a reason*; rather, what we might call the man's weighing of goods is being questioned. Health is not *so* important.

In speaking of a practical conclusion's being justified I am of course employing a fairly modest notion of justification, one that corresponds (roughly) to the third-person explanation of actions. A practical conclusion that is fully justified in this sense may not be justified *tout court*—for as well as intelligibility and rationality there are such matters as whether the agent's ordering of goods is a correct or proper ordering. Thus the answer to 'Why are you eating the Vice-Principal?' might be 'It's good for me: all that protein!', but this could scarcely be said to give a sufficient reason. Whether an agent's ordering of goods is itself a matter of practical rationality in a broad sense is a further question, one that we will be looking at later on (pp. 79–81). What needs to be willingly conceded is simply this: that the modest 'justification' I have been talking about doesn't rule out *all* kinds of criticism. In the case of inductive arguments, a conclusion may be questioned because of further evidence, evidence that wasn't mentioned in the original premises, and this despite the fact that the argument was as it stood a good inductive argument. The conclusion of a practical argument is similarly defeasible: it may be defeated e.g. by the 'further' consideration that the Vice-Principal is (or was) a human being.

The conclusion to be drawn from the discussion that has occupied Sections II and III of this chapter appears to be this: Hume may have been right that a set of beliefs won't produce an action without benefit of an active want; but he was wrong to think, if he did, that one cannot justify a practical decision simply and solely by reference to a set of beliefs. After all, it is also true that a set of premises won't entail a theoretical conclusion without benefit of a rule or rules of inference; but to justify a theoretical conclusion you need only point to the premises.

IV.

We have seen that, where a person is acting with some goal or intention, the reasons she gives in justification of her course of action will typically be statements, true or false. Among such statements, those supplying desirability characterizations have a special status. As for what the person wants or is aiming at, this is something that is typically made manifest in what she does (where doings include sayings)—i.e. in the fact that she takes *these* statements for her practical premises, and draws *this* conclusion (among various conclusions that might rationally be drawn). These results are fairly modest, in that they leave much still to be said on the subject of what makes someone good *qua* human agent. In particular, more needs to be said about desirability characterizations, and especially those which relate to what is good.

I have argued that it is a sort of *a priori* truth that there exist answers to 'Why do you want that?' that count as sufficient and adequate, and hence as justifying: if there were not, the language-game of asking for and giving practical reasons would have no point, and the word 'Why?' as it occurs in that game would be a mere noise. In addition, following Anscombe, we have seen that demands of intelligibility and interpretability constrain what answers to 'Why?' can count as sufficient and adequate, and that the constraints here relate, unsurprisingly, to what is humanly normal or natural. Of course, the humanly natural includes much that we wish to discourage, such as temper tantrums, and *these* traits and behaviours typically fail to supply the agent with practical reasons that count as good ones; this is partly because of the social nature of the language-game, but it is also because a trait or behaviour may be humanly natural and yet be bad for the agent himself. The notion of a good reason for action connects with what is good for you more closely than it does with what you desire; and the concept of a desirability characterization (as introduced by Anscombe) relates, obviously, to something's being an intelligible object of desire, rather than to something's being good—though of course statements about what is good constitute an important class of desirability characterizations, e.g. 'Guinness is good for women like me'.

Now in saying that the concept of a desirability characterization doesn't as such relate to what is good, I am going against what Anscombe herself says at various points, e.g. when she assimilates the questions 'What do you want that for?' and 'What's the good of it?' (*Intention*, p. 78). Anscombe, following Aristotle and Aquinas, takes goodness to be the object of wanting in the sense in which truth is the object of judgement. Here we encounter the Thomist thesis that whatever is desired is desired under the aspect of the good (*quidquid appetitur, appetitur sub specie boni*). This need not amount to the claim that a rational agent always aims at the *realization* of some good thing, for one way of bringing an end to 'Why?' questioning is with an answer giving, not a further intention, but rather a motive, such as gratitude: as, 'Why do you want to send her a present?'—'Because she looked after my cat last week.' As Anscombe argues,[17] such motives are genuinely 'backward-looking' in that they rest upon reasons relating to what has occurred, not relating to what is to come about as a result of one's actions. For an allegedly forward-looking reason such as 'In order to show my gratitude' presupposes the idea of gratitude, which, however, can only be understood *via* such reason-giving statements as 'Because she looked after my cat last week'. Still, one who does something out of gratitude may perhaps be said to 'desire something under the aspect of the good', in so far as she returns good for good, and in doing so manifests a good character (and, we may add, is aware of that fact).

But what about the motive of revenge? 'Why do you want to kill him?'—'Because he killed my daughter'. Here, the reason given supplies a desirability characterization, i.e. it brings an end to 'Why?' questioning in an intelligible manner; but can the agent be said to desire something under the aspect of the good? If Anscombe is right,[18] backward-looking motives are to be understood as relating to the ideas of good *or harm*, and it is the idea of harm that is evidently crucial to the motive of revenge, not that of good. The agent wishes ill upon another person. Whether the motive of revenge can be a good *motive*—whether, that is, a reason like 'He killed my daughter' can serve to justify an act of revenge—is another (complex) question, one that we encountered in Chapter 1 (pp. 35–6). What seems clear is that the motive of revenge poses a problem for the Thomist thesis, in so far as it does not appear to present an end under the aspect of the good, though it certainly presents an end as 'somehow desirable'.

Another problematic case is exemplified by the reason-giving statement, 'In order to win'. In a game of chess, this statement surely brings an end to 'What for?' questioning. Certainly, 'What do you want to win for?' is an odd question, inviting the reply, 'You're meant to try to win!', which would be a sort of tautology, and so hardly apt for specifying some goal of the agent. Could 'In order to win' be said to present an end under the aspect of some good? Only in a very attenuated sense, i.e. by virtue of the fact that its counting as a good reason rests upon the fact that playing chess is pleasant (for many people)—rather than by virtue of the fact that it's good if *I* win the game (why not the other player?).—It is quite possible that Anscombe did not have statements like 'In order to win' in mind

[17] Anscombe, *Intention*, p. 20.   [18] Ibid., pp. 20–1.

when she coined the term 'desirability characterization'; nevertheless, such a statement is apt to bring an end to 'Why?' questioning, and appears not to present an end under the aspect of the good.

Finally, there is the case of pleasure. Answers to 'Why do you want to do that?' such as 'For the fun of it' or 'For pleasure' are very often sufficient answers, but it is far from clear that they present ends under the aspect of the good. However, this is a topic I will be dealing with more fully later on. For present purposes, I hope merely to have indicated some problems with the Thomist view that whatever is desired is desired *sub specie boni*. Let us then return to the topic I broached a few paragraphs back, namely, that of the relationship between good reasons for action and what is good for the agent.

The topic of what is good for a person is connected to the topic of what a person needs. You can of course need things that relate, not to your own good, but to some other person's (or animal's, or thing's) good; thus a doctor might say, 'We need more bandages over here'. The sort of need or necessity that relates to some such good has been dubbed 'Aristotelian necessity', since Aristotle defines it thus: the necessary is that without which good cannot be or come to be.[19] In fact, our concept of a need is perhaps better understood as that without the satisfaction of which bad will be or come to be. A person can't be said to *need* piano lessons simply on account of the fact that learning the piano is a good, nor to *need* a set of weights on account of the fact that weight-lifting gives one strong arms, which are good to have. But you can be said to need insulin if you are diabetic, or to need money to travel to your grandfather's funeral, for diabetes is an illness and it is a shame not to be able to attend a close relative's funeral. There is evidently no hard and fast line to be drawn between things that are good to have and things which it is bad not to have; but as so often, the lack of a hard and fast line here doesn't mean that the distinction is 'merely subjective', or anything of the sort. For simplicity, I will in what follows sometimes speak of someone's needing what it would be good for them to have as well as needing what it would be bad for them to lack.

Now although I have claimed that the concept of a good reason for action is more closely tied to what is good for you than it is to what you

---

[19] See Aristotle, *Metaphysics*, ch. 5, 1015a20–5.

intelligibly desire, there is evidently an important connection between these latter two things—between needs and wants. We have already seen that there are limits of intelligibility on what a person can be said to want, and some of these limits derive from what people need. This shows up in the fact that although we can conceive of human beings who never played music or who never wore clothes, we cannot really conceive of human beings who never pursued what they took to be good for them. Why not? Such creatures would very likely die out, but species *have* died out because of being ill-fitted to survive, so we can hardly appeal to the Theory of Evolution if we wish to call such people inconceivable. If there are grounds for this claim, they surely relate to what is presupposed by the possibility of ascribing wants to people at all. To understand or make sense of the behaviour of a creature, as was argued in Chapter 1, requires one to respond and react to its behaviour in ways that are at bottom instinctive and pre-linguistic. One has to be able, e.g. to see some behaviour as that of *trying to get an apple*. If none of the behaviour of a group of creatures simply strikes us as this or that (trying to get an apple, being in pain . . .), then the concept of wanting something or other will not get a foothold, any more than it does in the case of kettles or oak trees. And it seems likely that notions of what is good for creatures, of what enables them to thrive, and of what they need, will underpin a lot of our basic responses to and interpretations of their behaviour. Think of the connections between *hunting, catching, eating, food*, and *nourishment*. Wants, ends, and needs are here interwoven in a single phenomenon. We can see this animal's movements as *hunting* because of what in a broad sense 'surrounds' it, this being what enables us to see the activity as having a *telos*, i.e. the predator's catching its prey; we can see that as *catching* (as purposeful in the way that catching is) because of what the predator then does with its prey; of the various things the predator does with its prey the important one is *eating*, on account of the natural history of such animals, and of animals generally; and in calling that *eating* we invoke the idea of the animal's deriving something it *needs*, in the form of nourishment.

The example of hunting shows the connection between an animal's wants and its needs, rather than between its wants and what it *takes* to be its needs. But in the context of understanding an animal's behaviour this difference is less than it seems. For non-human animals, there is almost no distinction at all; and when it comes to human beings, though people can be wrong about what they need and what is good for them, it is what they are trying to get and what reasons they would give for trying to get it that are important for understanding their actions—such 'understanding' is of the whole gamut of behaviour, linguistic and non-linguistic. And it couldn't be that people were by and large radically mistaken about what was good for them, any more than they could be radically mistaken about which substances are edible. It is, if you like, an empirical fact that human beings, like other animals, want and pursue those things they think they need—but this empirical fact serves as one of the hinge propositions of the language-game of describing one another's behaviour. (It is thus like 'Human beings can see' in relation to the language-game of colour-ascriptions; see Chapter 1, pp. 19–20.)

We thus see how wants and needs are connected, and why it appears inconceivable that there should be tribes of people who never wanted what was good for them. The connection between what human beings want and what is good for them helps to explain why 'It's good for me' is a desirability characterization, i.e. a statement apt for bringing an end to a series of questions of the form, 'Why do you want X?' After all, the questioner must partake sufficiently of your own form of life to be talking to you in the first place, and his own grasp of what good and bad reasons for action are will have to derive from his own humanity. In asking for your reasons, his aim is to be able to interpret your actions, to make sense of them. Such interpretation presupposes that you are the sort of creature that generally desires what you take to be good for you in preference to what you take to be bad for you—if, that is, you are a normal specimen; and that you *are* normal is (necessarily) the default position.

V.

Desirability characterizations supply *prima facie* good reasons for action, but it is possible for there to be a clash between what an agent intelligibly desires and what is good for him. This is, as it were, a clash between desirability characterizations, for 'X is/would be good for me' itself gives a desirability characterization, a fact which received some elucidation in the last section. Since it is a human being talking, this last statement amounts to 'X is/would be good for me *qua* human being', and the traditional Aristotelian account of matters accords a central place to this statement, by arguing roughly as follows.

The aims attaching to particular activities are necessarily subordinate to that aim, or those aims, that a reflective and wise person might be able to mention in answer to the question, 'How should I be living, in order to be a good human being?' The latter question always makes sense; and if the answer to it, which may be long and complex, entails that e.g. doing well as a journalist is incompatible with doing well as a human being, then 'X would forward my career as a journalist' cannot, all told, function as a good reason for action. For the life of a journalist is merely a certain sort of human life; journalistic activities will be but a subclass of the activities constituting a person's life as a human being; and considerations to do with journalism are therefore subordinate to ones to do with human life as such.

According to this Aristotelian account, it could be said that desirability characterizations in many cases give only provisional answers to the question 'Why?' An answer like 'X would forward my career' will count as adequate within the context of an enquiry which assumes the innocence of the career alluded to, and this assumption is itself a perfectly intelligible one for an enquirer to make, in the typical case. But the range of the enquiry could be extended so as to drop that assumption.[20] The enquiry could, for instance, become one about the different careers a person might follow. Extending the terms of reference of this enquiry in this way would in the end lead those involved to the point of asking, or being asked, 'How does such-and-such contribute to your leading a good life as a human being?' The range of the original enquiry cannot *always* be sensibly extended in this way: if you ask 'Why do you want to get a new kettle?' and I answer 'The old one is broken', it wouldn't be a sensible way of continuing the conversation for you to ask, 'But why do you want to drink tea at all?' Drinking tea is one of those 'things it is human to do' (see pp. 59–60, above), and in that sense is not a general *aim* of mine at all, any more than is walking. The particular goal of drinking tea on a particular occasion does not point towards a generic goal, *to drink tea*—nor to a generic goal, *to get pleasure* (for reasons we will encounter in Chapter 3). And of course it couldn't be made out that tea-drinking was as such inimical to human flourishing, unless new evidence showed it to be bad for the health, say.

---

[20] *Could* be extended. There is no requirement that an enquiry be forever extended in this way (see pp. 68–9, above).

Now there is surely much truth in the Aristotelian account. But there is a question that clearly needs to be addressed, namely: How are considerations relating to the good of *others* meant to figure in human practical reasoning? The traditional answer is: in order to be a good human being (good *qua* human agent), you must have character traits that involve your having the good of others among your goals. This I think is true. But why is it true? Is it because we are social animals, and so are meant to be concerned for one another's welfare, in the way in which a honey bee is meant to cooperate with the other bees in finding suitable flowers? If this were the whole answer, then ethics would seem to be derivable from biological teleology, which it is not. Such practices as killing the runt of the litter might benefit the species from a biological perspective, but could never benefit it from an ethical perspective.

Our concept of human flourishing does not *determine* the shape of our ethical concepts; rather, there is a complex symbiotic relationship between the two. As was argued in Chapter 1, the language-game of asking for and giving reasons for action is a social phenomenon, involving diverse human interactions—and it is from this language-game that the standards of goodness and badness in practical reasons derive. Thus it is this language-game that determines what counts as good practical reasoning for an individual person, whether or not he or she gets called to account by the rest of us. But it is accountability before the rest of us which is crucial to the 'altruistic' nature of good practical reasoning, and so to the 'altruistic' strand in our concept of a good human being[21]—since a good human being is good *qua* human agent. To be sure, none of this would be possible, any more than would language itself, were human beings not by nature social and gregarious creatures, characterized by those capacities for sympathetic reactions and responses to each other that were examined in Chapter 1. But what all this shows is that the Aristotelian account needs supplementing: the 'final end' of leading a good life for a human being does, as Aristotle says, involve the ethical virtues, but this very statement involves concepts (*good life, ethical virtues*) with roots not only in our biological nature, but also in our linguistic intercourse with one another. Here we see one aspect of the importance of language for human life.

---

[21] Cf. pp. 12–15, above.

With this linguistic supplementation to Aristotelian theory in mind, we may return to the claim that some of one's ends are necessarily subordinate to others, all of them being subordinate to the final end of leading a good life for a human being. Aristotle wanted to argue that there was a highest and best form of human life, one devoted to philosophic contemplation. This is a view I shall be examining later on; for now, it is the *structure* of Aristotle's account that I want to endorse, a structure which allows talk of a good or bad ordering of ends, independent of whether there is just one form of the Good Life (which in fact I doubt). Some ends necessarily count as more important than others, the latter being subordinate to the former, and a person's habitual actions will often manifest an ordering of ends, good or bad—e.g. their actions may manifest putting journalistic success before honesty, or vice versa. The task of showing *which* ends are important for a good life must be carried out case by case, and the results will not look like proofs, but will rather appeal to a potential plethora of facts about human psychology, human institutions, human history, anthropology, etc. How much detail is put in will depend on the kind or level of ignorance or puzzlement in the enquirer, so that a philosopher who asks 'Why should honesty come before maximizing pleasure?' would seem to be troubled by a different sort of lacuna than is the person who asks 'Should telling my children the truth come before giving them wonderful and fantastic tall stories (the Tooth Fairy and co.)?' Even if a person never explicitly asks herself the very general question, 'How should I live?', she will show that she is addressing that question in her life if it is characteristic of her to ask or ponder such particular questions as that about truth-telling when they arise. The habit of such pondering is reflectiveness, and it yields, or at any rate moulds, habits of action, and hence character.

VI.

But reflecting on such questions as these is made harder in a culture where confusion prevails as to what ethical enquiry *is*. One of the main confusions in our own culture concerns the status of one's desires, and the relation of these to one's needs. We have already encountered the picture of a person's desires as above or below rational criticism or justification, and as being a sort of highest court of appeal in the deliberations of any rational agent. This radically flawed picture of desire is associated with certain tendencies of thought within our culture, notably those of utilitarianism and classical liberalism.

It is no accident that the classic exponent of these two tendencies was one and the same person, John Stuart Mill. Mill's famous 'proof' of the Principle of Utility rests on the idea that happiness is intrinsically desirable because universally desired. Happiness he defined as pleasure and the absence of pain—pleasure and pain being, as Hume had already said, the two springs of human action. Empiricist that he was, Mill (again like Hume) construed pleasure as a mental state authoritatively known only to the subject, the same therefore being true of happiness. The sovereign status within utilitarianism of 'I want' was thus assured, and it has always been a main problem for utilitarians how to prevent utilitarianism from collapsing into mere egoism. In the course of his 'proof', Mill devotes one clause of a sentence to this problem: ' . . . each person's happiness is a good to that person, and the general happiness, therefore, a good to the aggregate of all persons'[22] ('good' has already been explained in terms of desire). Turning to Mill's liberalism, this likewise accords a central place to people's wants. It is thanks to Mill that we have liberalism's defining principle, often referred to as the 'harm principle': that people are to be allowed to do whatever they want so long as they don't interfere with other people doing what *they* want.[23] The principle can be seen as a politically stabilized version of Aleister Crowley's so-called Law of Thelema, '*Do what thou wilt* shall be the whole of the Law', a 'law' which if adopted by any group would lead pretty soon to the dissolution of the group—something presumably perceived by Mill.

---

[22] Mill, *Utilitarianism*, ch. 4.

[23] Or in Mill's words, the principle 'that the sole end for which mankind are warranted, individually or collectively, in interfering with the liberty of action of any of their number, is self-protection. That the only purpose for which power may be rightfully exercised over any member of a civilised community, against his will, is to prevent harm to others. His own good, either physical or moral, is not a sufficient warrant' (*On Liberty*, ch. 1). (i) The phrase 'individually or collectively' is crucial: Mill does not merely think that it isn't the *state's* business to interfere with people's private doings, or that the evils of *state* interference will always outweigh the evils resulting from people's being allowed to do what they want in private. As he goes on to put it, 'Over himself, over his own body and mind, the individual is sovereign.' (ii) The use of the terms 'harm' and 'good' might suggest moral criteria lying outside the conceptual circle of desires, pleasure, pain, etc. If such criteria were indeed intended, then Mill's official theory would be contradicted; but in fact Mill was, like later utilitarians, willing to supply or imply reductions of concepts like *harm* to concepts lying within the circle.

It can be asked whether Mill's 'harm principle' is only an improvement on Aleister Crowley in virtue of this stabilizing feature. Is it really possible that the grand old man of British liberalism is just the cleverer cousin of the self-styled Wickedest Man Alive? Well, the sorts of desires imputed to his fellow men and women by Mill were not the sorts of desires which Crowley and his followers either felt or pretended to feel.[24] Mill's optimism about human nature probably prevented his taking seriously the possibility that human beings might desire rotten and despicable things, in any great numbers; and to the extent that they did desire such things, Mill would have put this down to bad education and bad social arrangements. But that line of thought naturally leads to a crucial qualification of liberalism, one which restricts the range of desires mentioned in Mill's Principle to *good* and *sane* desires; and it is a familiar point that Mill shows himself drawn to this sort of qualification, and to the concomitant idea of a human nature with objective standards of flourishing. The problem is that this Aristotelian idea is not, on the face of it, consistent with Mill's utilitarian and empiricist premises.

Why should Mill's Principle be restricted so as to refer only to good, sane desires? The reason is simple: there cannot be any intrinsic reason why the pursuit of bad or crazy desires should not be interfered with. There may be extrinsic reasons, such as that one will do harm by the *means* one adopts to hinder other people's actions; but this will be a case-by-case matter, and there is no reason to think that interfering with others *must* have bad side effects. As things are, we do in fact discourage and hinder drug addicts from using drugs, for instance.

Does the liberal principle survive if it is rephrased as stating that people are to be allowed to do whatever they want so long as (i) they don't

---

[24] In fairness to the Great Beast, he seems in some moods to have leant towards a more Millian position. Tim Maroney (Gnostic Priest, initiate of the Ordo Templi Orientis, Neo-Pagan Witchcraft, and the Golden Dawn) tells us that 'one view which one often finds in [Crowley's] writings, and is accepted by most of his followers, is that one must respect not only one's own will but the wills of others. All the wills are magically arranged so that there is no conflict between them, just as (so it was believed in Crowley's day) the stars are arranged so that they never collide. The personal will and the will of all are mystically joined as a whole which is also the basis of individuality in a paradoxical way. Collision between wills would indicate that one or the other person was not doing their True Will. At other times Crowley said that the only error was to believe that others existed at all and that they had wills that could be violated.' Source: http://larabell.org/mirrors/maroney.org/CrowleyIntro/Do_What_Thou_Wilt.html.

interfere with other people doing what they want and (ii) what they want is in any case decent and sane? I do not think so. For once we have allowed (ii) we have undermined (i). The rationale for (ii) is that it can't always be wrong to interfere with others who act upon bad or crazy desires; and this rationale would require us to alter (i) in its turn, so as to be restricted to other people's decent and sane desires. We then no longer have a political and ethical *principle*, but rather a quasi-tautology along the lines of, 'Don't interfere with people who are behaving all right anyway, unless perhaps they themselves are interfering with people who are behaving all right'. (The 'perhaps' is necessary, as any liberal would surely admit; e.g. it may not be okay for you to interfere with a parent's silly interference in certain of his offspring's innocent doings.)

As for utilitarianism, it too could only be remedied by measures that undermined it as a moral theory. Just as the possibility of bad desires poses a problem for classical liberalism, so the possibility of nasty pleasures poses a problem for classical utilitarianism, and these two problems in fact become one for those modern forms of utilitarianism which substitute 'desire-satisfaction' for 'pleasure'. As we shall see in Chapter 3, the goodness of a type of pleasure, or of a 'pleasure-experience', can be nothing intrinsic: it is necessarily a function of the goodness of the activity, state, or fact in which pleasure is taken. But this means that there is such a thing as bad pleasure—in particular, pleasure taken in bad things. Utilitarians could only make allowance for this by dropping the axiom that pleasure is intrinsically desirable, and enjoining us to maximize only *good* pleasure. This would leave it without the necessary single currency for utilitarian calculation, since it seems that the goodness of the activities, etc., in which pleasure is taken will have to be understood on Geach's 'attributive' model, with an open-ended diversity of activities to each of which the concept *good* applies (where it does) in virtue, roughly, of background teleological standards. At any rate, the only hope of rendering the different pleasures commensurable would seem to lie in detecting a corresponding commensurability among the various activities, etc.—and the most obvi-ous way of managing *this* would be by adopting the Aristotelian notion of an architectonic end for man. By which stage we have left utilitarian theory behind completely.

Liberalism and utilitarianism are not just theories developed by phil-osophers; they are, as I have said, tendencies of thought within our culture, even if their most coherent expression has come from the pens of philosophers. Each tendency may be regarded as stemming historically from that post-Enlightenment individualism and empowerment of the common man which is, in the West, associated especially with the development of democratic styles of government. Every regime has its myths and fables, and democratic regimes are no exception. Absolute monarchy justified itself by the theory of the divine right of kings; representative democracy justifies itself by the theory that the People's will is necessarily for the best. For modern democracy, unlike its ancient forebear, defines itself above all as giving people what they *want*, where this aim is deemed to be intrinsically, and not merely instrumentally, good.[25] And 'what people want' is not meant as shorthand for 'what people want for the community'—electors are not called upon to justify or explain their desires. Indeed, since a politician only gets into power if voted in, the politician's rhetoric has inevitably developed in the direction of promising to give people what they want *for themselves*. In this way, what is given sovereign status is people's wants, where there is and can be no reference to the reasons they have for those wants.

An election or referendum results in a collective decision to do one thing rather than another. With respect to this decision the devotee of democracy faces a dilemma, similar to the one famously put forward in Plato's *Euthyphro*, where it is asked whether acts are pious because the gods love them, or the gods love them because they are pious. The democrat faces the following analogous dilemma: Is the decision the best one because people voted for it, or did people vote for it because it was the best decision among the possible decisions? As with the classic *Euthyphro* dilemma, each horn has its problems. The first horn makes anything willed by the People the right thing as a matter of definition, while the second horn accords incredible knowledge and wisdom to the electorate. The only way to avoid the dilemma, and thus to reject each of its horns, is by admitting that democracy is a (fallible) means to an independently specifiable end—namely, the well-ordered and just running of society. What *that* amounts to must be a matter, not of brute desire-satisfaction, but of people's getting and doing what, as human beings and citizens, they need to get and do. But if there is no general acknowledgement of this

---

[25] H. L. Mencken was more specific; he defined democracy as 'the theory that the common people know what they want and deserve to get it good and hard'. (Mencken, *Notes on Democracy*, 1926.)

fact concerning the proper purpose of democracy, and thus no general acknowledgement among voters of the proper reasons for voting, then it is hard to see how a democratically elected government could govern well unless accidentally—e.g. by virtue of there being people in government who have knowledge and wisdom *despite* having got there by the route they did.

VII.

I began this chapter by considering the question, 'What sort of life should I lead, in order to be a good human being?' This led us on to the topics of practical reason and of wanting. A major aim of this chapter so far, it could be said, has been to put wants in their place—a place defined in relation to *reasons*, and especially reasons to do with what is good, for oneself or for others. The idea of good action which goes with this account explains that notion especially in terms of good reasons for action, as also with good reasons for wanting things. And the natural model of responsibility that goes with all this states that in the *central* case a person is responsible for what he intends, either as ends or as means, intention being understood in terms of reasons (i.e. in terms of possible answers to the question 'Why?'). Responsibility is important for ethics above all because of the connection that holds between the reasons for one's actions and one's accountability before others, something that is a consequence of the social nature of the language-game. But there is a rival model of responsibility, associated with the position which Anscombe dubbed consequentialism. A consequentialist must deny much of what I have alleged so far; and for this reason, as well as for the reason that consequentialism is prevalent in our culture, it is to this moral theory that I now turn.

The term 'consequentialism' has come to mean any moral theory for which the value of an action is solely a function of the value of its consequences—'value' being understood in various ways, notably (for utilitarians) as having to do with the amount of pleasure produced. But the view which Anscombe was interested in delineating, although closely associated with utilitarianism, was a view primarily about intended versus foreseen consequences, and also about the *range* of consequences attributable to an action. In 'Modern Moral Philosophy', she mentions Sidgwick as having made the move of denying '*any* difference between foreseen and intended consequences, as far as responsibility is concerned'; and she suggests 'that *this* move on the part of Sidgwick explains the difference between old-fashioned Utilitarianism and that *consequentialism*, as I name it, which marks him and every English academic moral philosopher since him' (p. 36).

As a matter of history, Sidgwick was not, I think, the first philosopher to have assimilated foreseen and intended consequences. Bentham had already done so, and the idea goes still further back. It is expressed, for example, by Benjamin Franklin's comic creation, Miss Polly Barker, who when defending herself in a New England court on a charge of bearing illegitimate children, addresses the court thus:

And on the other hand, take into your wise Consideration, the great and growing Number of Batchelors in the Country, many of whom, from the mean Fear of the Expence of a Family, have never sincerely and honourably Courted a Woman in their Lives; and by their Manner of Living, leave unproduced (which I think is little better than Murder) Hundreds of their Posterity to the Thousandth Generation.[26]

The form of Polly Barker's argument will be familiar to modern readers. We find it more starkly expressed in the following passage:

To fail to do beneficial research is as wrong as doing harmful research. To fail to release a drug which will save 100,000 lives is morally equivalent to killing 100,000 people. To fail to develop a drug which will save 100,000 lives is morally equivalent to failing to release it. We may not be able to point to those people whose lives would have been saved but their lives are no less valuable because they are in the future or they are anonymous.[27]

Not for these writers the restraint of Polly Barker's phraseology, 'little better than Murder'; no, for them, what we have is something on a par with murder. It goes without saying that the equivalences asserted by Savulescu and Devolder are not embodied in our legal system. Charges of mass murder are yet to be made against those who fail to develop life-saving drugs, partly, no doubt, because of the difficulty of 'pointing to' the people in question, as the authors coyly express the analogous difficulty *vis-à-vis* the victims.

---

[26] Benjamin Franklin, 'The Speech of Miss Polly Barker', in *The Autobiography and Other Writings*, ed. O. Seavey (Oxford: Oxford University Press, 1993), p. 249.

[27] J. Savulescu and K. Devolder, 'The Moral Imperative to Conduct Stem Cell and Cloning Research', *Cambridge Quarterly of Healthcare Ethics* 15(1): 7–21.

Both the above-quoted passages illustrate how two claims are typically joined together:

(DSE) There is no morally significant difference, as far as responsibility goes, between intended consequences and foreseen (or foreseeable) consequences;

(NR) If B wouldn't have occurred had you done A, then by not doing A you cause, or help cause, B.[28]

The reason why these two claims are connected in the minds of consequentialists is, I think, that the kind of responsibility which is serving as a model is responsibility for *negligence*. By this I mean that what gives these two claims any plausibility at all, especially (NR), is a certain picture of responsibility—namely, the sort of responsibility which may be engendered by a surgeon's failing to wash her hands, or a motorist's failing to take care near a pedestrian crossing, or a journalist's failing to confirm that somebody really did say what has been attributed to him. In these cases, the surgeon, motorist, and journalist may be called to account for occurrences they did not intend, such as a patient's death, or a pedestrian's injuries, or the ruining of someone's reputation; and in all these cases, the bad occurrences are imputed to them because of their failing to do something. The various omissions can properly be cited as among the causes of those occurrences; that is to say, such an omission will be among the first things, quite possibly the first thing, to be mentioned in answering, 'Why did such-and-such occur?'

Now what such cases evidently have in common is that the negligent person is meant to be doing something (e.g. confirming an attribution), and he is not doing it. But how is it determined *which* things are those things that a person is meant to be doing? Various features of a situation can determine this: your job, the activity you're engaged in, your relationship to another person, your physical proximity to another person, and so on. The list of features apt for making something your business is probably open-ended. But it is because the situation a person is in has some such feature that the person is called to account—not simply because

---

[28]   DSE = Doctrine of Single Effect; NR = Negative Responsibility. The phrase 'Doctrine of Single Effect' is constructed by analogy with 'Doctrine of Double Effect'. The traditional Doctrine of Double Effect is the best-known form of the view that the intended effects of an action are to be distinguished from its merely foreseen effects when it comes to responsibility.

he did not do a certain thing. And this connects with our earlier account of 'good' as attributive. In 'a good F', the concept 'F' will involve some sort of goal, or function, or role, or characteristic mode; hence being a good doctor, or a good parent, or a good neighbour, is a matter of doing what can reasonably be expected of a person with that goal, or function, or role, or characteristic mode.[29] If you do *not* do something that is essentially involved in being a good F, that means that if you are an F you will fail to be a good one. Of course, if the reason for your not doing that thing lies outside you, and so doesn't relate to your aims or your character, then you are not to blame—e.g. if you were yourself prevented by another from doing it. On the other hand, 'I didn't *know* I was meant to do that' will usually not be an excuse, since in the typical case knowing what is involved in being a good F is itself one of the things that is involved in being a good F (for fairly obvious reasons); hence, in the relevant sense, knowledge or ignorance are among the things that can bear upon a person's character.

These remarks constitute a sketch of our concept of negligence as it is actually employed in our lives. They do not, of course, provide grounds for believing either (DSE) or (NR), above. Rather, the everyday notion of negligence is inflated by consequentialism—defined as it is by (DSE) and (NR)—into a grand theory of moral responsibility. This theory happens to be of particular use when it comes to criticizing those who won't join a crusade, for if you have made a case why something should be done, it helps to be able to accuse those who won't assist you in doing it of malice, or obstructionism, or the nearest thing in your conceptual scheme. As George W. Bush said about those countries unwilling to join in his Iraq adventure, 'You're either with us or against us'.[30] The tone of Savulescu/ Devolder's assertions, like Bush's, could be called *pre-accusatory*. This tone is a concomitant of a feature of consequentialism that has been more than once remarked upon, namely that it has a tendency to divide all actions open to an agent into the obligatory and the forbidden. (Look at the title of Savulescu/Devolder's article.)

---

[29] As in a court of law, the phrase 'reasonable expectation' works perfectly well—not despite, but *because of*, its being vague; it does not open the door to an anarchic proliferation of requirements. Once again, the social language-game of asking for and giving reasons is the setting for all this, and is no more characterized by an insane onus of justification than (*pace* Descartes) is the language-game of theoretical enquiry. See Chapter 1, p. 11.

[30] In full: 'You're either with us or against us in the fight against terror'.

None of this, so far, is meant as refutation. For that, we need to look more closely at (DSE) and (NR). Since proponents of (DSE) almost always rely on (NR) to arrive at their substantive conclusions, I think it worth focusing on the latter.[31] (NR) is relevant to (DSE) because it brings many occurrences within the range of *things brought about by an action*; and it does this by relying on a counterfactual model of causation, such that 'x caused y' is explained as meaning or amounting to 'If x hadn't happened, y would not have'. What is to be remarked about this model of causation is that, unless it is further qualified, it enormously inflates the class of cause-effect relations. The Big Bang is a cause of the egg's boiling; Smith's birth is a cause of his death; and, since we are allowed to include negative conditions, my dog's not jumping out of a fourth storey window to land on top of the man below is a cause of the bank robbery (since the man was on his way to rob a bank). Tough-minded philosophers may reply, 'Yes, all these are strictly speaking causes, or perhaps better, causal conditions, of the events in question—so what?' To which the reply is that the real question has just been shifted elsewhere, as so often in philosophy; for what we now want to know is why an investigation into a fire mentions a cigarette on the floor rather than the presence of oxygen, or why a doctor's not washing her hands is mentioned in a post mortem rather than the patient's having lived in London.

(DSE) and (NR) are typically used in accusatory or pre-accusatory contexts. But they would work as well in supplying grounds for rejoicing and self-congratulation, precisely on account of that inflation of the class of effects of an action which I have mentioned. After all, if I can be cited as a contributory cause of any death that I fail to prevent, shouldn't my *not* killing somebody be called 'saving his life'? If it weren't for the fact that I didn't kill my brother yesterday, he wouldn't be alive today! As far as practical deliberation goes, perhaps an agent should just balance his awfulness off against his evident bounteousness . . . Just as the accusations entailed by Savulescu/Devolder's account would be divorced from any feasible practice of blame or punishment, so the congratulations likewise entailed by it would be divorced from any feasible practice of thanks or reward. Also relevant here are those human reactions of resentment and gratitude whose importance for this topic was noted by P. F. Strawson.

---

[31] For some discussion of DSE, see Teichmann, *The Philosophy of Elizabeth Anscombe*, pp. 112–26.

As Strawson argued, there is in general no higher level of rationality by reference to which the range of what we resent or are thankful for may be radically reduced, or (we may add) radically extended.[32] Indeed, an obviously simplistic counterfactual theory of causation couldn't be an element in any 'level of rationality' at all.

Once again, the anthropocentric nature of our concepts comes to the fore. Notions of praise and blame have their roots in the lives actually led by human beings. But the same also goes for notions of cause and effect: the reason why a cigarette is cited as cause of a fire rather than the presence of oxygen has to do with human interests—in this case, the interest we have in preventing fires (which will rarely be effected by creating oxygen-free environments, given our need for oxygen). Both routes to prevention and routes to production play a role in determining what we call a cause, as does the idea of what's *meant* to happen. A sprinkler system is meant to come on in the event of a fire; eyelids are meant to close properly; doctors are meant to take steps not to harm their patients. The senses of the phrase 'meant to' in these examples are different, but related. It is not hard to see why we want to track down things that are not doing what they're meant to be doing, since we rely on these things in leading our lives and forming our plans.[33]

Consequentialists appear to view causation as 'the same everywhere', and thus as susceptible of the sort of simple account exemplified by (NR). But causation is not the same everywhere, and although counterfactuals are certainly *relevant* to causation, they cannot be the whole of it. But in any case one can argue as follows: assume that the whole truth about causation is given by a counterfactuals-based theory, so that (NR) must be true; why, then, should moral responsibility be tied to the (known) effects of one's actions? It would seem, rather, that the vast—nay, infinite—class of the 'effects' of my actions must strike anyone as having very little to do with *me*.

The point here is not that it is terribly difficult to know what the total effects of your actions will be. You don't *need* to know such a thing, given the wildly expanded notion of 'effect' on offer, and the idea that you *would* need to know it in order to be quite certain of the moral worth of your

---

[32] Cf. Chapter 1, pp. 15–16. Strawson's article is 'Freedom and Resentment', in *Freedom and Resentment and Other Essays* (London: Methuen, 1974).

[33] Cf. Chapter 1, pp. 22–3.

actions leads to some very odd results. We are now, it is true, in the domain of all those far-flung 'consequences' of an act which a consequentialist will not hold against an agent, being so hard (or impossible) for the agent to guess at—so that our topic is no longer moral responsibility. Nevertheless, the typical consequentialist is committed to this claim: that it is not certain that Hitler's actions as Führer were morally dreadful, since it is possible that the future total history of mankind would have been even worse had he not done what he did. Of course, Hitler showed some very nasty characteristics, of the sort which can be fairly safely predicted to have bad consequences in the relatively short term; but for the consequentialist, character traits are secondary to actual outcomes in the moral scheme of things. It is the total history of the world that really matters.

Now the idea that there is a possibility, even a tiny one, that the Nazi regime was a good thing is just idiotic. There is an instructive parallel to be drawn here with Mill's treatment of arithmetical necessity. Mill's empiricism led him to diagnose our faith in the truth of $7 + 5 = 12$ as arising from the large number of occasions where we have experienced seven things and five things making a total of twelve things.[34] And that means that, although very unlikely, it is not impossible that the next batch of seven and five things will in fact fail to add up to twelve. $7 + 5 = 12$, if taken as expressing a universal proposition, is at best highly probable. A similar conclusion must be drawn concerning 'The Holocaust was an evil event' if the nature of evil is explained in standard consequentialist terms. Mill was wrong about arithmetical certainty, the consequentialist is wrong about certainty in the moral sphere—and in each case, the diagnosis is that the philosopher is *looking in the wrong place*, something that in its turn can be explained by the impulse to philosophical generalization: Mill had an over-simple 'one size fits all' conception of knowledge, while consequentialists have an over-simple 'one size fits all' conception of causation.

VIII.

One of the main attractions of utilitarianism and consequentialism is the fact that these theories address themselves to large-scale problems, such as battery farming, or third-world starvation, or (in Bentham's day) prison

---

[34] J. S. Mill, *A System of Logic Ratiocinative and Inductive* (1843), bk II, ch. 5; esp. sec. 6.

conditions. Classical utilitarianism was as much a political movement as a philosophical one, and nineteenth-century utilitarians proposed numerous measures to those in power, i.e. to those whose job it was to deal with the problems of society, or with many such problems. But of course it is not only politicians who concern themselves with the large-scale problems of the world, and the existence of charitable organizations shows one obvious way in which non-politicians get involved in tackling such problems.

The word 'charity' comes from the Latin *caritas*, which roughly means *love*—or as Hume might have put it, *benevolence*. Acts motivated by charitable or benevolent feelings belong to a different category from that to which belong acts motivated by a sense of obligation: although 'ungenerous' is certainly a criticism, it is not the same sort of criticism as 'dishonest'. As critics of modern utilitarianism have pointed out, the inclusion of charitable acts among obligatory ones indicates an impoverishment, and a person who saw his ethical relations with his fellow human beings as exhausted by notions such as obligation and duty, and acted accordingly, would himself be emotionally impoverished. Nevertheless, even if I am not under a personal obligation to give money to charities, or to develop life-saving drugs, I may have certain responsibilities *qua* member of a group with certain responsibilities; and it is this consideration, I think, that gives sense to talk of 'what we owe', e.g. to people living in the third world, or to those who will come after us. I said above that it will be in virtue of certain features of a person's situation that he can be said to have been negligent, and to have *failed* to do something (as opposed to simply not having done it). This idea can be extended to groups of people, such as those on a committee or on a board of directors—after all, many act-descriptions only make sense as predicated of collective acts (e.g. 'repealing a law'), and it is frequently the job of a particular group to carry out acts of this sort, so that failure to do so constitutes group negligence.

There is a strong argument to the effect that, given modern conditions, the people of a country (say) can be seen as having certain collective responsibilities to people in other countries. These responsibilities would not arise from any decisions or background conventions, any more than does the individual responsibility you have to help the person next to you in the café who is choking on a fishbone. In the latter case, the relevant feature of the situation is physical proximity; and it can be argued that there is an analogous feature of the situation we find ourselves in as people well aware of and not at all cut off from those in need in other countries. The argument would need, I think, to stress those two facts: that the information is there and the power to do something as a group is real. For one might say that, in the individual case, physical proximity is important precisely because it goes with immediate knowledge and opportunity (I can't help but see him choking, and I can hit him on the back at once).

The difficulty arises at the level of individual action. How can I do something that is intended to contribute to a group action unless there has been something like a group decision to perform that action? But there need not have been an actual decision. A general movement can serve as a background against which my own action can come under the relevant description—a movement such as a general boycott, or a general attempt to raise the money to buy a field. There won't always be such general movements afoot, however; and where there is not, individual actions like sending money, or indeed trying to start a movement, fall into a different category—they are, or are more like, acts done purely from charitable or benevolent motives. Hence the sort of Aristotelian approach in ethics which is argued for in this book is not disabled from including in its account of the good life goals relating to large-scale problems, including ones that can only be achieved by groups of people. A human being is a social animal, and human flourishing, as has already been argued, necessarily includes a strong strain of altruism. Reasons for action include reasons for group action, and good human agents will often see their agency as tied to the agency of other people. The capacity to do so may in many instances derive from a more general capacity, that of seeing oneself as part of a community—and perhaps also, for that matter, as part of history and as part of the natural world. In Chapter 4, I will be looking at how the capacity to see yourself in these ways can be involved in leading a good life, how in fact it can be a source of human happiness.

3

Pleasure and Pain

I.

How are pleasure and pain relevant to ethics?

A simple answer would be: 'Pleasure is good, and pain is bad; and ethics has to do with what's good and what's bad.' But even this simple thought would probably go hand in hand with a further one: namely, that creatures typically pursue pleasure and avoid pain (if they can). Pleasure and pain, that is, have a crucial connection with action, and since it is clear that morality is of practical, and not merely theoretical, import, philosophers have tended to agree on the importance of pleasure and pain for ethics, even if this basic agreement hides a mass of disagreements as to the natures of pleasure and pain. Even those philosophers who have thought of moral motivation as pure and impartial in a way that *excludes* any idea in the agent's mind of what it would be pleasant to do would nevertheless agree that pleasure and pain are of huge ethical significance; for such philosophers would very likely see them as the chief forces capable of diverting us from the Moral Way.

The above remarks have yoked pleasure and pain together as if they were opposites, in some sense of that word. And this has been the dominant view of matters in philosophy as far back as Aristotle, who opposed *hēdonē* and *lupē*.[1] Because the primary use of the English word 'pain' is in application to a kind of physical sensation—as in 'lower back

---

[1] See Aristotle, *Nicomachean Ethics* (Cambridge, MA: Harvard University Press, 1975), VII. xiii.1.

pain'—the opposition of pleasure and pain by English-speaking writers has encouraged, or been a natural corollary of, the view that pleasure is a sort of sensation. We have already come across the conception of mental states, such as emotions, as akin to sensations, these being thought of as self-intimating episodes of consciousness, with a certain duration, typically having a certain intensity, and with an intrinsic 'character' knowable authoritatively by the subject. And we found this conception to be quite inadequate, certainly as applied to the emotions. The 'sensation' model is no better as applied to pleasure, though it is perhaps yet more tempting to apply it to pleasure than it is to apply it to such things as pride or offence.

According to the view in question, pleasure is a certain inner state, one that accompanies the various activities, thoughts, etc., that are found pleasant by the person doing the acting, thinking, etc. Whether this inner state gets called a 'sensation' is of little account, and there are many philosophers who would prefer a more up-to-date term: 'quale', plural 'qualia'. A rose by any other name would smell as sweet, and much the same goes for ideas, impressions, sensations, qualia, or whatever you want to call them. The key features are those just mentioned: pleasure-states (the story goes) are self-intimating episodes of consciousness, with a certain duration, typically having a certain intensity, and with an intrinsic 'character' knowable authoritatively by the subject. Their connection with outward behaviour is contingent, in the sense that these inner states have an intrinsic character or nature that is independent of any behaviour. Even a functionalist will assert this last; for although a functionalist definition of 'pleasure' will amount (roughly) to 'that state (typically) produced by such-and-such causes and (typically) producing such-and-such behavioural (and other) effects', the state *in itself* will be e.g. a brain-state, which it is logically possible should produce quite other behavioural effects from those normally produced.[2]

It is not hard to see why the view of pleasure as an inner state should have proved so popular. In fact, there are a number of reasons.

First, there is the quite general tendency to regard psychological expressions as denoting inner states or processes going on in the subject

---

[2]   As with David Lewis' imaginary 'mad pain'; see Lewis, 'Mad Pain and Martian Pain', in *Readings in Philosophy of Psychology, Vol. I*, ed. Block (Cambridge, MA: Harvard University Press, 1980), pp. 216–22. For a diagnosis of the functionalist impulse, see Chapter 1, pp. 22–3.

and authoritatively known to him. This tendency itself has at least three sources: (i) the construal of linguistic meaning on the model of name and bearer, so that e.g. 'pleasure' must refer to a thing or entity if it is to be a meaningful expression (an entity with a certain independent nature, that is the same entity on the various occasions of reference); (ii) the idea that first-person authority about psychological states is to be explained by reference to a 'private theatre' to which the subject alone has access; (iii) the quasi-methodological approach to psychological questions by which the person who wants to discover the nature of (e.g.) thinking tries to do so by seeing what's going on when he's thinking, with the result that anything he finds is bound to be an episode of consciousness.

Secondly, among things that are found pleasant or pleasurable there is a large and important class of sensations (impressions, qualia, what have you)—e.g. sensations of taste, sex, warmth, and intoxication. It is then natural to think of these sensations as themselves somehow constituting one's pleasure; which however makes immediate problems for the view that pleasant activities etc., are accompanied by a particular sensation (pleasure), since all the sensations just mentioned are evidently quite different from one another.

Thirdly, there is the recognition that a person can habitually go in for something and enjoy it, but can also habitually go in for something and *not* enjoy it; which appears to show that pleasure is not a matter of what a person does or even how she does it, but of 'what is going on inside her'.

And finally, answers to 'Why do you want to do that?' such as 'For fun', or 'For the pleasure of it', are very often sufficient and adequate answers—they supply desirability characterizations, in Anscombe's phrase. The aim of the person would then seem to be: pleasure. The alternative would surely be: to go in for an activity having the property of pleasantness—which sounds absurd, especially since *whether* an activity is pleasant is for the agent to say, there being much diversity in what different people find pleasant. ('Chess-playing is not *in itself* pleasant'.) One does the thing in order that doing it produce in one the state of pleasure; this appears to be the explanation why 'For fun' supplies a desirability characterization, and why one has authority as to whether one has succeeded in getting any pleasure. Pleasure thus appears as a state of the subject, authoritatively known to her, and produced by various outer or inner causes.

II.

Here then are four sources of the idea that pleasure is an 'inner state'. I will be looking at the last two later on in this chapter. What of the first, the general tendency to regard psychological expressions as denoting inner states or processes? In Chapter 1 I sketched how as human beings we are struck, in an instinctual way, by syndromes of behaviour, syndromes occurring in one another but also in animals—and how these syndromes are the subject-matter of many of our psychological concepts. These facts account for various features of those concepts, e.g. their irreducibility to any set lists of independently describable behaviours, their connections with human reactions (such as the characteristic reactions to another's rage or misery), the way in which we teach psychological terms to children when they are learning to talk, the close connection between the psychological and the ethical, and even the special role of the first person (*very* schematically: a first-person avowal of an emotion, e.g. is itself a criterion of the person's feeling that emotion, and thus has a different status from a second- or third-person ascription of the emotion). If all this is right, then the 'inner state' picture cannot be generally adequate.[3] And when it comes to pleasure, it is clear that there are syndromes of behaviour familiar to us as the expressions of pleasure, as also of pain, enormously various and multi-faceted though these be—e.g. smiling and laughter on the one hand, weeping and slumping on the other.

Now a post-dualist philosopher, such as a functionalist or physicalist, will very likely think himself immune to some of the classic criticisms of the 'inner state' account, such as are implicit in (ii) and (iii), above (p. 97). In fact, as has been noted,[4] physicalists who put faith in what neuroscience can tell us about psychology often unwittingly betray dualistic assumptions; and this is not wholly surprising, given the picture shared by dualists and physicalists, of the inner state (be it immaterial or material). Even so, it is true that functionalism and physicalism merit their own treatment. Much could be said on this topic, but I will restrict myself to a single form of objection. It is an objection that relates to our reactions to other people's psychological states, e.g. their pleasure or pain—reactions

---

[3] The fullest treatment of these issues in modern times, or indeed ever, is of course that of Wittgenstein. See his *Philosophical Investigations* (*passim*).

[4] Chapter 1, pp. 29–30.

whose status cannot be given due recognition by functionalism/physical-
ism, any more than by traditional dualism.

Imagine that a friend of yours goes for a brain-scan—maybe he has been
suffering from headaches. The results of the scan come back, and appear to
show that he has no brain. Naturally, your friend, who is not a little
disconcerted, is summoned for a second scan, and subsequently a third
one and a fourth, using different scanners. But each time the results are the
same: no brain. An incision into the skull appears to reveal that it contains
nothing but rather watery blood. What is your reaction?

If mental states are just states of the central nervous system (physicalism),
or alternatively are whatever internal states realize certain functional roles
(functionalism), then it is dubious whether your friend can experience
anything at all. Your friend, in fact, seems to be none other than that
character from recent philosophy, the Zombie. This character is usually
described as being physically and behaviourally 'just like us', but as lacking
mental states, mental states being conceived along traditional dualist
lines—i.e. as sensation-like episodes in a private realm. But the Zombie
we are now dealing with is a physicalist or functionalist Zombie. He
appears just like us, and behaves just as we do, but lacks mental states,
conceived along physicalist/functionalist lines—i.e. as physical and/or
functional states (typically internal). We can assume that continued investigations, plus what is sometimes called 'our best scientific theory',
together fail to point to any internal states of your friend that could
be identified as beliefs, or desires, or perceptions, or pleasure, or pain.
If physicalist or functionalist theories are right, you would be rational to
think, 'Oh well; it doesn't really matter what I do to him, or to *it*. He can't
really feel pain, or anything else for that matter—I could chop off his arm
for meat . . . ' But of course you would do no such thing, not because of
some residual doubt about the results of the scans, nor because it would
make this thing before you less efficient as a machine, but because he (not
'it') is your friend, is a human being (a somebody), is talking to you about
these distressing results, is obviously afraid, is looking you in the eye. There
is no question but that he is afraid, and if you chop his arm off, there will be
no question at all when he screams in agony that it *is* agony. What there is
inside your friend's *skull* is simply a red herring. A person who could
blithely saw a screaming man's arm off, as one might saw off a branch of a
tree, would be a psychopath; he would be someone whose grasp of reality
is defective, not someone who knows something the rest of us don't.

I don't think that this little story can be objected to on the grounds that it is physically impossible for a creature to exhibit behaviours of the sort we are imagining without there being some internal mechanism. Such physical impossibility may be admitted. The question is whether there is a conceptual possibility of someone's lacking a brain, and moreover lacking any internal state which mediates between 'input' (like having an arm chopped off) and 'output' (like screaming). And while the whole issue of conceptual possibility and impossibility is a vexed one, it is to be noted that functionalists and physicalists characteristically rely on a theory of causation according to which there is a Humean distinctness of cause and effect that is meant to point to the conceivability of an event's lacking its usual (and even scientifically requisite) cause,[5] even—it would seem—to the conceivability of its lacking *any* cause. (Not that we need describe the brainless person in such terms: the cause of his smile, e.g. could be your giving him a hug.)

What our story of the brainless person serves to bring home is how psychological concepts are anchored in human reactions and interactions—a by now familiar theme.[6] And for our present purposes, this is of more acute relevance to the ordinary concept of pain than it is to that of pleasure, in the sense that there is a rather definite human impulse to help those who are in pain and suffering, including your imaginary brainless friend. There is no very definite natural reaction to another's pleasure, but instead a large range of possible reactions, from sympathetic pleasure through indifference to disgust or even alarm. This variety corresponds to the variety of things *in which* people can take pleasure, and points to the proper home of the phenomenon of pleasure: not in one's private mental theatre, but in one's activities, broadly construed. (This view of things will be elaborated later on.) To be sure, there are many and various things capable of annoying people, and as we shall see, there is a case for opposing pleasure not to pain, but to displeasure or annoyance. But if it is pain we are talking about, be it physical or mental (i.e. anguish/depression/grief...), an asymmetry of the sort I have described does exist; and it is

---

[5] The motive for this is to allow the physicalist or functionalist to dissociate the allegedly crucial internal state from any merely behavioural manifestations. Lewis' 'mad pain' is a case in point; see n. 2 above.

[6] The story and its implications are more fully discussed in R. Teichmann, 'The Functionalist's Inner State', in *Wittgenstein and Contemporary Philosophy of Mind* , ed. S. Schroeder (Basingstoke: Palgrave, 2001), pp. 24–35.

arguably the source of that desire, on the part of some utilitarians, to enjoin the minimization of suffering, rather than the maximization of pleasure (even where calculation of the latter involves taking 'pain' as having negative value). The thought 'Suffering is bad', however inchoate, has a certain force or urgency, connected with the human impulse to help. This force is lacking from the thought 'Pleasure is good', since, as I have said, there is no analogous typical human reaction to manifestations of pleasure.

Pleasure and pain, I have been arguing, are not inner states, either of the traditional dualist variety or of more recent physicalist/functionalist varieties. The expression 'inner state' is not an ordinary English expression, of course, and it is possible, even probable, that in some contexts it could be used appropriately of pleasure or of pain, as of other psychological states— so long as it didn't carry the theoretical baggage I have been associating it with, whether dualist or physicalist. But if pleasure and pain are not inner states in the sense or senses intended, what are they?

III.

I will defer giving an answer to this question for the time being. Instead, I want to return to those simple assertions with which this chapter began, namely, 'Pleasure is good' and 'Pain is bad'. These assertions are as philosophically problematic as they are natural to make; and they figure centrally in our ethical thought. But what do they mean?

If pleasure is a good thing, it seems it must be an intrinsically good thing, as opposed to being instrumentally good. The question 'Why do you want what's pleasurable?' has something absurd about it, and that would not be the case were pleasure merely good as a means to some further end. The concept of something *good in itself* is, however, a rather puzzling one. Earlier on, I gave a (very) potted history of twentieth-century philosophical thought about 'good',[7] in which figured the two theories of Moorean intuitionism and post-Moorean subjectivism—the latter more of a 'theory-cluster'. Moore does in fact think that pleasure is good, especially aesthetic pleasure and the pleasure of friendship; and for him, goodness is what it is (and not another thing) and one can't really say much else that is positive. A subjectivist, on the other hand, is likely to say that the statement 'Pleasure

---

[7] Chapter 2, pp. 56–7.

is good' expresses a pro-attitude towards pleasure—not only one's own pleasure, but also that of other people and animals. This pro-attitude, being a feeling or emotion, can be neither rationally defended nor rationally criticized. J. J. C. Smart, in his contribution to *Utilitarianism: For and Against*, seems to adhere to this line.[8]

What of the third view of 'good' which I mentioned, according to which it functions, at least frequently, as an attributive adjective, i.e. as a fragment of longer phrases: 'good F', 'good for so-and-so', 'good at ϕ-ing', etc.? It is not immediately clear how 'good' could be functioning attributively in the statement 'Pleasure is good', or for that matter in the statement 'Pleasure is a good'. Good as what?—or good for what? Well, one possible answer to this last query is: good for human beings (and perhaps more generally, for animals). A life without pleasure, it could be said, is not a good life; children deprived of all pleasure when growing up will be maladjusted, unhappy, and quite probably psychologically disturbed. But isn't something similar true of pain? Isn't a life with little or no *pain* liable not to be a good life? This could either mean a life where physical injury, etc., fails to produce pain in the person—such people tend to die young—or alternatively an extremely sheltered and cosseted life—this being a recipe for producing a spoilt, soft, and morally flabby individual. Isn't pain in fact necessary for leading a good life, or rather the right kind and amount of pain? It is true that this line of thought doesn't present an immediate problem for the view that pleasure is a good, for perhaps both pleasure and pain are goods (if of the right kind and amount). Nevertheless, a problem lurks here.

At this point we need to introduce a point that will assume much importance later in the discussion: namely, that 'It's pleasant' very often gives a desirability characterization, i.e. a sufficient and adequate answer to 'What do you want that for?' If we are to explain the sense of 'Pleasure is (a) good' in terms of the fact that pleasure is good for human beings, connecting this fact with the capacity of 'It's pleasant' to supply a desirability characterization, then we will face the question: Why does 'It's painful' *not* give a desirability characterization, given that pain would seem also to be good for human beings? For we would surely hesitate to call 'X is painful' a characterization of X as desirable, even in a case where the

---

[8] J. J. C. Smart, 'An Outline of a Utilitarian System of Ethics', in Smart and B. Williams, *Utilitarianism: For and Against* (Cambridge: Cambridge University Press, 1973). See in particular sec. 1, p. 7.

pain is character-building: to answer the question 'Why do you want that?' by saying 'Because it hurts', or 'Because it's distressing', is not a way of rendering one's aims or actions intelligible. Hence the fact that masochism is recognized as deviant, as a trait that needs to be made sense of.

Against this it might be pointed out that the *function* of pain is to signal that something is wrong, for instance that a part of the body has been injured; while the function of pleasure (at any rate of physical pleasure) is, if anything, to signal that things are as they should be. The pleasures of food, sex, warmth, etc., are obvious examples. But this way of putting things is liable to lead us to classify pleasure as a sensation, in the sense in which physical pain is a sensation, and such a classification is misguided, as was argued in the last section. Perhaps it is correct to say that the function of the pleasurable sensations associated with certain bodily states and activities is to signal that things are as they should be. But this still leaves untouched all those pleasures that are not those of bodily states and activities, concerning which it can't be claimed that the function of the pleasurable sensations is to signal that things are as they should be. The only *sensations* you have when sprinting, or reading about the Second World War, or attending an auction, may not be pleasant sensations at all, but either neutral or painful.

So there seem to be difficulties with alleging that pleasure is as such good for human beings, certainly if by claiming this it is hoped to explain why 'It's pleasant' (often) supplies a desirability characterization. But the main and overriding objection to the idea that pleasure is good for human beings is that people can take pleasure in all sorts of things, good, bad, and indifferent. There are extremely common pleasures that serve no practical ends and make no obvious contribution to human flourishing, such as going on funfair rides or polishing one's furniture; worse than that, there are very common pleasures that are actually inimical to the good of others and/or of oneself, such as the pleasures of cruelty and dissipation. And, *pace* the utilitarians, it is not as if in these cases there is something bad, some torture, say, plus something good, the pleasure of the sadist. The fact that he enjoys it does nothing to mitigate the badness of what a sadist does.[9]

---

[9] There are parallel points to be made about pain, distress, etc. Remorse involves some sort of distress or anguish (whose object will be something one has done), and such distress or anguish is not simply an unfortunate side-effect that wouldn't occur in an ideal world. Subtract the pain and what you have isn't remorse. But, given its surroundings (human life, human nature), remorse is a good thing.

Thus we find that there is a case for saying: if pleasure is a good, in so far as a life that lacks it is deficient, then so is pain—in which case, we won't be able to explain why 'It's pleasant' supplies a desirability characterization in terms simply of its being a good for human beings, since 'It's painful' never supplies such a characterization. Simultaneously there is a case for saying: pleasure is *not* quite generally a good, since people take pleasure in all sorts of things.

Why then *does* 'It's pleasant' supply a desirability characterization? And how, if at all, does its doing so connect with the thought that pleasure is (a) good?

Desirability characterizations were discussed in the last chapter,[10] but let us remind ourselves of what they are. If someone says 'I want some string', they can be asked what they want it *for*. They might reply, 'I want to tie up this present'. The question 'But why do you want to do *that*?' wouldn't usually be asked by anyone who knows the ways of the world; but it could for all that be informatively answered. That answer might in turn provoke the question, 'And why do you want that?'—and so on and so on. At a certain point we will get an answer to 'Why?' that presents an end as simply desirable in itself. This answer will supply a desirability characterization. The question 'Why do you want that?', asked of such an end, will be futile, frivolous, or uncomprehending.

What determines whether a given end-description counts as a desirability characterization? It might be alleged that the process of asking 'Why?' only comes to a halt when the enquirer feels satisfied with the reasons given, and that this is a subjective matter. But in fact dissatisfaction with reasons can itself be unreasonable, in the practical just as much as in the theoretical domain. Conversely, the adequacy of a given reason for action, or of a given end, are not matters which it is in the power of the agent to decide. 'Why are you removing your socks?'—If I were to answer this question by saying, 'So as to add them to the cassoulet', I would not, without further explanation, supply an adequate reason for my actions. And the phrase '...so as to add socks to the cassoulet' does not in itself present some end as desirable. The reasons for this have to do with (i) the public nature of the language-game of giving and receiving reasons,

---

[10] Chapter 2, Section III.

together with (ii) a shared notion of what is normal, natural, and intelligible for human beings.

Given that there are fairly objective criteria for what shall count as a desirability characterization, it seems clear that one example of such a characterization will be 'X is pleasant'. 'But why do you want what's pleasant?' certainly has the appearance of a silly question. The end presented as thus desirable might be that of drinking another glass of champagne, or of going for a walk on a summer's day. These are examples of activities, but there are also passive pleasures, such as the pleasure of being driven in a fast car. And perhaps there is also such a thing as being pleased by, taking pleasure in, some fact, such as having come into an inheritance. In what follows, I will be using 'is pleasant', 'is pleasurable', 'is fun', etc., as more or less interchangeable, despite the differences between the uses of these expressions. These differences (I hope) will not be germane to our enquiry.

Now those philosophers who follow Aristotle and Aquinas would say that whatever is desired is desired under the aspect of the good, a thesis that received some attention in Chapter 2 (pp. 74–6). If you desire to have an operation for gallstones, which involves pain and the risk of infection or death, this will be because the operation may be viewed under the aspect of the good at which it *aims*—namely, good health. When it comes to your ends, as opposed to the means you adopt towards those ends, such ends (e.g. good health) will be desired unqualifiedly under the aspect of the good, i.e. *as* goods. There is room for error about where ultimate goods are to be found, i.e. about what things they inhere in, but if you err in this way that just means that your aim is off-target, not that you are aiming at something other than the target. The target, in the relevant sense, will always be some genuine good. Thus the Thomist.

A person's goal or end is what they would give as the final answer in a series of answers to the repeated question, 'Why do you want that?' It would thus seem natural for a Thomist to equate the goodness of an end with its desirability, in Anscombe's sense: for a desirability characterization brings an end to such repeated asking of 'Why?' An example of a desirability characterization, as we have noted, is 'X is pleasant'. So it appears that to desire something because it is or would be pleasant, and not as a means to anything further, is to desire that thing under the aspect of the good, and *as* good. But we should at any rate pause before attributing such a claim to Elizabeth Anscombe, despite her adherence to the Thomist view of desire just outlined. Having said that it isn't one of her aims (in *Intention*) to examine the concept of pleasure in any detail, she goes on:

Nor should an unexamined thesis 'pleasure is good' (whatever that may mean) be ascribed to me. For my present purposes all that is required is that 'It's pleasant' is an adequate answer to 'What's the good of it?' or 'What do you want that for?'[11]

The difficulty we face, and which lurks behind these remarks of Anscombe's, is the following: should we explain the notion of a desirability characterization via that of what is good, or vice versa? In other words, do all answers that terminate a series of 'Why?' questions by counting as adequate and final manage to count as such because they allude to what is good, or do ends count as good because in citing them as ends one furnishes final and adequate answers to the question 'Why?'? The word 'good' is certainly *capable* of being used in a substantive sense, a sense that is independent of the notion of a desirability characterization—e.g. where it occurs attributively, in phrases like 'good barometer', 'good at spelling', etc. But it might be argued that if we are to speak of final ends as good, or as desired under the aspect of the good, then we had better tie the sense of 'good', used thus, to that notion. For, as we have seen, there are difficulties in construing 'Pleasure is a good' along the lines of 'Pleasure is good for human beings'.

The present proposal, then, is to take seriously Anscombe's apparent assimilation, in the quotation above, of 'What's the good of it?' and 'What do you want that for?', and to see what she says about desirability characterizations as an *explication* of the Thomist thesis that whatever is desired is desired under the aspect of the good. According to this line of thought, to allege of 'X is pleasant' that it presents X under the aspect of the good is simply to say that it supplies an adequate answer to 'Why do you want X?', an answer that renders the agent's purposes and behaviour intelligible. There are, as I argued in Chapter 2, problems with the Thomist thesis taken quite generally, and the present proposal is not so much intended to save the thesis as to follow a philosophically promising path for our enquiry into pleasure and pain.

One advantage with this approach is the following. To concentrate on the notion of a desirability characterization is to concentrate on questions to do with the *justification* of aims and actions. If 'X is pleasant' supplies a

---

[11] Anscombe, *Intention*, pp. 77–8.

desirability characterization, then it gives a *prima facie* good reason for pursuing X. Only a *prima facie* good reason, for, as with any desirability characterization, there may be other considerations that count against pursuing X, and that override the reason given. One such consideration may be 'But if you pursue X, you will be acting badly'—pursuing X being a manifestation of some vice, some kind of defect of character. But the force of such an objection surely rests on the fact that 'eschewing vice' is itself a form of desirability characterization: 'Why should I be a good, as opposed to bad, human being?' appears to be a question in the same class as 'Why should I be healthy?'[12] The *interest* of 'X is pleasant' is that it is a reason carrying some weight, even if that weight can be overridden. And this is something we can assent to without committing ourselves to the view that pleasure is a good, in some more substantive sense of that term.

IV.

At this point, we must return to the question of the *nature* of pleasure. In Section I, I looked at some of the problems faced by an account of pleasure as a sensation, or quale, while in Section II, I briefly criticized functionalist and physicalist accounts. If these accounts are mistaken, where should we look instead?

Aristotle famously defines pleasure as 'the unimpeded activity of our natural state'.[13] In modern times, the philosopher who can be most credited with resurrecting an Aristotelian account of pleasure is arguably Gilbert Ryle.[14] Ryle's critique of the 'sensation' theory of pleasure is coupled with a positive account, according to which we need to look at such whole phrases as 'take pleasure in'; we can then see that 'Mary takes pleasure in riding' basically means 'Mary enjoys riding', or 'Mary likes riding'. To enjoy riding is not to do two things simultaneously, riding and enjoying;

---

[12] It may be pointed out that physical health is necessary for the achievement of many possible ends, whilst being a good human being is not. Being a good human being may even be said to have the character of *closing off* avenues that would otherwise be available to a person (by stealing, lying, etc.). But these facts do not indicate the greater intelligibility of 'Why should I be a good human being?' as compared with 'Why should I be healthy?'—at any rate if the arguments of the previous two chapters to do (i) with the social character of reason-giving and (ii) with the concept *good human being* are cogent.

[13] Aristotle, *Nicomachean Ethics*, VII.xii.3.

[14] G. Ryle, 'Pleasure', in his *Dilemmas* (Cambridge: Cambridge University Press, 1969), pp. 54–67.

it is to do one thing (riding) in a certain way, or against the background of a certain set of habits, or something along those lines. Enjoying is conceptually related to preferring, going in for, trying to get, etc.

What may be termed the Aristotelian account of pleasure avoids many of the pitfalls of the various 'inner state' models; and it is consonant with the general approach to psychological concepts which I have been adumbrating in this book. (See, e.g., the last paragraph of Section I, above.) But if one adopts the Aristotelian account, one faces a special problem with the thought that 'X is pleasant' supplies a desirability characterization. The root of the problem is this: that on the Aristotelian view, enjoying is a very close cousin of *wanting*.

Jeremy is asked: 'Why do you want to play pushpin?' He replies: 'Because playing pushpin is pleasant.' But the latter seems in effect to mean, 'Because I like playing pushpin'; and isn't this dangerously close to 'I want to play pushpin'? Our original question surely asked for a description of playing pushpin that would make sense of wanting to go in for it, a description that would render the desire to go in for it intelligible. 'I like playing pushpin' doesn't seem to give information about the activity of playing pushpin, so much as about the agent's propensity to play pushpin—which, it might be said, is the very thing we wanted to be made intelligible.

Of course the concepts of enjoying and of wanting are not the same. You can want to do something you won't at all enjoy, such as unblocking the drains. And while 'These people are aiming to satisfy their wants' has the air of a tautology, 'These people are aiming at pleasure' does not. This is why people who only or largely pursue pleasure form a quite specific class of people, that of hedonists. So 'I am in this instance pursuing pleasure' appears informative as an answer to 'Why?' But what is it to pursue pleasure, over and above pursuing what you want?

It is only in a rather strange sort of case that someone might adduce the pleasantness of an activity as itself a means to some further end. A man following a self-help programme might decide to pursue pleasure so as to reduce his overall stress levels, or so as to indicate to others his right to do things simply for his own sake (assertiveness training)—or for yet more *recherché* reasons. But by and large, when 'X is pleasant' is given as the answer to 'What do you want that for?', it doesn't characterize X as a means to some further end. Could the following be true: that in telling us she finds something pleasant, what a person typically means to tell us is nothing more than that she has no further end in view when she goes in for it? To say that the person aims at pleasure as an 'end in itself' would be a misleading way of putting things; the truth is that she simply pursues the activity *not* with any further end in view. A connection could be made with those theories of art which assert that the essence of the 'aesthetic attitude' is its disinterestedness—the fact that one does *not* view the art object as a means to anything further. Such theories would seem to trade on the basic fact that art is for pleasure, along with the fact that 'X is pleasant' has the character we have just alleged of it. But more importantly for our present discussion, the force of 'X is pleasant' now looks to be very similar to that of another kind of answer to 'Why?'—namely, 'For no particular reason'. This latter kind of statement does not show, if an action is in question, that the action wasn't intentional: the statement does not refuse application to the question 'Why?', in Anscombe's phrase, but it does (of course) indicate that there is no reason for the action, e.g. no further end in view. And indeed sometimes there is not much to choose between the answers 'No particular reason' and 'Just for fun', if asked 'Why are you doing that?'—for example, when drawing a face in the margin of your essay, or when tapping out the rhythm of Ravel's *Bolero* on the car steering-wheel.

If these thoughts were along the right lines, then 'X is pleasant' would in fact appear to be unsuited to play the part of a desirability characterization. When given as the answer to 'Why are you doing that?', it would be tantamount to 'No particular reason'[15]; and so when given as the answer to 'Why do you want to do that?', it would surely have much the same force. It wouldn't supply one's *reason* for wanting something; it would simply report, or be an expression of, one's wanting that thing, and wanting it not as a means to any further end.

But this account can't be right as it stands. For Jeremy might habitually choose to play pushpin, with no further end in view, and yet get no pleasure out of it. We would perhaps call him 'addicted' to pushpin. So there must be more to finding something pleasant than *merely* going in for it with no further end in view. The fact that addictive or compulsive behaviour can be utterly devoid of pleasure may help to explain part of the

---

[15] As an idiom, 'For no particular reason' perhaps carries connotations of casualness and light-heartedness, and so is not *simply* the expression of one who performs a voluntary action but for no reason. This does not materially affect my point.

attraction of the old idea of pleasure as a conscious experience. What, after all, is the *difference* between an addiction that gives pleasure and one that doesn't? It's natural to suggest that the difference lies in something going on in the agent in the first, but not in the second, case—especially since nothing in the agent's habits or preferences seems to distinguish the cases.

To this it might be replied that we are looking in the wrong place for the relevant preferences. It's sometimes said that addictive behaviour is less free than non-addictive behaviour, and Harry Frankfurt has suggested that we look to a person's 'second-order desires' to determine the extent of this freedom.[16] Second-order desires are desires as to what (first-order) desires to have. If you desire to give up cigarettes, then you will form the second-order desire never to desire a smoke—but if the cravings keep coming, and you succumb to one, your action is not an expression of free will, for Frankfurt. Now if Jeremy regularly regrets his bouts of pushpin, expatiates on the worthlessness of the game, and so forth—all of which in Frankfurt's book betokens a clash between first-order and second-order desires—if Jeremy does these things, then we might be the more inclined to call him a pushpin addict, or at any rate weak-willed when it comes to pushpin. But, to repeat, none of this goes to determine whether or not Jeremy, when playing pushpin, actually gets pleasure from it, enjoys it, has a nice time. The state of his second-order desires doesn't help us with this question. If the addict Jeremy *continues* to get a kick out of the game, he could say 'Pushpin gives me pleasure' in honest answer to the question, 'Why do you want to do *that*?'; and if he doesn't, he couldn't. And this does suggest that 'X is pleasant' is informative in a way that 'No particular reason' is not.

Moreover, we could cite those possible, if unusual, scenarios which I touched on above, in which the pleasantness of an activity is aimed at as a means to some further end. If 'X is pleasant' were like 'For no reason', surely it could never be given as a reason in a bit of means–end deliberation?—unless, that is, doing something for no particular reason could be aimed at as a means to a further end! And while some of the Existentialists might have made out that this could be attempted, in so far as they thought that the aim of becoming truly Free was to be achieved by acting groundlessly, and so put forward a reason for doing reasonless things, aiming at

---

[16] See H. Frankfurt, 'Freedom of the Will and the Concept of the Person', *Journal of Philosophy* 68(1) (1971): 5–20.

pleasure as a means (to stress-reduction, say) clearly doesn't involve the paradoxicality or irrationality that the Existentialist programme appears to.

V.

If 'X is pleasant' does give information about X itself, what kind of information does it give?

A desirability characterization is a statement that renders it intelligible why one should want something, and which suffices as an answer to 'Why do you want that?' And there are very few statements, if any, that are *guaranteed* to play such a role. (By 'statement' I mean 'statement-type', rather than 'particular utterance'.) For (i) there may always be defeating considerations; and (ii) the context may render the statement itself unintelligible. As to (i): if I say, 'This is nutritious, that's why I want to eat it', I fail to give a sufficient or adequate reason for my desire if what I propose to eat is my own arm. As to (ii): if I say, 'That would be pleasant', I fail to be fully intelligible if what I propose to do is fill the bathtub with bits of string. There are limits on first-person authority concerning pleasure. If you say you find something pleasant or fun, but those who share your form of life can't see what on earth it is that *could* be pleasant about the thing in question, then the onus is on you to explain where the pleasure lies. I don't mean you have a 'duty' to explain this; just that the verdict as to whether your statement 'It's pleasant' made any sense depends on whether you can explain yourself. In this respect the concept of pleasure is like that of wanting, the nature of which was discussed in Chapter 2.

The statement that something is pleasant is thus subject to certain public standards of assessment as regards its intelligibility. If the statement 'It's pleasant' is challenged, then sometimes the fact that the challenge is not met leaves the statement in limbo: namely, when the context renders the statement *prima facie* unintelligible. Hence 'X is pleasant' might or might not succeed in supplying a desirability characterization. If I say I find some activity pleasant, and you ask me 'But how is it pleasant?', I can start describing the activity in more detail. My purpose then is to make *you* see something; that is, my purpose is that a certain phenomenon should begin to make sense to you, the phenomenon (roughly) of a human being's freely pursuing something for its own sake. A similar case is that of finding something interesting. 'What's so interesting about biology?' is a challenge that is to be met, if it can be, by further description of biology. The person might for example say that animal organs and behaviours are amazingly well-fitted to their functions in ways that biology describes illuminatingly, or that a study of different animals' biologies shows how animals are similar to or different from us in various ways . . . etc. There may or may not come a point when the listener says, 'I begin to see why you find it interesting'; he may just shrug his shoulders and mutter, 'What a waste of time'. But if he *does* say, 'I begin to see why you find it interesting', he is not thereby expressing a dawning interest in biology: my description of biology was not intended to elicit sympathetic feelings in my audience, so much as to get him to *see* the point of certain activities. Similar remarks go for explaining how some activity is pleasant.

An important point to note is this: that in expatiating on what it is about some activity that makes it pleasant, i.e. that renders intelligible your finding it pleasant, you need not be supplying descriptions of some end you have been aiming at. It may not be one of my reasons for going in for stamp-collecting that I want to experience a certain sort of satisfaction or excitement, for instance, even though I might mention the satisfaction of completing a set or the excitement of finding a rare stamp as examples of what makes stamp-collecting fun. 'Finding such-and-such a rare stamp will excite me' need not figure even implicitly in any practical deliberations of mine. It is true that if I mention various features of stamp-collecting in my account of the fun of the hobby, then I usually imply that I myself am drawn to stamp-collecting at least in part because it has those features—in *some* sense of 'because'. But I might mention aspects of stamp-collecting that are valued by other collectors, or even just aspects that I guess my interlocutor will see something in. This will at any rate be so when the question 'But what is the pleasure of it?' is a question primarily about the activity, and not (as it might be from the lips of one's life coach or psychoanalyst) a question primarily about the character and motives of the person of whom it is asked.

We get the same picture with queries about more straightforward matters of fact. If Sue asserts that p and Bill asks her for grounds for this assertion, he will be satisfied (or he ought to be) if he is given grounds why *he* should believe that p, and these may or may not be the grounds which led Sue to believe it. For Sue, p might be an item of general knowledge, something she learnt at school years ago; and it would be absurd for Bill to demand that she be able to remember the occasion when she learnt this fact, and that she must remember having had good grounds for taking her teacher's word for it. Despite the fact that Sue probably can't oblige with such demands, she may well be able to *find* reasons in favour of her assertion, if only by going to a reference book.

Returning to our main topic: if one says 'It's pleasant' or 'It's fun' (etc.) in answer to 'Why do you want to do that?', this answer does typically bring an end to 'Why?' questioning. But it also allows for the challenge, 'But what *is* the pleasure of it?' Of course, that question may be stupid, e.g. if the activity is well known to be the recreation of countless people. But it may not be stupid; and when that is the case, there is a sense in which questioning has not been brought to an end. Nevertheless, questions intended to elicit propositions that occurred (implicitly or explicitly) in the agent's practical reasoning *have* probably come to an end; for as we have noted, to say wherein the pleasure of something consists is not necessarily to give one's reasons for going in for it, in the sense of 'means–end' reasons for aiming at it. At the same time, a failure to give a remotely adequate answer to 'What *is* the pleasure of it?' will tend to cast retrospective doubt on the intelligibility of the claim 'X is pleasant', and so cast doubt on its capacity to bring 'Why?' questioning to an end (i.e. to be a desirability characterization).

We are now in a position to see how 'X is pleasant' can, after all, be a desirability characterization. Let us first retrace our steps. Our main worry was that 'X is pleasant' amounts roughly to 'I like or enjoy X', and that the latter looks like a too close cousin of 'I want X'. In pursuit of an account of this statement, 'X is pleasant', we then considered the view that pleasantness can be understood in terms of going in for something just for its own sake (i.e. not as a means to anything further). On such a view, 'X is pleasant' might indeed manage to bring an end to iteration of the question 'Why?', but only in the sense in which 'For no particular reason' might also bring an end to such questioning; on this view, 'X is pleasant' could hardly be said to present an end as somehow *desirable*. But in any case, the view in question turns out to be inadequate, for two reasons: first, because one can, if unusually, pursue pleasure as a means, and second, because addictive or compulsive behaviour is also gone in for habitually and not as a means to anything further, though it may well bring no pleasure.

And at this point it will be useful to state what it *is* that distinguishes pleasure from mere addiction, something we are now in a position to do. The difference comes out in answers to the question 'What is the pleasure of that?' The *kinds* of thing a person can say to render intelligible his claim 'X is pleasant' are different from those things he might say if addicted to something which gives him no pleasure. They are also different from the kinds of thing one might say to explain an activity's[17] interest, or worthwhileness, or even decency. In all these cases, a desirability characterization—'It's fun', 'It's interesting', 'It's worthwhile', etc.—points towards an account, an open-ended set of explanatory remarks, as to what *constitutes* the fun, interest, worthwhileness, or whatever. 'Constitutes', not 'produces': pleasure and worthwhileness are typically not *produced* by those features that get mentioned in showing how something is a pleasant or worthwhile thing to go in for. This connects with what I have argued, that such features needn't be cited in the practical reasoning (implicit or explicit) of the person who is doing something 'because it's pleasant'.

But these considerations surely indicate that a 'desirability characterization', as Anscombe defines it, need not give the description of the person's end under which he was aiming at it. You *can* aim at and pursue pleasure, but if you say 'X is pleasant' in answer to 'Why do you want to do that?', you do not thereby show that you were aiming at X as a means to something called 'pleasure'. Your answer brings an end to 'Why?' questioning because, in the typical case, you imply that in doing X you have no further end in view; but what this amounts to is this: that you indicate, without actually giving, a species of rationale, which rationale is not to be taken as entering into any means–end deliberation, but which would (if given) enable an enquirer to make sense of your going in for X—by virtue of features of the activity itself. This species of rationale is what determines that *pleasure* is the relevant concept, e.g. as distinct from *interest*, *decency*, etc.; and it is what makes your answer, 'X is pleasant', a more substantial one than 'For no particular reason'.

We can now answer a question that was left hanging earlier, whether 'X is pleasant' properly speaking characterizes X itself, or the agent and his proclivities. It was because it appeared to do the latter that doubts arose as to its capacity to function as a genuine desirability characterization. The correct answer to the question seems to be: 'It does both.' For 'X is pleasant', as we said, amounts roughly to 'I enjoy X' (which gives information about the agent), while at the same time committing the speaker to

---

[17] For simplicity, I speak here as elsewhere of 'activities', meaning to include also passive pleasures.

the possibility of answering the challenge, 'But *how* is it pleasant?' And this challenge is to be met, if it can be, by giving a certain kind of rationale, a rationale that would typically mention features of X itself. In saying 'X is pleasant', one simultaneously points towards a kind of human phenomenon and locates oneself within a given instance of that phenomenon, as agent or patient. The range of this 'human phenomenon' is the range of human pleasures, an enormous range, whose members are linked by a host of family resemblances, including resemblances in respect of such diverse behaviours as: smiling, laughing, acting energetically, acting relaxedly—even (on occasion) moaning or screaming.

For Anscombe, the reason a person has for doing something needn't be related to some end he was aiming at; for it may relate instead to what she calls *motives*, such as the motive of revenge or the motive of patriotism. The first of these is an example of a backward-looking motive, given by some such reason as, 'I killed him because he killed my brother'; while the second is an example of an 'interpretative' motive (or 'motive-in-general'), given by some such reason as, 'I joined in the singing out of love of my country'. The explanation 'I did that for fun' looks to have the same sort of function as an explanation that cites an interpretative motive. Anscombe says that to give an interpretative motive 'is to say something like "See the action in this light"'; and 'to explain one's own actions by an account indicating a motive is to put them in a certain light'.[18] By 'an account', she means a fuller description of the action and its surroundings, one which is meant to enable an interlocutor to 'make sense'—a certain sort of sense—of the overall phenomenon. And this also seems to be what is going on when someone answers the question, 'What *is* the pleasure of it?'

A reason like 'Out of love of country' does not present any *end* the agent has. But we might nevertheless say that it is capable of presenting a proposed *action* as somehow desirable—that in that sense it embodies a desirability characterization. Similarly with 'It's pleasant': this statement gives a desirability characterization, as Anscombe says, but it does so (typically) in rather the same way as does a reason citing an interpretative motive. Perhaps indeed we should say that the typical force of 'It's pleasant' just is that of an interpretative motive.

---

[18] Anscombe, *Intention*, p. 21.

What then is it to pursue pleasure? How is it possible to be a hedonist? As the word is ordinarily used, a hedonist typically aims at sensual pleasures; and in that sense, aims to have various sensations, of taste, sight, touch, and so on. Here is another source of the temptation to regard pleasure as itself a sensation. But presumably it is possible to pursue pleasure for pleasure's sake even where the pleasure is cerebral or social in nature. (Consider the person who loves partying, not for the sake of anything he might imbibe or ingest, but simply for the company.) The conscious pursuit of pleasure involves self-knowledge: knowledge of what one enjoys, how much one enjoys it, how to get what one enjoys. If a person devotes time and mental energy to bringing about opportunities for those activities he enjoys, conceiving of them *as* activities he enjoys, then he can be said to pursue pleasure for its own sake (or: these pleasures for their own sakes). The self-consciousness with regard to pleasure that distinguishes such a person from others may (though it need not) go with a lifestyle involving more occasions of pleasure—i.e. more occasions when 'For pleasure' and the like give reasons for action. But the force of this statement as a reason is the same for the hedonist as it is for others. This force, as we have seen, is akin to, if not identical with, the force of statements giving interpretative motives, such as 'I did it out of love of country'.

One who pursues pleasure can on occasion *fail* in that pursuit, for he may find only disappointment or boredom. There seems to be a disanalogy here with, e.g., doing something out of love of country: although failure is possible, it is hard to think of cases where the kind of failure is such as could be reported by the phrase, 'What I did turned out not to be patriotic after all'. And this surely relates to the fact that the concept *enjoying* X involves the agent himself, his behaviour, responses, etc., etc. Enjoyment has characteristic manifestations, as we have noted; and as Ryle would have said, these manifestations correspond to adverbs, not to verbs—enjoyment is not itself an activity, but is a matter of how a thing is done or suffered to be done. Whether someone is enjoying something can very often be seen in how he is doing it. So if in answer to the question 'Why?' somebody replies 'For pleasure', his statement may be, as it were, contradicted by certain subsequent facts about *him*.[19] The same doesn't

---

[19] Are such facts *reported* by one who says 'I'm not enjoying this after all'? Presumably not, if 'reporting' is something done on the basis of observation (of behaviour, etc.). Rather, the

hold of such a reason-giving statement as 'Out of patriotism'—or at any rate, it doesn't hold in quite the same way.

For there are ways in which statements giving interpretative motives can be undermined by subsequent facts about the agent. An example is when a person's subsequent actions lack genuineness or authenticity. Imagine that during a general strike I decide to show my respect for and solidarity with the strikers by giving a clenched fist salute to likely-looking passers-by. I find, however, that whenever I do this I feel fraudulent and silly. In answer to 'Why the clenched fist?' I would have said, 'I'm doing it out of solidarity with the workers', thus giving an interpretative motive; but my statement is undermined rather as 'For pleasure' may be undermined, by what I find to be the case when I give my salute. What I discover has to do with me myself, and its relevance to my earlier statement has to do with the *concept* of solidarity. An expression of solidarity is only adequate if it is genuine, as opposed to contrived, stilted, half-hearted, or the like, and this is in part a matter of the extent to which the agent himself can 'identify with' what he is doing. To be sure, I succeed in giving clenched fist salutes, and even in signalling solidarity with the workers; but I find that in doing these things I am not, after all, shoulder to shoulder, marching under the same banner. These metaphors fail to ring true, and since symbolic gestures depend upon such metaphorical meanings, my gesture is a flop, and hence undermines or renders futile my earlier declaration, 'I will do this out of solidarity'. There are some parallels here with pleasure, I think. One of them is this: that in giving the salute, I was not aiming at some independently specifiable outcome, called 'solidarity'; in much the same way, a person who does something for fun isn't aiming at an outcome called 'fun', or 'pleasure'.

We have seen that there is a sense in which it could be said that pleasure is a good: namely, where the notion of a 'good', as it appears in this context, is tied to that of a desirability characterization—a characterization of an action as 'somehow desirable'. And it must be admitted that, so construed, 'good' is not functioning as it does in, say, 'good knife', 'good parent', or 'good for the digestion'. Moreover, if we thus explain this use of 'good' by reference to desirability characterizations, while at the same time drawing a parallel between the motive of pleasure and interpretative

---

utterance will itself be one of the criteria of non-enjoyment, just as 'That hurts!' is one of the criteria of pain, along with wincing, moaning, and so on.

motives, then (it might be objected) there is surely nothing to stop us from saying things like 'Patriotism is a good', 'Solidarity with the workers is a good', and the like. For if 'For pleasure' can bring an end to 'Why?' questioning, can't 'Out of patriotism' or 'Out of solidarity'?—and for essentially similar reasons? At any rate, given that such statements cite interpretative motives, it follows—if Anscombe's account is correct—that they don't, even implicitly, cite independently specifiable ends, as a means to which one adopts the course of action in question; so to that extent there seem to be grounds for thinking of a statement like 'I clenched my fist out of solidarity with the workers' as supplying a desirability characterization, i.e. as an answer apt to bring an end to 'Why?' questioning.

Perhaps part of the answer to this problem lies in the success or otherwise that may attend attempts to spell out what I have been calling the *rationales* associated with the relevant concepts. 'What *is* the pleasure of it?' asks for a certain kind of rationale: it asks for a description of doing X that will make sense of one's going in for it for its own sake, etc. One can similarly ask for a description of the activity of expressing solidarity with the strikers that will make sense of going in for *it*. And it may be demanded of such a rationale that (e.g.) the merits of the strikers' case be satisfactorily outlined. That is arguably a part of what is involved in 'making sense of this activity'. And just as 'For pleasure' may fail to supply a fully intelligible desirability characterization if a request for a rationale cannot be met, so 'Out of solidarity' may fail, and for similar reasons.

Still, this very parallel between pleasure and solidarity would mean that 'Pleasure is a good' and 'Solidarity is a good' belong in the same boat. And yet it seems possible that a person might want to throw doubt on the pointfulness of *any* expressions of solidarity, without thereby appearing insane. He might just regard all this chatter about solidarity as an excuse for pious strutting. Such a person would respond to the statement 'Out of solidarity', not so much by continuing the series of questions, 'But why do you want to do that?', as by denying altogether the statement's *prima facie* reason-giving force. Clearly, this could not sensibly be done in the case of the statement 'For pleasure'. The phenomenon of pleasure plays too large a role in human life; it is indeed essential to any recognizable form of normal human existence. It is this fact, perhaps, that serves above all as justification of the saying that pleasure is a good.

VI.

If the account of pleasure that has been given here is correct, then the significance of pleasure for ethics has to do especially with *good (and bad) reasons*—just as was found to be the case with emotions in Chapter 1 and with wants in Chapter 2; though the role of reasons in each of these three cases is not exactly the same. In the case of pleasure, the role of reasons comes out in (i) the sort of answer that can be given to 'What do you want (to do) that for?', and (ii) the sort of answer that can be given to 'What is the pleasure in that?' The first sort of answer ('It's pleasant') purports to give a desirability characterization, while the second sort purports to supply what I have been calling a rationale. The first sort of answer presupposes the possibility of an answer, however banal or obvious, of the second sort. And given the possibility of such a rationale-supplying answer, 'It's pleasant' supplies a good reason for doing what one is doing.

In Chapter 2, we encountered the idea that there are 'things it is human to do', activities that are characteristic of human life, and which feed into our notion of human flourishing—walking, talking, listening to music, drinking tea, etc., etc. Aristotle's definition of pleasure as 'the unimpeded activity of our natural state' thus makes a lot of sense; for where there are adequate answers of kinds (i) and (ii), this adequacy derives from the fact that someone is doing a humanly natural or normal thing, typically for its own sake and with no further end in view. That they take pleasure in what they are doing is something manifested in what they do and say, i.e. in characteristic behavioural signs and also in the kind of rationale they (can) give for what they are doing. The unimpeded engagement in natural human activities, characterized by such manifestations, may well be regarded as a *prima facie* human good.

Prima facie only, of course—for error and human defectiveness can enter in, both as regards the agent's ordering of goods and because the range of what is humanly natural inevitably encompasses activities that count as vicious, given especially the social nature of the language-game of giving and demanding reasons for action. The actual extent of human viciousness is an empirical question, and history seems to lend considerable support to those thinkers who have seen human nature as peculiarly twisted or tainted. But this is a topic for another occasion.

More needs to be said, however, about the relation of reasons to pleasure and to pleasant activities. We have seen how emotions like pride and fear have characteristic objects, where the object of an emotion is typically meant to give a reason for it. The object of Arnie's fear may be the big dog on the other side of the street, in virtue of his belief that the dog is (or could well be) dangerous. Can one speak of the object of pleasure, as one can of the object of an emotion? Gilbert Ryle writes:

> Pleasure and distaste do not require diagnosis in the ways in which sensations may very well require it. The fact that I have come to like some things and dislike others has an explanation and of this explanation I may or may not be ignorant. But when I have just been amused by some particular joke, the question 'What gave me that pleasure?' does not await an answer. For of course I already know it was that joke, if it was that joke that had amused me.[20]

Now it is true that if a person is amused by a joke, he will know 'straight off' that it was the joke that amused him, and not (say) the speaker's red socks; and this may suggest that here we have something akin to an object of fear, about which a person is an authority. The assertion 'I'm scared because there's a big dog over there' may be faulted if there is no dog, and also if there is a dog but it is quite safe—but it cannot, without alleging self-deception of some sort, be faulted by a remark like, 'No, it's because it's getting dark that you're scared'. And self-deception is necessarily the exception: a special case has to be made for it.[21] Fear thus has a cognitive aspect, one relating in the paradigm case to what a person takes to be dangerous.[22] But there seems to be no analogue of such a belief, or 'cognitive content', in the case of being amused at a joke. The only candidate would be the belief that the joke was funny; but one doesn't have to be an out-and-out subjectivist to find such a 'belief' a bit fishy. You could be mistaken in taking a certain dog to be dangerous, but you could hardly in the same sense be mistaken in taking a certain joke to be funny. At any rate, if there is room for a mistake here, it would presumably have to do with (hypothetical) general agreement in response to that joke, and the fact that you were out of step with such agreement. And while this might show you to have a defective (or just eccentric) sense of humour, it is not relevant

---

[20] Ryle, 'Pleasure', p. 59.

[21] Cf. Chapter 1, p. 6.

[22] The phrase 'takes to be' is intended to cover more than just *belief*, where the latter involves straightforward truth or falsehood. The cognitive aspect of an emotion may sometimes be more like a 'picture' than like a belief; even so, there will be room for error. See C. Calhoun, 'Cognitive Emotions?', in *What is an Emotion?*, eds C. Calhoun and R. C. Solomon (Oxford: Oxford University Press, 1984).

to our present enquiry. For you obviously don't find a joke funny *because* you believe that most other 'normal' people would also find it funny. Your amusement is not based on any belief at all; and although there is such a thing as being amused, or more generally pleased, by the (putative) fact that such and such, about which a person can indeed be mistaken, Ryle has actually chosen an example where this is not the case—an example where one might be inclined to speak of the *cause* of a person's amusement, not the object.

The reason why it might look odd to call a joke the cause of your amusement is precisely the one Ryle mentions, namely, that you don't have to speculate about why you are amused, nor rely on general knowledge (as you do when judging e.g. the cause of your sweating). You *just know* what it is that amused you. But in fact this does not show that the concept of cause is here out of place. For what we have may well be what Anscombe dubbed a 'mental cause':

As e.g. when we give a ready answer to the question 'Why did you knock the cup off the table?'—'I saw such-and-such and it *made me jump*.'[23]

The phenomenon of mental causes presents an obvious challenge to Humean models of causation, according to which there can be no such thing as 'direct' knowledge of cause and effect.[24] So much the worse for such models; there evidently *is* such a thing. As Anscombe points out, effects of mental causes, known immediately as such by the subject, include involuntary and voluntary actions, and also thoughts and feelings. But the fact that something is a cause of a feeling, say, does not rule out its also being a reason for, or object of, that feeling:

The object of fear may be the cause of fear, but, as Wittgenstein remarks, is not *as such* the cause of fear. (A hideous face appearing at the window would of course be both cause and object, and hence the two are easily confused.)[25]

If being directly knowable does not distinguish cause from object, what does? The object of a feeling, as we have seen, figures in what purports to

---

[23] Anscombe, *Intention*, p. 16.

[24] Mental causes were mentioned in Chapter 1, p. 7. For further remarks on the subject, see R. Teichmann, *The Philosophy of Elizabeth Anscombe* (Oxford: Oxford University Press, 2008), pp. 14–16, 30–3, 234–6.

[25] Anscombe, *Intention*, p. 16. She cites para. 476 of *Philosophical Investigations*, which simply insists on the general distinction between object of fear and cause of fear.

be a (good) reason for that feeling; or, where it fails to do so, the feeling gets classified as irrational or not fully rational. If a hideous face appears at the window unexpectedly, one can indeed cite a reason for being scared, namely that a horrid man is lurking outside, with an evident interest in what's going on in this room. (As remarked earlier, such a statement may be faulted for being factually false, but that is another issue.) At the same time, one's reaction of fear is an involuntary reaction, not within one's control, and (in these circumstances) sudden and unexpected; and these features make us lean towards the classification 'cause'. There is in fact no hard and fast distinction between reasons and mental causes (cf. *Intention*, pp. 23–4).

The blurred boundary between cause and object is especially to be found with those psychological categories associated with involuntary, or not fully voluntary, behavioural manifestations. For with such categories, the behaviour may lead us to talk of a 'cause', while the cognitive aspect of the psychological state (or whatever we call it) leads us to talk of 'reasons'. And we can of course distinguish two possible questions—e.g. 'Why did you jump?' and 'Why are you scared?' Returning to Ryle's example of amusement, we can similarly distinguish 'Why did you laugh?' from 'Why are you amused?' But amusement and laughter are so tightly connected that the natural inclination to speak of laughter's being caused carries over to amusement—though at the same time, in so far as 'Why are you amused?' means the same as 'What's so funny?', answers can often be given, by way of explanation. This 'explanation' will not be explanation of how you come to be in a state of amusement; rather, it will aim at *making sense* of the joke, and of your finding it funny. In other words, it will endeavour to enlighten the person asking the question, by supplying a *rationale*. His question is really more of a 'How?' question than a 'Why?' question—it means 'How is that funny?' There are various kinds of answer to such a question.

The whole topic of humour is an incredibly deep one. Like the human enjoyment of music, the human enjoyment of jokes—and of course humour covers a lot more besides jokes—can seem extremely puzzling. Why do we go in for these things? And what am I asking for when I ask this 'Why?'? Nor is this a matter of 'mere' intellectual curiosity, for both music and humour are surely central components of the good life for many people. Since our topic is pleasure, a pertinent question would be, 'What are we taking pleasure *in* when we are amused?'—or, 'What are we *enjoying* when we are amused?' Is it that we like to laugh? Well, yes—but that is by no means the whole of it. Laughter, however, does seem to me to be at the heart of the concept of humour, and its being an involuntary form of behaviour lends weight, as I have said, to the idea of amusement's having a cause—something embodied in phrases like 'I was tickled by what he said'.[26]

Music and laughter both exemplify the need, when giving an account of pleasure, of using a suitably extended concept of 'activity'. It helps to begin by thinking about *bona fide* activities, such as riding, which a person can enjoy doing; but if we call *listening* (to music or to jokes) an activity, we are clearly allowing some activities to be passive, as it were. A key point is that you can be asked 'What are you doing?', or e.g. 'Why are you sitting there?', and can answer, 'I'm listening to this string quartet (or: that raconteur)'—thus giving a description under which what you are doing is intentional. 'Why are you doing *that*?' is then answered by 'For pleasure'—or more likely, by 'It's beautiful', or 'He's hilarious', or some such.

Listening is a form of attending, and the concept of attention is a peculiarly difficult and elusive one. But without stopping to examine it more closely, we should note that it is possible anyway to hear or overhear a tune or a joke without having been listening out for one. Aristotle's *energeia*, standardly translated 'activity', is not tied to intentionalness in the way that 'activity' typically is, but rather to a notion of (being at) work, where 'work' = *ergon*; and hearing does count as an Aristotelian activity of our nature. But just as one can enjoy hearing a tune, so one can enjoy feeling a cool breeze on one's face, or enjoy the sensation of acceleration as the plane takes off, or enjoy the extreme heat of a spicy curry. Are these all examples of the unimpeded activity of a natural state (capacity)? It would seem that care is needed not to inflate the concept of a natural capacity: vomiting is a manifestation of a natural capacity, a very useful one, and a person can certainly go in for it unimpededly—but not typically with much enjoyment. But a thorough examination of what Aristotle's definition of pleasure amounts to, and of how far his account is defensible, would take us too far afield. What seems indubitable is that the concepts of

---

[26] The phenomenon of laughter can itself appear ludicrous from a detached point of view. The Chambers Dictionary definition of *laugh* certainly brings a smile to the face: 'to express, by explosive inarticulate sounds of the voice, joy, scorn, etc., or a reaction to tickling, etc.' A Martian would have hard work filling out these *etceteras*; we human beings can do this, though not exhaustively, courtesy of a repertoire of instinctual capacities of reaction and judgement, of the sort that were discussed in Chapter 1.

pleasure and of enjoyment apply to hearing or overhearing a tune largely on account of the person's desire, or willingness, to go in for the same or a similar experience again, her manifestation of the familiar signs of pleasure (such as also attend the activity of listening), her explanation of her reactions—and so on. In general, we should not be surprised to find a fair degree of open-endedness and indeterminacy in the concept of pleasure, as also in the concept of pain, where that is understood as the complement or opposite of pleasure—what Ryle calls 'distaste' in the above quotation. As for the physical sensation of pain, that is a whole topic to itself.

VII.

In Chapter 2, I mentioned liberalism and utilitarianism, two theories, or theory-groups, which in various ways pervade our culture. The moral right to do what you want, and the intrinsic desirability of pleasure—here are two ideas that for millions of people have the status of dogma. Both ideas are susceptible to the same sort of objection, an objection that appeals to the proper location of the key concepts—*wanting* and *pleasure*—within the space of reasons. 'Why do you want that?' and 'What is the pleasure in that?' are questions that (in many if not all contexts) call for answers. And this connects with the fact that neither wanting nor pleasure can be understood on the model of sensations or quasi-sensations.

A famous tag asserts that *de gustibus non disputandum est*: there is no disputing about tastes. The Latin *gustus*, like its English equivalent 'taste', has a primary application to the activities of eating and drinking. (*Gustare* = to taste.) To enjoy the taste of your food is to enjoy certain sensations, and about these there is indeed no sensible disputing. If I detest what you relish, this is simply and succinctly accounted for by the fact that we have different sensations, and although such sensations can be described, to give such a description is not to give a rationale of the sort that can be questioned or criticized. But the principle that there is no disputing about tastes is taken to be relevant to a much wider range of pleasures than just those of the table. It is a principle that we find enunciated again and again in discussions of art and the arts, where the term 'taste' also has a home. That the same term can be used in connection with buns and bordeaux as in connection with sculptures and symphonies shows the depth of the illusion, that all pleasure is a matter of nice sensations.

The question 'What is Art?' would take us into distant realms from which we would in all likelihood never return. My own view is that *art* is as much a family resemblance concept as any; but one can see why it has seemed natural to think of the defining purpose of art as being that of giving pleasure. What perhaps speaks most for this view is a historical fact: that while serving, and continuing to serve, many and various further ends, art has come to occupy a characteristic place, at least in the West—that of being an object of what Kant calls disinterested contemplation. We listen to music, read poems and novels, go to plays and films, all with no further immediate ends in view. In other words, we pursue these experiences for their own sake, in some sense of that phrase. And this, as we have seen, is a part of what it is to pursue a thing 'for the pleasure of it'. As usual, there are exceptions; architecture is thought of as an art form, though essentially geared to producing objects with a particular function or functions. But its status as art form arguably derives from the fact that the design of buildings can incorporate, and has incorporated, features that are ornamental and 'useless'; and structural features of buildings come to be looked upon with the same eye. It is surely significant that architecture is regarded primarily as a *visual* art. And of course people do visit great cathedrals simply to contemplate their beauty.

Given what has been said so far about pleasure, the claim that art is for pleasure might lead us to ask, '*What* are you enjoying when you enjoy art?', and also specific questions of the form, 'What is the pleasure in experiencing work W?'—and similar questions. And such questions are answerable, at any rate when made sufficiently concrete.

With the motif passed through many vicissitudes, which takes leave and so doing becomes itself entirely leave-taking, a parting wave and call, with this DGG occurs a slight change, it experiences a small melodic expansion. After an introductory C, it puts a C sharp before the D, so that it no longer scans 'hea-ven's blue,' 'mead-owland,' but 'O-thou heaven's blue,' 'Green-est meadowland,' 'Fare-thee well for aye,' and this added C sharp is the most moving, consolatory, pathetically reconcil-ing thing in the world. It is like having one's hair or cheek stroked, lovingly, understandingly, like a deep and silent farewell look. It blesses the object, the frightfully harried formulation, with overpowering humanity, lies in parting so gently on the hearer's heart in eternal farewell that the eyes run over. 'Now for-get the pain,' it says.[27]

[27] Thomas Mann, *Doctor Faustus*, trans. John E. Woods (New York: Vintage, 1999), p. 55.

This description of Beethoven's op. 111 piano sonata as it nears its end might conceivably be given as part of an answer to 'What do you enjoy about this music?'—though it would more likely be given in answer to 'What do we enjoy about this music?'—or more likely still, in answer to 'How does this music manage to be so affecting?', the question effectively being addressed by Mann's imaginary musician, Wendell Kretschmar. For the justice of the description is best appreciated by those who can already hear it in the music, at least to some extent. Shared form of life will not be quite enough. But the point remains that there is such a thing as explaining what there is in some experience that *makes sense* of valuing it and of going in for it; and if there exist explanations of this sort, it follows that it is possible for there also to be descriptions of pieces of music that make sense of loathing or being bored by them.

Somebody might admit that there is this (possibly modest) degree of objectivity in matters of musical taste, while sticking to the idea that there is no real point in disputing over disagreements. For he might think that what is being described e.g. by Wendell Kretschmar is, or belongs to, a world that is self-contained—the world of music (or the world of Beethoven, perhaps). This world has its own standards, it does not connect with human life more generally. Music, such a person may argue, may have rights and wrongs internal to it, but from outside it can only be regarded as just another pursuit—rather as there are rights and wrongs internal to golf, while from without it is just another game. Helping himself to Hume,[28] he may admit that there are people who count as experts or afficionados in music, by dint of their experience, discrimination, lack of prejudice, etc., and whose preferences therefore go to determine a standard of taste—but he may say, 'Nothing much hangs on this, however; such people may feel passionate about music and make it central to their lives, but that is just how they are. Music cannot *improve* anyone, not even great music.'

An obvious problem with this line is that, if a description like Kretschmar's of the op. 111 does count as eloquent and just, if it does ring true, then it is hard to see how such music as op. 111 could *fail* to be capable of improving a person. Kretschmar's description is not couched in intramusical language, but in language that connects it with human life, and in such a way as to make quite plain that what is being described is, if the

---

[28] See D. Hume, 'Of the Standard of Taste'.

description is just, something of deep human significance. That language is operating metaphorically, it might be said. But metaphors can be true or enlightening, just as can *pictures*, e.g. of human beings or animals, of the sort that were discussed in Chapter 1 (Section IX).

A person can be improved by being enlarged—as they may be enlarged by thinking, understanding, and knowledge. Once again, these things are not just 'inner states', for they are necessarily manifestable in word and deed. They are part of human life. A conception of improvement that limited it to 'producing more morally good actions' would belong to the sort of utilitarian framework that is bound to trivialize the significance of art, either by seeing it as instrumentally valuable only (yielding the limited species of 'improvement' just mentioned) or by seeing it as a source of nice or nasty sensations, *alias* pleasure or pain, and so not as such liable to improve at all. But although this utilitarian conception of improvement is inadequate, it is true that psychological and moral improvement in a person will have outward forms. By its fruits you shall know it.

A person's involvement with, and attachment to, a certain kind of art will have manifestations of a diverse kind. This is especially true in the case of music. But it is not hard to think of various characteristic such manifestations. Consider how some kinds of music and not others can be used to whip up ideological frenzy (marching songs), or to stimulate lacrimal glands (Disney), or to accompany a burial service (T. L. de Victoria). Or recall the success of those attempts to put off the more anti-social varieties of teenager from hanging around shopping centres, by piping classical music through speakers installed there. Of course, you cannot just read off the value of a kind of music from the sorts of behaviour or emotional state it naturally encourages or discourages, or the sorts of behaviour or emotional state it 'goes with' or not—things are not so simple. But you can do something not very far from that, in virtue of facts about the emotional content of music.

It is impossible to deny that musical experience is somehow connected to human emotion, though many philosophers have fallen at the first or second hurdle in attempting to say what exactly that connection is. 'Emotive' descriptions of music are in some sense metaphorical, but they are not so metaphorical that it is an open question whether a piece describable as calm is on the whole more likely to be calming, or a piece describable as frenzied is on the whole more likely to excite. These are fairly simple examples, and the range of musical experience is so wide that there is a strong case for speaking of the existence of emotional states peculiar to that experience; but even these are not ineffable, nor so disconnected from non-musical life and emotion as to nullify the point of the present remarks. I have spoken of the idea that music may improve a person, and if this is true, then it must surely be through *habits* of listening (and/or playing, singing, studying, extolling . . .) that a person improves, or for that matter degenerates. A continuous exposure to heavy metal will not have the same sorts of psychological effects as a continuous exposure to plainchant. And exposure to music that has a single, specific emotional message will not have the same sorts of effects as exposure to five centuries of European music with a correspondingly wide emotional palette.[29] These of course are empirical statements, and there are those who would smilingly ask for the statistical evidence, just as they might ask for statistical evidence that continuous exposure to violent movies is liable to corrupt, or that umbrellas do in fact keep you dry. The effects of exposure to music are probably different, and more diffuse, than those of exposure to movies. And when music sets words, the total effect will often if not usually come about through a blend of musical and verbal action. It would be an unsubtle person who scoffed at the very idea of such effects.

The question can be put in the form of a dilemma. If music is important in the way that those who love it say it is, then the effects of music are deep ones: music gets to you, it affects your inner being, it is not just a recreation. Alternatively, music is not really so important, and musical experience is recreational only—essentially a form of aural tickling. Most people with any real interest in music would, one hopes, opt for the first horn of this dilemma (and it's not clear why we would want to listen to those without any interest in it). But anything that affects people in the deep sort of way described under the first horn looks as if it must be something with genuine psychological, and hence ethical, power—and that means power for good or for ill. Plato was not crazy to think that music matters at a political level, even if his proposals for regulating it, like other proposals put forward in the *Republic*, are a tad totalitarian. Thomas Mann, from whom I quoted above, also saw the importance of music for extra-musical human life, in a way that typifies German thought on this matter; and so did Tom Stoppard, whose play *Rock 'n' Roll* presents

---

[29] Also known as 'classical music'—a genre of music in roughly the sense in which the non-sonnet is a genre of poetry.

Western rock music as having been a force for political and cultural liberation for dissident Czechs in the 1960s. Stoppard's case can, I think, be questioned, since history shows that a yearning for things Western has often been directed at Coca-Cola, jeans, and the Hollywood movie *qua* comestible—in a word, elements of a *lifestyle*[30]; and it is arguable that rock 'n' roll had the same political significance in the Cold War as did these other products, and not the intrinsically liberating character that Stoppard sees in it. But Stoppard could not have written a plausible play with the message, 'Coca-Cola was a force for political liberation', and the very fact that there is a possible debate here about the political significance of a certain kind of music does show something about the status of music. Indeed, a play could be written as a counter to Stoppard's, depicting rock 'n' roll as a manifestation, even an expression, of an amoral and apolitical capitalist hegemony. Perhaps there would be truth in both plays.

I have focused on music, among the arts, not only on account of its intrinsic interest, but also because it is peculiarly tempting to regard the pleasure we take in music as constituted by certain sensations, or alternatively as having for its object certain sensations ('I enjoy the *sounds*'). This conception of musical experience utterly fails to square with the actual significance of music in human life. The pleasure of listening to music, like other pleasures, relates to what the listening person does and is, and how she does it and is it, so to speak. This is why music does *not* occupy a completely isolated domain, cut off from the rest of life; the unity of the person herself sees to that. In general, pleasure is not a thing that you aim to get and have, like money or a new possession. Getting money or a new possession does not (in itself) alter who you are—but to a very great extent, you are what you enjoy. The notion that pleasure *is* a gettable thing is perhaps particularly at home in, if it is not a product of, an affluent and acquisitive society, where a special status is assigned to *getting what you want* (money, cars, satisfaction . . . rock 'n' roll again). But musical pleasure is no more a gettable item than is knowledge or understanding. The parallel is not accidental.

---

[30] For more on this important concept, see Chapter 4, pp. 135–6.

4

The Good Life

In Chapter 2, I said that the two central questions of ethics, 'How should I live?' and 'What sort of person should I be?', could both be answered in similar fashion: 'Lead the life of a good human being'. The almost tautologous nature of this answer derives in particular from the equation, or association, of 'good human being' with 'good human agent'. But although the answer tells us very little, it does nonetheless point to a substantive enquiry, into what *constitutes* the life of a good human being. The first thing we might want to ask is: Is this the same thing as a good life for a human being?

It appears not. For many a good human being has suffered much evil, either natural evil or evil at the hands of others (sometimes *for* being a good human being); and surely the life of such a person is far from ideal, and could hardly be called a good life. This is certainly true if 'good life' means, roughly, a life which might (rationally, properly) be wished for. Nobody sane would wish to be put into the position of being flung into gaol for having opposed the Nazis, for instance—in an ideal world, the Nazis would never have come to power, and it would never have been necessary to oppose them. Philippa Foot discusses the situation of just such brave individuals when looking at the question how being a good or virtuous person connects with being *happy*; and she writes:

In the abstract what they so longed for—to get back to their families—was of course wholly good. But as they were placed it was impossible to pursue this end by just and honourable means. And this, I suggest, explains the sense in which they did not see as their happiness what they could have got by giving in. Happiness in life, they might have said, was not something possible for them.[1]

For Foot, as for Aristotle, being virtuous, eschewing evil, is a necessary but not a sufficient condition of being happy (or *eudaimōn*)—in the sense of 'happy' where it makes sense to 'identify happiness with human good'.[2] This last qualification is important, for, as Foot says, '*happiness* is a protean notion', and the English word has various connotations in different contexts, including ones of contentment or of cheerfulness. But if we identify happiness with human good, and if 'good' here functions as more than an emotive term, and more than a term merely expressive of what one desires, then we are identifying happiness with the sum total, as it were, of things it is good for a person to have or do or be, where these include things it is bad to lack (necessities) and things it is just good to have. Happiness in this sense is the same as flourishing. Our concept of human flourishing is complex, and, as I have argued, differs from e.g. that of health especially in its inclusion of elements deriving from the nature and purposes of practical reasoning.[3]

Ethical virtue is necessary, though not sufficient, for human flourishing. But much more remains to be said concerning the nature of human flourishing or happiness. The good life is the happy life, and the wise one seeks after true happiness. What then is true happiness?

I.

Two dichotomies present themselves. The first is that between a conception of happiness as individualistic and a conception of it as socially conditioned; the second is that between a conception of happiness as an ongoing process (or as supervenient on such a process or processes) and a conception of it as an achievable end-state. It is tempting to think that these dichotomies present philosophical dilemmas—that is, that an individualistic conception excludes a social conception and that a 'process' conception excludes an 'end-state' conception. Everything depends upon the meanings of the relevant terms. What better way to proceed than by starting with Aristotle.

---

[1] Philippa Foot, *Natural Goodness* (Oxford: Clarendon Press, 2003), p. 95.
[2] Ibid., p. 97.   [3] See pp. 59–61.

Aristotle may be depicted as thinking that happiness (*eudaimonia*) is (i) individualistic and (ii) an end-state. He argues, famously, that the highest happiness is to be found in contemplation (*theōria*), and gives a number of reasons in support of his view. In the following passage we find him giving reasons that rely for their force on (ii) and then on (i):

And again we suppose that happiness must contain an element of pleasure; now activity in accordance with wisdom is admittedly the most pleasant of the activities in accordance with virtue: at all events it is held that philosophy or the pursuit of wisdom contains pleasures of marvellous purity and permanence, and it is reasonable to suppose that the enjoyment of knowledge is a still pleasanter occupation than the pursuit of it. Also the activity of contemplation will be found to possess in the highest degree the quality that is termed self-sufficiency; for while it is true that the wise man equally with the just man and the rest requires the necessaries of life, yet, these being adequately supplied, whereas the just man needs other persons towards whom or with whose aid he may act justly, and so likewise do the temperate man and the brave man and the others, the wise man on the contrary can also contemplate by himself, and the more so the wiser he is . . . [4]

To begin with Aristotle's individualism, as I have dubbed it, we can surely admit that self-sufficiency has some sort of value in human life. What is not so clear is whether the greater self-sufficiency of any given activity *ipso facto* shows it to be an activity of greater importance for human flourishing than some other activity. For we need to ask what sort of value it is that is enjoyed by self-sufficiency. A natural answer is this: to the extent that an activity can be pursued without the help of other people (and, we may add, with the minimum of material means), to that extent one's pursuit of it is immune to the vagaries of fortune, in the form of changes in other people's inclinations, capacities, and so on. Such an activity is *safer* than one that enjoys less self-sufficiency. Now this feature of the contemplative life has indeed been extolled in different times and places throughout human history. We find versions of the idea in Buddhism and Stoicism; and in combination with a dualism of mind and body, the idea often goes with a general claim that the material world is less pure, less reliable, and more generative of error and defect, than the world of the mind.

I doubt if Aristotle's motivation in citing self-sufficiency has much to do with mind–body dualism, and although immunity to the whims of fate

[4] Aristotle, *Nicomachean Ethics*, trans. H. Rackham (Cambridge, MA: Harvard University Press, 1975), X.vii.3–4.

may play a role in his thinking, it doesn't seem that he is prey to any Stoical desire simply to avoid disappointment and suffering. Rather, he is surely putting before us a picture of the best and most admirable human being as one who is in a certain sense *complete*—as having resources that are in themselves adequate to living a good life. Such completeness may be thought of as a kind of moral strength, the strength of independence. A child is dependent, and dependency in an adult often appears as a sort of childlike state; and like St Paul, Aristotle may have thought that growing up is meant to involve putting childish things behind one.

Nevertheless, independence from others is necessarily limited. This is partly a matter of human vulnerability and the inevitability of decline in old age, but more deeply it is a matter of our concept-scheme. What concepts might human beings have developed of human flourishing? The answer to this is doubly constrained: by what it is to be a human being, and also by the social character of language, and of the reasons that are given, through language, for adopting some ends and not others. These themes will by now be familiar. Human flourishing, the sort that in Foot's phrase is identical with human good, could not be such that e.g. stealing and getting away with it is conducive to flourishing; but nor could it be such that a general unwillingness to cooperate with others is conducive to flourishing. The life of the hermit may be a good life, but it could not be so *in virtue of* the hermit's unwillingness to cooperate with others, even if choosing to be a hermit necessarily involves detaching oneself from opportunities to cooperate with others.[5] If the contemplative life is a good life, it is not so *in virtue of* its not needing other people, in the sense in which, as Aristotle says, justice needs other people. (It is interesting that he asserts this also of courage, and even of temperance; but these seem to be virtues that Robinson Crusoe might have displayed.)

For one thing, there is a huge range of human goods that cannot be achieved without human cooperation. A life of contemplation lived among others requires an infrastructure: houses, roads, shops, money, bridges . . . and these things could not be created or maintained without the joint efforts of groups of people. The philosopher himself must rely on the word of others, and if others are dishonest, he may have to spend time that might have been spent philosophizing in chasing up the necessities

---

[5] Here we encounter a form of the distinction between intended and foreseen consequences.

of life. None of this is to say that contemplation is not a human good, and perhaps the highest human good. It is simply to say that *human good* cannot be a thoroughly individualistic notion, and nor therefore can *human happiness*.

'Individualism' is also the name of a cultural phenomenon of the modern world, not irrelevant to the present argument. This phenomenon is connected with two other '-isms' that have already featured in this book: Millian liberalism and utilitarianism.[6] Modern individualism finds expression in such interconnected claims as: that each person is the best and only judge of his or her happiness; that happiness may be found in more or less any way of living; and that a society is well-ordered in which people are encouraged and allowed to find happiness in whatever way they wish. The conception of human happiness that is implicit in these claims is liable to be one according to which happiness is an inner state, authoritatively known to the subject, with an intrinsic 'character'... i.e. a conception according to which happiness is a sensation or quasi-sensation, or is somehow made up of states that are sensations or quasi-sensations. We have already seen how this sort of conception fares in the case of pleasure, and it seems clear that it stands an even slimmer chance of getting things right in the case of human happiness. There may be reasons for thinking that, very often, a person is the best judge of how happy she is, but these reasons will have to do with the person's self-knowledge—a knowledge that comes from honest reflection on one's doings, one's character, how others see one, and so forth. Self-knowledge, like all knowledge of this kind, is an achievement, and sometimes it is a difficult one. People often deceive themselves about their doings, their character, and how others see them—and to say, 'But even so, they must know if they're happy' is not only wrong-headed but irresponsible. For if adhered to in real life, this proposition would lead to a dereliction of the duty of looking after those near you.

The reasons why individualism has come to pervade our culture are complex. Among historical causes, one might cite increased affluence (in the West), which together with democratization has made possible the

---

[6] There are dangers attendant upon using the '-ism' suffix in philosophy, notably that of imagining that it brings clarity and precision to a discussion when it does no such thing—see Chapter 5, pp. 176–8. In using the words 'liberalism', 'utilitarianism', and (especially) 'individualism', I mean on the whole to signify broad trends of thought. These words should not be thought of as pseudo-technical terms and are intended to wear their vagueness on their sleeves.

pursuit of individual goals on a hitherto unknown scale, goals pursuable without regard to the requirements traditionally imposed by family and community. I hesitate to weigh up whether such profound changes have been for the better of for the worse 'over all'—if such a question even makes sense. My concern here is rather with certain ways of thinking that have gone with these social changes, ways of thinking which can be thought of as having the function—to speak anthropologically—of justifying and upholding people's practices. An interesting notion in this connection is that of a *lifestyle*.

One evening in the 1950s the playwright Arthur Miller was having dinner with two friends. All three men were concerned and depressed at various local failures of community spirit. In answer to a question of Miller's about how people would come to think of their own lives, one of them, Richard Cloward, gave his opinion thus:

'The question is going to be lifestyle,' he replied.
I had never heard the expression before. 'What's that mean?'
'There will be competing styles of life, symbolic and essentially meaningless differences in clothing, speech patterns, tastes in food, cars, and so forth. The class struggle is over for now, and maybe even the conception of rank-and-file organizing. People are less and less interested in common action, which even now is getting to seem strange and kind of pointless. Identification will be more and more in terms of style—the self-image will be politically neutralized that way. It's going to be style-conscious, not class-conscious.'[7]

At the time, Miller says, the notion seemed to him an empty one, and it was only gradually and later on that he saw the point of Cloward's remarks. The 1960s ushered in what might be called the glorification of lifestyle, lifestyles being rather like commodities, to be picked off the shelves (on the basis of our old friend, subjective preference) and thereafter adopted as one's own. Were a lifestyle to be defined only in such material terms as dress, food, and design of car, it would be an age-old phenomenon, and to most or many of its elements the tag *de gustibus non disputandum est* would apply. But (i) to define *yourself* in these terms, as Cloward was implying, is to succumb to a kind of infantilism, and (ii) lifestyles typically include more than just these matters of taste—they can include political affiliations, religious beliefs, attitudes to work and leisure, and much more: the whole gamut of social mores, you might say.

[7] Arthur Miller, *Timebends* (London: Methuen, 1988), p. 363.

The point here is not that a splintering of society into subcultures is necessarily a bad thing, for after all, a subculture may adhere to better standards than the main culture—so may many subcultures, at least in principle. The point is, rather, that where beliefs and mores get to be regarded as items in the same category as clothes and food, to be chosen according to personal taste, then we are back with a picture of human ends as above or below reason, a picture that is both philosophically mistaken (as has been argued in previous chapters) and socially disastrous—at any rate, if genuinely believed by many people. To throw in another '-ism', what we tend to get at this point is relativism, a trend of thought that has produced the term 'judgemental'. As might be guessed from the fact that this term is used pejoratively, relativism has a tendency to go with double standards. Consider the indignant saying, 'Such-and-such a group want to *impose their morality* on other people'. The danger of self-refutation here is acute, since the saying appears to be relying on a 'moral' principle, that one ought not to impose one's moral principles on others. (To avoid the danger, the relativist must make out that *his* moral principles are not intended to be 'imposed' on anyone.) Apart from the issue of self-refutation, there is the fact that if groups were not allowed to impose their morality on others there would be no laws, judges, juries, and policemen; but those who use this phrase are generally of such conventional views that they would simply lack the courage to embrace genuine anarchism.[8]

Here is a kind of paradox: that an ethos according to which each of us is free to pursue his or her own individual goals is by no means guaranteed to produce a rainbow society, a rich embodiment of diversity—being in fact quite as likely to produce widespread fashions in thought as well as in styles, fashions whose worth is rarely put in question since, after all,

---

[8] The phrase is typically employed when attacking Christian morality. Thus A. C. Grayling writes: 'It is time to demand of believers that they take their personal choices and preferences in these non-rational and too often dangerous matters into the private sphere, like their sexual proclivities. Everyone is free to believe what they want, providing they do not bother (or coerce, or kill) others . . . it is time to demand and apply a right for the rest of us to non-interference by religious persons and organizations—a right to be free of proselytisation and the efforts of self-selected minority groups to impose their own choice of morality and practice on those who do not share their outlook.' Grayling, *Against All Gods* (London: Oberon Books, 2007), p. 16. Note the phrase 'their own choice of morality'—cf. 'their own choice of wallpaper'. (Elements of a lifestyle.) The gist of this passage seems to be that the majority view ought to prevail; for to 'apply a right to be free of proselytisation' is presumably to stop the 'self-selected minority' from saying things on matters about which the majority ('the rest of us') are at liberty to speak. What a majority does can never be 'proselytisation'.

'Everyone's entitled to their own opinions'. The psychological fact is that human beings will tend to clump together, do and think like the herd, unless in their formative years they are given a stiffer message than 'Do and think what you like'—namely, 'Do what's right and think what's true'. Individualism in fact breeds conventionality.

A particularly cynical version of relativist conventionality is displayed by journalists who describe ethical or political debates in terms of the strategic value of expressing a view, the assumed strategy being to win the argument (or wield influence, or get elected, or . . .). For journalists infected by relativist thinking, the idea that political views are going to be true or false will appear simply quaint. Debates and discussions get to be looked upon as games, e.g. power-games, with the journalist playing the role of a sophisticate who knows better than the politicians whose behaviour he is delineating with such detachment. The expression of a view may even be called a *mistake*, not on account of its being false, but on account of its seeming eccentric or unfashionable or out-of-date, e.g. to an imagined Joe Public. A key concept in this connection is that of the gaffe. When a politician is said to have made a gaffe by asserting something or other, what this usually means is that he has said something that may offend, or appear ridiculous to, somebody—especially somebody he would do well, in worldly terms, to impress. Where the party he ought really to be impressing is the electorate, or some other numerous body, the politician's offence will thus be that of going against *les convenances*. Were the politician to defend his remark by saying, 'But I wanted to speak the truth, not to get ahead in my career', the accusing journalist will probably think this impossibly disingenuous, and in any case will long ago have seen through all talk of truth in these matters.

So much for cultural individualism, and its sister trend, relativism. What I have called Aristotle's individualistic conception of happiness is of course pretty unrelated to what a proponent of cultural individualism might say on the topic of happiness. But in passing from a discussion of the former to a discussion of the latter, I have not simply been falling foul of an equivocation attaching to the vague term 'individualism'. Somewhat similar considerations may be adduced against Aristotle's invocation of self-sufficiency (*autakreia*) as may be adduced against the modern idea that each is the best judge of his or her happiness, and that different varieties of happiness and lifestyle are all 'equally good' (so long as you don't hurt other people). Those considerations derive above all from the social character of the language-game of asking for and giving reasons, especially reasons for action, something which both constrains and feeds into the concept of human flourishing.

None of this rules out a certain pluralism about human happiness, that is, a view according to which there are different and incompatible ways of life, each of which may embody a form of true happiness. And although the concept of a happy life is socially constrained, this fact does not, I think, mean that a way of life cannot be called happy which is in no way directed to the good of others. Perhaps the life of the contemplative hermit embodies one such form of human happiness, even though it is obviously a way of life (like some others) such that if everybody went in for it, the human race would die out. The criterion, 'If everybody did that . . . ', is not a suitable one for determining which ways of life are good ones; and part of the reason for this has to do with the *division of labour* that is necessary for the flourishing of a society or group. Such division of labour is clearly required when it comes to incompatible tasks like feeding and defending a city, for instance: those engaged in guarding the walls and fighting off invaders can't also be engaged in growing and marketing vegetables and rearing animals. But soldiers and farmers are at any rate doing things directed at the good of themselves and of others—not so your typical hermit. How then can a hermit's life be called a good life?

In the hermit's case, it may be possible to argue that a society flourishes *in which that sort of thing goes on*. The hermit's life, in other words, may in fact be conducive to the good of the group, *qua* group, even though no individual (other than the hermit) benefits in any direct way from his doings, and even though the hermit need not be *aiming* at the flourishing of the group. Here would be a case of division of labour, the 'labour' being that of maintaining a sort of flourishing of the community: some follow the solitary life, others bring up families, etc., etc. Whether we can speak this way will of course depend entirely on the nature of the hermit's activities. Perhaps he is doing mathematics, or history, or evolutionary biology. Perhaps he is coming to terms with his wicked past and is devoting himself to solitary penance. Perhaps he is engaged in prayer and meditation—or philosophy. Isn't it possible for someone to think, e.g., 'It is good to know that such people exist, that this goes on, especially since the rest of us are mostly chasing after trinkets'? Couldn't you even say that a person *does* benefit from the doings of hermits or scholars or philosophers or non-publishing poets, in so far as he belongs to a society which includes them? Don't you benefit, after all, from the fact that your society includes, and has included, saintly or heroic men and women, though their deeds were for the immediate good of others, others who are perhaps long dead? It is possible, after all, to be rightly proud of your country or your culture, or for that matter rightly ashamed of it; if you are proud of it, a natural expression of such pride is a sort of thankfulness, e.g. that certain deeds were done, and a person who is thankful for something presents himself as having in some way benefited from that thing. As a human being you are part of something bigger than you—some *things*, rather. Knowing that this is so may well be a key to human happiness, and it is a theme we shall be returning to.

II.

So far I have been looking at the first of the two dichotomies mentioned at the start of the previous section, namely the dichotomy between conceptions of happiness as individualistic and conceptions of it as socially conditioned. What of the second dichotomy, relating to the question whether human happiness is (or supervenes on) a process, or is instead some kind of end-state? In the above quotation from the *Nicomachean Ethics*, we found Aristotle writing that

> it is held that philosophy or the pursuit of wisdom contains pleasures of marvellous purity and permanence, and it is reasonable to suppose that the enjoyment of knowledge is a still pleasanter occupation than the pursuit of it.

Since he has already characterized happiness as consisting in a certain activity (*energeia*)—namely, activity in accordance with virtue[9]—and since he is arguing that true happiness consists in contemplation, alias 'the enjoyment of knowledge', Aristotle must regard the enjoyment (as opposed to the pursuit) of knowledge as an activity, in his sense. It is at once an activity and an achievable end-state. This is not a paradox, still less a direct contradiction; and if Aristotle's account of matters is correct, it would seem that human happiness may be viewed both as a process and as an end-state (so long as 'process' is understood in a certain way). Nevertheless, one might question the assertion that the pursuit of wisdom is less pleasurable than its attainment,

---

[9]   Aristotle, *Nicomachean Ethics*, X.vii.1.

especially if this is meant to imply a general preference for attaining things over pursuing them. There is, after all, the familiar view that in many arenas of life it is the pursuit, the travelling, the exploration, that really counts. Here in fact we encounter a certain deep tension within human nature, between the impulse to do and the impulse to rest. The tension arises in particular because activities like pursuing, travelling, and exploring are ones that seem almost by definition to be done *not* for their own sake: surely they all aim at some species of completion?

We have already encountered the question 'Why do you want that?', by repeating which we can in principle arrive at an agent's overall aim. 'Overall aim' is in fact a context-relative sort of expression, and what counts in one deliberative context as an overall aim may properly be seen as provisional, or as a means rather than an end, in another. Despite this, there is, as I have argued,[10] much sense in Aristotle's characterization of human ends as subsumable under an overall end, that of leading a good human life, or at any rate the life of a good human being (for external factors may make it impossible to lead a good human life, i.e. a good life for a human being). If there are many ways of leading a good human life, Aristotle's thesis is to be used, not for homing in on the Best Possible Life, but for ordering and ranking ends within a specific form of the good life— a task which no doubt enjoys a certain measure of indeterminacy. Now if Aristotle is right that man's overall goal and final end is happiness, it might seem that nothing can be intrinsically (non-instrumentally) good except this happiness, and that actions performed courageously, or out of love, or in noble self-sacrifice, are just means to a certain end, that of being happy. Interpreted thus, Aristotle's ethics is in danger of excluding the possibility of genuine altruism, and the defence of Aristotle on this score is well-known and surely correct: happiness, or flourishing, is not to be thought of as something *produced* by virtuous activities, etc., but rather as *consisting* in those activities. Virtuous activities themselves typically either aim at certain things for their own sake, or have backward-looking or interpretative motives that do not aim at anything further at all. In both cases, answers to 'Why?' terminate with statements whose adequacy depends ultimately on their human intelligibility, and which count as ethical statements

---

[10] See pp. 79–81.

because of their connection with human good in general—not just with the agent's own good.

We do not ask ourselves 'How should I live?' in the midst of our activities, when an unhesitating confidence is often a prerequisite of doing the right thing in the right state of mind. We ask it when reflecting on our life, and on the habits of action which we have, or could adopt. *This* is the sense in which our many and varied ends can be seen as subsumed under the architectonic end of leading a good life, or of being truly happy.

It is tempting to think that Aristotle's account provides an answer to the worry that was voiced a couple of paragraphs back, a worry arising from the existence of two impulses, to do and to rest. 'Surely', it might be said, 'human happiness can only be conceived of as a state of rest if that means a state arrived at or perfected—more specifically, the state of being a good and virtuous human being, unthwarted by external factors. But such a state itself consists in having a set of habits of thought and deed, habits that are manifested in activity. In ethics, to be is to do, and to do is to be.' This answer would aim to show how there is, after all, no contradiction between the two notions, doing and resting, as these notions are to be employed in this enquiry. But the worry I have in mind will not be eased in this manner, however much truth there is in the answer itself.

To see the nature of the problem, consider the fact that many virtues only exist because the world contains things that are awry—deficiencies and excesses, evils both natural and man-made. Thus courage is needed because human beings often face dangers of one sort or another, threats to life or to the goods of life. In other words, courage is needed to avert evil. Honesty is needed because telling the truth and keeping your word are internal norms of the practices of language and of promising, practices needed by human beings; but honesty is accounted a *virtue* because of the possibility of dishonesty, and the reality of incentives to dishonesty—a reality which opens the door to things that are evils, both in virtue of the fact that the practices of language and promising are goods, and in virtue of the characteristic motives of those willing to be dishonest. Incentives to dishonesty are one form of temptation, and as Foot puts it, the virtues 'are *corrective*, each one standing at a point at which there is some temptation to be resisted or deficiency of motivation to be made good'.[11] (This goes for

---

[11] Philippa Foot, 'Virtues and Vices', in *Virtues and Vices* (Oxford: Blackwell, 1978), p. 8.

courage as well as for dishonesty, of course, since running away from danger is a very natural impulse.) The reason the temptations in question are 'to be resisted' is that not resisting them opens the door to various evils.

In a world in which these evils did not exist there would be no need for, or possibility of, the virtues. A paradise in which we never faced threats to life, limb, or peace of mind, in which food and shelter were always plentiful, and in which human beings never desired the harm of others, would be a place without struggle and without a history. Compassion would be absent, since there would be no suffering to inspire it—there would be no need for the motives of charity or of self-sacrifice, no need for public-spiritedness or for efforts towards reform or amelioration—no place for a parent's tears of joy when a child returns home safely, no reason to give your cloak to a beggar. Life lived in such a paradise would lack many of those things that strike us as most noble and admirable in human beings, and many of those emotions that are part and parcel of love itself. Without bitterness, nothing would be sweet. Indeed, it is not clear that the creatures leading such a life could really be *us*.

But what is the problem? After all, earthly life is not a paradise, and there will always be possibilities of evil, and hence opportunities both for the virtues and for humanly recognizable forms of love. If there is a problem here, it might be said, it is a problem faced by certain traditional conceptions of heaven and the afterlife. (What is it to have a virtuous character in heaven?) Human life is to be pictured as an ongoing struggle, and human happiness is especially a matter of conducting that struggle well.

This is true. But to be good is, among other things, to hate cruelty, dishonesty, and avarice, to share in the grief caused by early death or a crippling disease, and so on. It is from such a mindset that good actions flow. So if to be truly happy involves being a good person, then human happiness, it seems, must go with a kind of chronic dissatisfaction with the world—chronic, because we do not live in a paradise and (whatever utopians and revolutionaries have thought) we lack the power to create one. And here is the tension I spoke of earlier, between the desire to do— i.e. the desire to struggle against earthly evils—and the desire to rest—i.e. the desire for those evils to have been conquered. If ever the evils were finally conquered, we would have a life without virtue, nobility, or human love, the very things from which the desire to struggle emanates, and which give that desire its universal depth and importance.

When Aristotle speaks of the life of practical virtue as less self-sufficient than the life of contemplation, he is pointing to a dependency of virtue on things which he takes to be somehow alien to happiness. And while one may object to the idea that interaction with one's fellow human beings can be regarded as alien to human happiness, the evils of the world against which the virtues are in a certain sense directed are indeed alien to happiness, if only because virtue consists in part in hating or wanting rid of those evils. But the virtues would not exist in a world without those evils. So the life of virtue does after all lack Aristotelian self-sufficiency, in a fairly radical sense. The question is whether this is any kind of mark against the life of virtue. As I said earlier on (p. 132), it is not clear that a lack of self-sufficiency is in itself any objection to a mode of living; and the problems surrounding the life of virtue which we have been looking at seem to relate rather to what I have called a deep tension in human nature, between the impulse to do and the impulse to rest.

This tension is felt when reflecting on one's own life, especially when reflecting on it as a narrative, with direction and development. It can also be felt when reflecting on the narrative of human history. A human life, unlike human history, has a basic and universal narrative ordained by nature, consisting of infancy, childhood, youth, middle age, and old age. These subdivisions may be somewhat arbitrary, in the sense in which the subdivisions constituted by a given colour vocabulary are arbitrary—for getting older is a *gradual* process. But the arc of a life, from birth to death in old age, evidently constitutes a natural narrative, albeit one that can be cut off prematurely. Human history is not like this. The narrative directionality of history is more a matter of how we interpret the past, interpretation being a species of *seeing as*. We see some kinds of period or event as more significant than others—the lifetime of an empire, say, or the invention of motorized transport. This does not imply a lack of 'objectivity' in history: historical explanations and classifications, like causal explanations and classifications,[12] employ concepts that are anthropocentrically anchored, but a main theme of this book has been that anthropocentrism does not repel objectivity. Nevertheless, there are interpretations and interpretations.

---

[12] See Chapter 2, p. 91.

One interpretation of the past which has often proved irresistible to historians is that which depicts social and cultural developments as embodying some kind of progress. On one such view, modern history shows a steady overall improvement in the West, both in people's ideas and in the conditions of society. But this optimistic picture of historical development involves a difficulty when it comes to assessing the preconditions of progress; for many of the developments that are seen as progressive and as heralding better things have themselves arisen out of conditions that fall well below the optimist's standards of enlightenment. Thus British parliamentary democracy did not burst forth fully formed, like Athena from the head of Zeus—an enormously complex and secure background of laws, officials, customs, technology, etc., is required for the existence of parliamentary democracy, and its birth was necessarily preceded among other things by the evolution of a stable monarchy, which itself began as a matter of some strongest man assuming power over other strong men, by force and threats of force (how else?). Again, many of the glories of high culture required a background of general wealth, and such wealth often came into being through struggles, competition, and the production of human misery on a pretty grand scale; moreover, there is a strong case for saying (as with parliamentary democracy) that the achievements of high culture could only have come about in this way.[13]

Now part of the problem here evidently has to do with the urge to categorize historical phenomena as either good things or bad things, a feature of history books that is comprehensively sent up in Sellar's and Yeatman's *1066 and All That* (e.g. 'The Norman Conquest was a Good

---

[13] It is important not to misstate this point. It would be an exaggeration to say that wickedness is an absolute prerequisite for any human civilization; it is enough to reflect that (i) we have an attachment to the *actual* form our civilization took and takes (with its pyramids, its Roman aqueducts, Shakespeare's bloody history plays, and the rest); (ii) in general, before there is a background of restraining laws and customs, it is strong and ruthless men that will tend to come to power, and so it has to be through their efforts that the stability evolves, embodied in restraining laws and customs, which is ultimately necessary for the flourishing of a civilization; and (iii) strong and ruthless *groups* of people will tend to dominate or even exterminate more peaceable groups, so the forms of civilization that endure will, at least very often, be those of the former kinds of groups. Of course, were there only men of good will, neither (ii) nor (iii) would hold: nothing about being virtuous in itself prevents you from creating wonderful civilizations. At the same time, we need to be sensible about what *counts* as being virtuous or vicious: we should not project anachronistic notions of what is morally and psychologically possible onto past events. A modern horror of physical violence, for example, would hardly aid you in understanding human interactions in seventh-century Britain.

Thing, as from this time onwards England stopped being conquered and thus was able to become top nation'). But, as we have seen, even quite humble things are incapable of simply being good or bad: something or someone will always be good *qua* this or bad *qua* that, good under one description or bad under another. This goes in spades for the complex and multifaceted phenomena of history. The correct response to a question like 'Was the Industrial Revolution a good or a bad thing?' is surely, 'It was a bad thing in so far as it had such-and-such features and effects, and a good thing in so far as it had such-and-such other features and effects'.[14] And this in turn tends to undercut a good many unqualified *wishes* relating to the past, such as, 'If only the Industrial Revolution had never happened!' As we shall see, it is significant that nothing practical hangs on what wishes of this sort you entertain, or on whether you entertain any at all.

But history is relevant to the future and to our plans and hopes for the future. Those plans and hopes will often be backed up by a certain reading of history. And if you do, for example, interpret history in terms of continual progress, then you may in principle end up facing questions as to whether some proposed (e.g. technological) development is really to be justified by the expectation of its contribution to the march of progress, or whether the evils attaching to that development rule it out. Of the *past* we can say, 'Though brute force and the lust for power are far from ideal, it's hard to see how Western civilization in its actual form, and of which we are so proud, could have got going without people going in for them; nevertheless, we need neither bemoan those early savageries nor rejoice that they happened.' However, when we turn from the past to the future, we move from a theoretical to a practical question. And if that question is posed in a general form, we seem to encounter something of a paradox: a static future looks as empty and uninteresting as a period without any history, but we would flinch from allowing present evils just so as to enable change, development, and (as you might say) topics of conversation for later historians. Here is a form of that tension I have spoken of: a tension between the desire for change, activity, novelty, development (doing), and the desire for peace, stability, and lack of conflict (resting). One can simply contemplate the past, but a mere contemplation of the future is not

---

[14] Christians have traditionally referred to Adam and Eve's fateful disobedience as *felix culpa*, or 'happy fault'—as in the Exsultet of the Easter Vigil: *O felix culpa quae talem et tantum meruit habere redemptorem*: 'O happy fault that merited such and so great a Redeemer.'

possible, at any rate for us human beings as a group; for we must again and again choose between doing and not doing.

III.

Parallel remarks can be made about an individual's life. A person can think that it was terrible to lose the use of his legs, but that if he hadn't he would never have met the nurse who became the love of his life—and so he might just wave away the question 'Are you glad or regretful that you lost the use of your legs?' He could say that the event was both good and bad, under different descriptions. But he could hardly take an analogous attitude to the fact that in doing or suffering some future evil he would very probably, at the same time or afterwards, enjoy some good. This fact cannot simply be contemplated—it must apparently be acted on, either by choosing the evil or by rejecting it. And one form of this dilemma, it appears, is the dilemma as to whether to choose change, activity, novelty, development (doing), or peace, stability, and lack of conflict (resting). A given, concrete dilemma of this form might be called a life choice. Is there a right road to follow here?

A phrase that needs to be attended to is: 'to choose evil'. When a historian says that once upon a time dreadful acts were committed, without which certain fine developments of culture would never have come about, he ought to mean that those who performed those dreadful acts did wrong, were vicious in doing what they did. They ought to have thought, 'I won't do *that*!' And this is what one of us now ought to think, presented with the same options. We ought not to choose evil, in this sense—even if we know, or believe, that certain conceivable fine developments of culture will only ever come about if someone or other chooses the evil in question. (The 'oughts' in the last three sentences relate to practical rationality, i.e. to the issue of being a good human agent—they cannot be understood in relation to a cosmic point of view, since there is no such thing.) The objection may come, 'If everybody always thought and acted as you did, there would never be historical developments of any sort!', but this is really the same sort of objection as, 'If nobody was vicious in any way, there would never be any opportunities for the virtues!' Both statements are falsified by the fact that Mother Nature can throw things at us: earthquakes and famine can generate historical developments, and also opportunities for courage, compassion, and the other virtues. Leaving natural evils out of it, however, the right response to the two statements is surely, 'There will always be bad, mad, and ignorant human beings in the world; and there will always be fine and noble people and things as well'. The attitude to take to such a world—i.e. to *the* world—is the same as that which ought often to be taken to past history. It is an attitude which eschews *if only* and *would that*, eschews wishes and regrets. For it is possible to hate cruelty while not hating this world in which cruelty exists—to hate the sin and not the setting. This is the attitude to take for a person leading a good life, who I earlier said was destined to a sort of chronic dissatisfaction. So he is; but it is recurrent dissatisfaction with particular people and events to which he is destined—not dissatisfaction with the world, or with human nature as such.

The attitude I am talking about is not one of resignation—to the world, or to the nastiness of the human race, or to both. It is rather the attitude (or activity) of contemplation.

It might seem that one who is faced with the sort of 'life choice' I mentioned a moment ago, between activity and rest, or struggle and peace, will not be much helped by the possibility of a contemplative attitude. For the choice in question will be a genuinely practical one, e.g. between having children or remaining childless. But something like a contemplative attitude may well come into play, and this connects with the fact that making a life choice need not be to 'choose evil'. Given that the 'evils' involved in choosing activity and struggle are something other than one's own bad actions—e.g. if they are the pain of childbirth, the inevitability of family rows in the future, and so on—then one cannot really be said to 'choose evil'. Faced with physical pain or with a family row, it will of course be rational to try to deal with it, or to wish it away; but in embracing a life that includes such things, it is best not to do so tremblingly or in a spirit of resignation, but as far as possible with confident certainty. In this way, the narrative of a human life and the narrative of human affairs (history) are similar. The bitter that is inevitably mixed up with the sweet may well be thought of as an object of reflection or contemplation.

If these thoughts are along the right lines, it seems that it will be characteristic of a (certain sort of) contemplative attitude that it regards some aspects of the past and of the future in a similar light. In thinking about past history, and also about one's own past, it is possible to take a dispassionate attitude to phenomena through a recognition of their place in a scheme of things in which good and evil are so intertwined that regrets are simply out of place. Of course, this does not go for all past events, but it is important that it does go for many. And a similarly dispassionate attitude is possible as regards the future, both of humankind and of oneself. There is no such thing as regarding the past and the future as *utterly* on a par: the very concepts of past and future, and their connections with thought and action, preclude this. A contemplative or reflective attitude is necessarily just one mode of thought about past and future, co-existing with and dependent upon other, more immediately practical modes of thought. But it is a mode of thought that appears to embody a kind of wisdom, and thus to be a source of happiness. For there is a sense in which it makes room both for the impulse to do and the impulse to rest. Someone may choose to have a family, being fully aware of the future struggles and difficulties entailed by that life choice, but may be able to regard those struggles and difficulties with a calm eye, despite the fact that other, less dispassionate attitudes will be brought to bear on the various concrete problems as they arise. Such a person chooses to *do*, and not to be safe—but is content with a scheme of things in which evil is mixed up with good, and feels no urge to struggle against that scheme. In so far as this contemplative attitude sees the future and the past in a similar light, it could—rather grandly—be called a contemplation of things *sub specie aeternitatis*.

I have been using the words 'contemplation' and 'reflection' pretty interchangeably. To the extent that the attitude in question has for its objects the activities and events of one's own life, past and future, our topic does seem to be that reflectiveness of which Socrates was talking when he said that the unreflective life was not worth living.[15] As the etymology of 'reflect' reflects, the attitude of reflectiveness is paradigmatically turned towards the agent: reflectiveness is reflexive. It leads, ideally, to self-knowledge. Contemplation is in this sense a more general notion than reflection, since the range of its objects is not restricted to a given life, indeed is more or less unrestricted. It leads, simply, to knowledge, or enlightenment—in the ideal case. Nevertheless, what I have called a contemplative attitude, one that is distinct from the practical attitude,

---

[15] According to Plato in *The Apology*.

and which eschews wishes and regrets, is, I have argued, a possible one to take up towards elements in one's own life.

We have seen some ways in which reflexive contemplation and self-knowledge might be a part of human happiness, especially by their making room for both the impulse to do and the impulse to rest. What reasons are there for thinking that contemplation in general has the same sort of significance? Aristotle's notion of contemplation (theōria) is more restricted than our notion of contemplation, having only eternal truths for its objects, and this in part explains the character of one of *his* arguments for the claim that contemplation is part of (the highest) happiness: namely, that contemplation is the activity of the highest part of a person's soul, and that we are most like the gods when we contemplate.[16] But the notion of a highest part of the soul would clearly need to be non-question-beggingly explained for it to help justify the honorific status assigned to contemplation, while something similar goes for Aristotle's claims about the nature of the gods, or of God (whose existence is in any case open to doubt). Something else that Aristotle says about contemplation, however, does seem important:

> Also the activity of contemplation may be held to be the only activity that is loved for its own sake: it produces no result beyond the actual act of contemplation, whereas from practical pursuits we look to secure some advantage, greater or smaller, beyond the action itself.[17]

One way of bringing out what Aristotle means is as follows: people can make money, they can sort out their mortgages, work conditions, and health problems, they can ensure that their family is well looked after—but then what? Enjoy yourself? Wait for death? The answer may come, 'But you can do what Aristotle also recommends—you can live virtuously. And didn't we agree that there will always be opportunity for virtuous action, in this imperfect world?' It is a riposte that does indeed address part of the problem. But two things need to be pointed out. First, if by 'acting virtuously' is meant all those ways of acting that any good person, however situated, will go in for, then these are not *activities* in the sense of pursuits with their specific goals. 'What shall I do in life?' cannot properly be answered, 'Be honest; show courage in adversity; help and support those near you . . .' At any rate, if this is the only and best answer, then it is

---

[16] Aristotle, *Nicomachean Ethics*, X.vii.2; X.viii.7, 13.   [17] Ibid., X.vii.5.

tantamount to, 'Just *live* (decently, of course)'—more of a quelling of the question than an answer to it. Hence the distinction between the questions 'What shall I do in life?' and 'How shall I live?'—though it is true that the latter can be interpreted so as to encompass the former. Second, if on the other hand by 'acting virtuously' is meant the adoption of certain virtuous ends as one's life goals, such as the relief of the poor or succour of the sick, then (i) these seem to be activities that 'secure some advantage', i.e. some good thing—which would make them activities *not* done purely for their own sake, in Aristotle's sense; and (ii) it seems an extreme view that holds that the *only* good answer to 'What shall I do in life?' is 'Dedicate yourself to good works'. But if there are other possible answers, what could they be?

In considering (i), we need to be sensitive to the different descriptions under which an activity can count as intentional. To dress wounds and administer medicine is to adopt means to a further end—namely, the health of the sick person. So dressing wounds is done not for its own sake, but to secure a good. But if a set of actions which includes the dressing of wounds, etc., is described simply as *curing the patient*, that gives an end, not a means to an end (in the ideal case). Of course, there is often or even usually some uncertainty as to whether a doctor will cure her patient, medicine being a fallible art; and for this reason, the act-description *curing the patient* will not generally be an appropriate one to give in answer to 'What are you doing?'[18] But to the query, 'Was Florence Nightingale performing actions just for their own sake, or with a further end in view?' it would seem arbitrary to reply, 'With a further end in view', having described the philosopher as doing something just for its own sake, if the sole difference between the cases related to the uncertainty of success. And anyway, is the achievement of knowledge and wisdom (by means of reading, talking, thinking, and so on) a thing so certain?

So perhaps such virtuous activities as looking after the sick should be thought of as done for their own sakes, just as much as is the activity of contemplating done for its own sake. At this point, however, Aristotle might ask why health is a good for the person cured. To be sure, it would be wrong to call health instrumentally good, in the way in which having money is instrumentally good; but it is clearly true that health enables one

---

[18] cf. Anscombe, *Intention*, pp. 39–40.

to live a human life, and to do 'things it is human to do', without the obstacles presented by disease and disability, and that this fact has an obvious bearing on health's being a human good. For the cured patient, the question 'What shall I do with my life?' once again comes to the fore, or should do if he or she is reflective. This, it might be said, is part of the hoped-for outcome of looking after a sick person. It is not just that one hopes that people who are once again on their feet should spend their time profitably—you might rationally hope that of anybody. It is rather that the point of curing the sick is connected in a deep way with the idea that a person's life is something to be led well, not badly. I am not advocating a virtue test that patients must pass in order to get treatment, or equal treatment with other patients—far from it. But it is a consequence of what I am saying that where a person who has been tended and cured goes off to lead a vicious or dissipated existence, that will count as a certain sort of disappointment for those who nursed him back to health. It will be a disappointment for *them*, for what he goes on to do is in some sense their business—his fate is now to a certain degree bound up with theirs.[19] In a similar way, a child can be a disappointment to her parents by going off the rails, despite the fact that they did not have a child *in order* for her to live a good life.

So there is a sense in which the goodness of looking after the sick presupposes the possibility of a person's leading a life well or badly, and that the proper purpose of looking after the sick cannot be fully understood without bearing that presupposition in mind. Aristotle could now ask us what 'living a life well' amounts to, and he might repeat his claim that it must be some activity which is done *purely* for its own sake, as looking after the sick, say, is not—given the sort of deep dependence of the point of the latter activity on the ability of patients to go on to lead good lives. If we tried to respond that the lives led by the cured should themselves be devoted to virtuous ends like that of caring for the sick, we would seem to be conjuring up a world in which everybody's life goals ideally relate to tackling the problems of the world—something which, as was suggested under (ii), above, looks excessively moralistic. Surely there is

---

[19] This very fact probably justifies an ethos in which it is *not* part of a doctor's or nurse's business to find out how a patient goes on to lead his or her life; for it is extremely important that medical professionals carry out their duties with impartiality, something that would be threatened by the entertainment of (quite natural) hopes or fears concerning the patient's future behaviour.

something worthwhile for a human being to do which is not just sorting out the world's evils, and which can, as it were, be enjoyed after all the sorting out—at the end of the day? And won't human happiness consist at least in part of an activity, or activities, that are worthwhile in this sense?

IV.

Before I can address this last question, it is necessary to consider an important objection that can be made to the foregoing characterization of the activity of looking after the sick, an objection which threatens the whole Aristotelian thrust of my discussion. In talking about the care of the sick, I have focused on the case of restoring people's health, and there is a very important kind of looking after the sick which is not this: namely, looking after the terminally ill, or the incurably disabled, or the insane. Those who look after these kinds of sick people cannot hope that their patients should go on to live good lives and flourish as human beings, restored by the care they have received. The point of such care has nothing to do with the possibility of patients going on to lead good lives. At the same time, this sort of looking after people may well be regarded as one of the finest of human activities, an expression in a very pure form of charity and loving kindness; and as such, it has been taken by some to show up an alleged inadequacy in an Aristotelian ethics that gives pride of place to human flourishing—for the hopelessly sick or insane cannot be called flourishing.

Raimond Gaita describes how in the 1960s he worked as a ward assistant in a psychiatric hospital where the patients 'appeared to have irretrievably lost everything which gives meaning to our lives'. One day, a nun came to the ward, whose utterly simple, natural, and uncondescending way of relating to the patients struck Gaita as revelatory.

Later, reflecting on the nun's example, I came to believe that an ethics centred on the concept of human flourishing does not have the conceptual resources to keep fully amongst us, in the way the nun had revealed to be possible, people who are severely and ineradicably afflicted. . . . In the nun's case, her behaviour was striking not for the virtues it expressed, or even for the good it achieved, but for its power to reveal the full humanity of those whose affliction had made their humanity invisible. Love is the name we give to such behaviour.[20]

---

[20] Raimond Gaita, 'Goodness beyond Virtue', in *A Common Humanity*, 2nd edn (London: Routledge, 2000), pp. 19, 20.

How should an Aristotelian respond to these thoughts?

The challenge posed to Aristotelian ethics resides in Gaita's placing side by side the flourishing human being and the ineradicably afflicted one, and insisting that as far as ethics goes—as opposed e.g. to biology—the first is in no sense superior to or of 'greater value' than the second. Gaita remarks that the most natural way of bringing out what he means is by saying that 'all human beings are sacred' (p. 23), a claim whose essential truth he regards as independent of religion or theology. The crucial thing is that the ethical status, so to speak, of the incurably sick is something that is best characterized in terms of the remarkable acts and attitudes of people like the nun, acts and attitudes which are revelatory:

> If I am asked what I mean when I say that even such people as were patients in that ward are fully our equals, I can only say that the quality of her love proved that they are rightly the objects of our non-condescending treatment, that we should do all in our power to respond in that way. But if someone were now to ask me what informs my sense that they are *rightly* the objects of such treatment, I can appeal only to the purity of her love. For me, the purity of the love proved the reality of what it revealed.[21]

Some philosophers would wish to object to Gaita's use of 'reality', and to his proposal that we allow as a real and genuine feature of the patients something that is in some sense dependent, not only on how another person (the nun) interacts with them, but also on how a *third* party (Gaita or another) perceives that interaction. (After the above quotation, Gaita continues, 'I have to say "for me", because one must speak personally about such matters.') But I do not wish to object to this feature of Gaita's view—what he says seems to me very possibly on the right track, and the whole phenomenon deserves a more detailed investigation than I have space for here. What I want to say, by way of an Aristotelian response to Gaita's challenge, is this: that the role played, in an Aristotelian ethics, by the notion of a flourishing human being is not such as to confer a particular (high) *value* upon flourishing human beings—whatever that might mean. The concept of a flourishing human being provides, rather, an anchor, or standard, in our ethical thought, one by reference to which a host of statements about what is good or fine or bad or base (etc.) are ultimately to be assessed. It is indeed precisely because the incurable patients in Gaita's account are human beings who fall so far short of this 'standard' that it makes sense to speak of them, and of the nun, in the way that Gaita does.

The nun, in his account, by her words and deeds showed humanly natural attitudes and reactions towards others, of the sort that were discussed in Chapter 1 of this book. Such attitudes and reactions, as we saw, provide a kind of bedrock for ethical thinking. Their paradigm objects are other human beings—not just flourishing ones. But the character of many of these attitudes and reactions depends on facts that have to do with whether another human being is doing well or ill, and in what ways. The *sort* of love that is described by Gaita as having been shown by the nun towards her patients is different e.g. from a love shown to a healthy and thriving person. There is obviously no simple 'scale of loves' here, but Gaita is surely right to see a love for the incurably insane as peculiarly selfless and giving, and yet as falling outside the conceptual remit of much ethical philosophizing—if not that of Aristotelian, then that of utilitarian philosophizing. I hope Cora Diamond will forgive my taking the following quote-in-a-quote out of the full context of her discussion; she here points out for us one very telling instance of conceptual poverty:

What I mean by 'stupid or insensitive or crazy' may be brought out by a single word, the word 'even' in this quotation: 'We have seen that the experimenter reveals a bias in favour of his own species whenever he carries out an experiment on a non-human for a purpose that he would not think justified him in using a human being, even a retarded human being.'[22]

Singerian utilitarianism does seem to lack the conceptual resources needed to keep the ineradicably afflicted amongst us, in Gaita's words. But the same is not, I think, true of an Aristotelian ethics—whatever Aristotle himself may have said or thought about the unflourishing.

As that last remark brings out, however, it is not from Aristotle, nor from ancient Greek thought at all, that we actually inherit the idea of the sick and vulnerable as especially worthy of our love and care. If we are Westerners, it is most likely from Judaeo-Christian thought that we inherit this idea. And of course the Western historical origins of hospitals, shelters, and soup kitchens are largely Christian. (Hospitals were originally religious

[22] Cora Diamond, 'Wittgenstein and Metaphysics', in *The Realistic Spirit* (Cambridge, MA: MIT Press, 1991), p. 23. Diamond is quoting Peter Singer's book *Animal Liberation* (London: Pimlico, 1995).

foundations.) The idea of love and care of the hopelessly afflicted is a very radical one, and is at all times threatened by its natural contender, the human propensity to honour and admire health, strength, worldly success, and power. What, if anything, can be said to explain or justify this idea?

Gaita is right, I think, to focus on the character and deeds of the loving person—the nun—and to see these as the clue to understanding what is in fact a *way of seeing* the afflicted, namely as sacred, or as 'infinitely precious'. Someone who can care for an insane person and respond to them, not as to an object or an animal, but as to a fellow human being—without feeling disgust, or boredom, or the call of Kantian duty—such a one may be said to have her spiritual eyes and ears wide open. Disgust, boredom, inner monologues, etc., are all in one way or another impediments to looking and seeing, and so to understanding, and this goes for relating to other human beings as much as for studying law or engineering. A truthful and three-dimensional picture of suffering and hopelessness will not be available from neurological studies nor from philosophical treatises like this one, but from first-hand accounts, either of those who have suffered themselves, or of those who have cared for them in that spirit of selfless attention of which Gaita writes. The Christian idea of the sick and hopeless is simultaneously an idea of a broadness of emotional understanding, one that is able to include the sick and hopeless in its view. That understanding has a kind of truth as its object: a kind of truth conveyable in language especially of a poetic or metaphorical character.[23]

If a Nietzschean or a eugenicist asks how such miserable specimens of humanity can be held up as *especially* important, at least part of the answer lies in a comparison, not between the flourishing and the unflourishing, but between the unruffled (or rarely ruffled) cheerfulness of an all-embracing sympathy, on the one hand, and the narrow impatience of those offended by aspects of the human condition, on the other. And if sickness and suffering are offensive, so must old age and death be. The broadness of view capable of embracing the former may also be able to embrace the latter with something approaching equanimity, but the eugenicist, as he starts to lose his hair, is more likely to be found researching the latest advances in cryonics.

---

[23] See Chapter 1, Section IX.

V.

In Section III, I described a certain sort of attitude to the future as akin to an attitude that is naturally taken to the past, dubbing that attitude 'contemplative', on account of its eschewing wishes and regrets, and imbibing good and evil together from the one cup. Gaita's nun evidently showed something like this contemplative attitude to her patients and to their suffering, a suffering that was both terrible and incurable, but that was borne by people whom the nun could love and care for as fellow human beings—happily drinking evil and good from the one cup. Could we then say that the nun was engaged in just that activity alleged by Aristotle to be the highest form of happiness, namely contemplation?

The object of contemplation is a kind of truth, and the one who contemplates aims at understanding things aright, with no further end in view. Now on meeting a new patient, the nun did not of course retire to sit and think about what she had seen and heard—at least, we do not imagine her doing that, or having to do that. But to interact with that patient in the way described by Gaita, the nun would be alert to the patient's needs and desires, and would be aiming at an understanding of those needs and desires, among other things. 'Surely not just for the sake of it, though! Wasn't she aiming to help the patient in practical ways?' The nun's aim was to look after and care for her patients; and *understanding* them was not a means to an independently specifiable end (looking after her patients), so much as something involved in, and manifested in, looking after them.[24] To be sure, such understanding could also be manifested in her later describing her dealings with her patients, assuming that she had adequate powers of linguistic expression. But we need not restrict the notion of understanding to the linguistic case, nor to some mental equivalent of language use ('pure thought'). Thought and language, as has been said earlier in this book, are interwoven with life and the activities of life. 'She is a very understanding person' is not primarily meant as praise for a person's intellect (and the point at issue is independent of whether this idiom is peculiar to English).

---

[24] Compare Wittgenstein on understanding a rule: such understanding is not to be thought of as a mental state producing certain behaviour, but (roughly) as an ability to do certain things spontaneously and without assistance (e.g. *Philosophical Investigations*, paras 150–6).

There seem to be many, in fact innumerable, activities which essentially (non-accidentally) involve or manifest understanding, and to improve at which is to increase one's understanding. What it *is* that you are understanding, in that you are doing something, varies from activity to activity, and so varies in extent, in depth, and in connectedness with other things. The study of fossils enlarges an understanding of the prehistoric past; playing poker enlarges an understanding of tactics within that game, and also (to a degree) of human psychology. Caring for the sick enlarges one's understanding of others, potentially at quite a deep level, and also of oneself. But of only some of these activities is it sensible to say that they are pursued *for the sake of* understanding. I said a moment ago that the nun did not aim at understanding her patients as a means to caring for them— but nor did she care for them as a means to understanding them! Her care for and interaction with her patients *embodied* a kind of understanding. Care and understanding were in a sense one. The activities of philosophy, on the other hand, (talking, reading, writing) can really be spoken of as being pursued for the sake of understanding, even while they themselves embody understanding—or come to do so. And it is philosophy that Aristotle has in mind when he extols contemplation. With philosophy, furthermore, the range and depth of the objects of understanding do serve to differentiate it from many or most other activities. That is to say, all this is true where philosophy is done for its proper end, and not for the sake of money, or rank, or fame, or kudos.

If it is understanding that is important, we might answer the question 'What shall I do in life?' by mentioning activities that non-accidentally and non-instrumentally involve understanding. But would we give priority to those activities that are done *for the sake of* understanding, like philosophy?—or would we rather give priority to those activities (perhaps including philosophy) which involve the kinds of understanding whose objects are themselves of importance? But what could constitute such 'importance'?

An explanation of the importance of a subject-matter, i.e. of certain possible objects of human understanding, will be something that can be given in answer to the question, 'What's the interest of that?' We encountered this question, and the answers that it can receive, in the last chapter, where I spoke of the distinction between giving a rationale and specifying an end or goal. To say what the interest of some subject consists in is to give a certain sort of rationale. Likewise, to say what the pleasure of some activity consists in is to give a certain sort of rationale; and the ways *in which* a subject or an activity can be either interesting or pleasant determine how 'important' it is. In fact, you can often ask of a single activity—philosophical study, for instance—either 'What's the interest of it?' or 'What's the pleasure of it?', and get much the same answers in reply, answers which, in the case of philosophy, would (one hopes) convey something of its importance. The person going in for the activity in question may have initially been asked, 'Why are you doing that?' or 'Why do you want to do that?', and may have answered, 'It's interesting', or 'It's fun', replies that give desirability characterizations. Such statements purport to bring an end to 'What for?' questioning, and thus present not means to ends, but ends: in the case of 'It's interesting' or 'It's fun', this doesn't mean that something called 'interest' or 'fun' is specified as the aimed-for result, as we saw in the last chapter, but rather that the activity is a certain sort of 'end in itself', to use the well-known jargon. To bring an end to 'What for?' questioning with these statements points to the possibility of further explanatory rationales.

And here we see what is wrong with the claim Aristotle makes about contemplation, quoted above: 'the activity of contemplation may be held to be the only activity that is loved for its own sake'. Many activities are loved for their own sakes, notably activities that are pursued for pleasure's sake, i.e. because they are pleasant or fun. That these things are typically and normally pursued for their own sakes follows from the nature of the concept *pleasure*. Indeed, Aristotle can here be quoted against himself: 'But agreeable amusements [*paidia*] also are desirable for their own sake; we do not pursue them as a means to something else'.[25]

This last statement comes in the course of a discussion of whether 'agreeable amusements' could constitute true happiness, with Aristotle declaring that they could not. It is clear from Aristotle's characterization of such amusements or pastimes that he is thinking of what Mill would have called lower pleasures, both philosophers taking 'bodily' pleasures to be lower than 'non-bodily' ones. As we have seen,[26] Aristotle insists that contemplation involves pleasure, and must do if it is to be a possible source of happiness—he has nothing against pleasant activities as such. All in all, what Aristotle ought to have said is this: many activities can be pursued for their own sakes, but those constitutive of true happiness must also aim at

---

[25] *Nichomachean Ethics*, X.vi.3.   [26] See p. 132.

understanding. Now this looks like a contradiction: we seem to have Aristotle saying that contemplation is pursued for its own sake and for the sake of something else (understanding, or the enjoyment of knowledge). This is more or less how I expressed matters a few paragraphs back when talking of philosophical activity; but I think that the appearance of contradiction can be shown to be mere appearance. The right account of things will turn out to be similar to Aristotle's account of becoming virtuous by performing virtuous actions,[27] and also similar to Wittgenstein's account of learning to read by reading.[28] How can you act bravely unless you're already brave? How can you read words unless you can already read? These questions are to be answered by pointing to the gradual nature of acquiring a capacity or disposition, which entails that there need be no *first* act of genuine bravery, no *first* act of genuine reading. In the same way, the person who reads, writes, thinks, and converses philosophically aims at increasing his philosophical understanding, though all this reading, writing, thinking, and conversing must already be (or rather, gradually become) philosophical activity—a manifestation of philosophical understanding. The main difference between philosophizing and reading would seem to be that people can be classified as completely competent in reading, as having as it were finished their training, while an analogous classification in the realm of philosophy does not exist. There are good reasons for this conceptual difference; though we should remember that a person can in fact always improve his reading skills, by expunging those few habitual misspellings or enlarging his vocabulary. But even more obvious is the fact that there is no limit to philosophical improvement—no end to philosophizing.

More will be said about philosophy and philosophizing in Chapter 5. But now is probably a good time to take stock, and to summarize our findings so far.

VI.

I began this chapter by introducing the notion of a good life for a human being, something that includes but is not the same thing as the life of a good human being. To want to lead a good life is to want to be truly

---

[27] Aristotle, *Nicomachean Ethics*, II.i.4; II.iv.1–5.
[28] L. Wittgenstein, *Philosophical Investigations*, paras 156–61.

happy, in the sense of 'happy' that allows us to say that happiness is identical with human good.

Two apparent dilemmas concerning the nature of happiness were then outlined: (i) happiness as individualistic versus happiness as socially conditioned, and (ii) happiness as process versus happiness as end-state.

(i) Aristotle's claim that happiness must be self-sufficient, or as self-sufficient as possible, was considered, and we found reason to doubt its truth, on account of the gregarious nature of human beings and the social character of the language-game of giving and asking for reasons (themes familiar from Chapter 1). Similar doubts were expressed about the claims of modern individualism, according to which each person is the best and only judge of his or her happiness. This cultural trend, and its sister trend, relativism, were anatomized. The possibility of a plurality of types of good life was mooted, a plurality partially explicable by reference to the division of labour that living in societies necessitates. Where the 'labour' is that whose notional goal is the flourishing of the whole society, I suggested that we could make room for the idea that good lives can be led e.g. by hermits and scholars, lives that could even be said to benefit others living in the same society.

(ii) This dilemma was diagnosed as arising from a deep tension within human nature, between the impulse to do and the impulse to rest (as I put it). An important form of this tension has to do with the fact that being virtuous involves struggling against various evils (doing), while in a world in which those evils had been conquered (and rest achieved) the virtues, along with other things constitutive of human happiness, would not exist. Of course such a paradise will never be so long as human life continues. But that observation doesn't really address the problem, despite its being of use to us. I then attempted to delineate a possible attitude to one's own future, or to the future of human beings more generally, one that is modelled, as it were, upon a dispassionate attitude to past events. This attitude involves accepting evil with good, where the two are inextricably intertwined, and waving aside all subjunctives and optatives—'If only . . . !', 'May it not be . . . !', and so on. I dubbed this attitude 'contemplative', in particular because it is not a *practical* attitude, even though it can be felt in the midst of, and indeed as part and parcel of, deliberations that are eminently practical. The possibility of this attitude enabled us to see how being virtuous need not after all entail being in a state of radical dissatisfaction with the world.

One form of this contemplative attitude, I argued, was that which can be shown by a person who, in a spirit of selfless attention, looks after the incurably sick in mind or body. Such activity, exemplified by the work of the nun in Raimond Gaita's account, embodies a kind of understanding, just as does philosophical contemplation—though it is obviously understanding of a different kind. Both these activities—care for the sick and philosophizing—are ones that are performed for their own sakes, at least in the ideal case; and there are many other activities that are performed for their own sakes. This is not surprising, given the variety of possible desirability characterizations, as given by e.g. 'It's fun' or 'It's interesting': for such statements (purport to) count as adequate and sufficient answers to 'Why?', and if intelligible, show the actions in question to have been done *not* with any further end in view. Justifying or explaining why one pursues some activity in one's life will therefore ultimately be a matter of providing what in Chapter 3 I called a rationale. And there may well be a case for saying that those rationales enjoy a special status which allude to the way in which an activity involves and enlarges one's understanding (and not all activities do that). But explaining the importance or significance of the *objects* of this understanding, i.e. its 'subject-matter', is really the same thing as explaining the point of the activity: there is in effect just one rationale, not two.

VII.

If it is possible to have a contemplative attitude to one's own future, an attitude that shares something with a dispassionate view of the past, then the most obvious challenge to the efficacy of that attitude must be the fact of one's mortality. Is it possible for a human animal, whose instincts are so geared to survival, to arrive at a state of mind that embraces the reality of death as easily as it embraces the reality of birth? Lucretius thought so; and he famously argued[29] that not to be alive in a thousand years' time can be no worse than not to have been alive a thousand years ago, something that nobody worries at. He used this argument, among others, in an attempt to show the irrationality of the fear of death. The argument relies on the idea of a symmetry of past and future, a symmetry that is meant to entail a

---

[29] Lucretius, *De Rerum Natura*, bk 3.

corresponding symmetry in the attitudes it is rational to take towards one's past and one's future. Despite the similarities, the contemplative attitude I have been discussing is to be distinguished from Lucretius' putatively 'rational' attitude to the future. How so?

Someone sceptical of Lucretius' argument might ask how it is meant to apply in the case of imminent death. If I know I will die in the next few hours, I cannot console myself by thinking, 'After all, I wasn't alive a few hours ago'—for I *was* alive a few hours ago. If I reflect in a more general way that there was a time when I was not alive, and that similarly there will be a time when I won't be alive, this is all very well, but it is the sort of reflection that a person might have who is not actually facing death, but is just thinking about it—as a child might think about one day getting married. Perhaps such general reflection helps those who are worried at the mere fact of death; but can it continue to help when the men in the firing squad are loading their guns? The content of one's worry, in such a case, is not *I will some day die*, nor is it very likely to be *I won't be alive in a thousand years*—it is *I am going to die in a few minutes' time*. The last 'worry' is different from the first two, and Lucretius seems only to be offering a cure for the first two. The problem is that, in the end, death *approaches*, and with it approaches the more immediate species of worry. We would like something to help us in the face of that worry.

The source of the difficulty is that Lucretius takes the ordinary self-concerned standpoint as the starting-point of his argument. From that standpoint, you couldn't care less whether you were around a thousand years ago. Indeed, an ordinary self-concerned person often couldn't care less what was happening a thousand years ago, full stop. Why bother? Ancient history butters no parsnips. Such a person may well feel the same way about the state of the universe in a thousand years, and about his own future non-existence at that distant time. But from the ordinary self-concerned standpoint, the events of the next few minutes, or days, or years, is of obvious interest. It is quite another sort of standpoint that is needed if we are to deprive death of its sting. I need to be able to think of my life, and of my death, as elements in a much bigger whole, or wholes: my family, my society, the human race, the natural world, the world. That is why it is indeed of relevance how things 'look' on a scale of hundreds or thousands of years. To think, in a totally general way, 'Thousands of years of life and activity precede me' is one thing, but to be able to fill in some of the actual detail of that enormous tapestry is another. For if a picture is given, you can get to see what kind of place you occupy in it; and, more importantly, you can begin to wonder at the picture itself. Here is one manifestation of the contemplative attitude: an enjoyment of the sort of understanding that Wittgenstein would call an 'overview' (*Übersicht*) of things. To wonder *whether* (or *how, why, who, when . . .*) and to wonder *at* are related phenomena: through the first we come to the second. Or in other words, through knowledge of the world around us we may arrive at a capacity for disinterested wonder.

But, as Aristotle would remind us, a capacity for viewing one's own life and death in this way is not just picked up or decided upon, for (where it exists) it is part of a person's second nature. You need to have some sort of training, and this typically means some sort of upbringing, if you are to be able to think of yourself in the way I have been sketching. The heroine of Edith Wharton's *The House of Mirth*, Lily Bart, looking back on her past, realizes that

[s]he herself had grown up without any one spot of earth being dearer to her than another: there was no centre of early pieties, of grave endearing traditions, to which her heart could revert and from which it could draw strength for itself and tenderness for others. In whatever form a slowly-accumulated past lives in the blood—whether in the concrete image of the old house stored with visual memories, or in the conception of the house not built with hands, but made up of inherited passions and loyalties—it has the same power of broadening and deepening the individual existence, of attaching it by mysterious links of kinship to all the mighty sum of human striving.[30]

Wharton is writing of the particular importance of *tradition* in constituting a person's setting, that setting being the picture in which the person may view herself as playing a part. A tradition in this sense, whether embodied in a bit of land or a house, or in 'inherited passions and loyalties', can be one of the worlds which a person occupies. But not every tradition is a world worth occupying. Hence the importance of critical reflectiveness, which enables you to assess your ends in life, but also the traditions to which you show and feel loyalty. To be rootless is typically a misfortune, but so is to have rotten roots, a condition that has for example been suffered by thousands of the sons and daughters of Germans who in one way or another were complicit in the terrible deeds of the Third Reich. Many of those younger Germans felt the necessity of cutting themselves

---

[30] Edith Wharton, *The House of Mirth*, bk II, ch. 13.

off from the traditions of their country, of their nationality, even of their family. Starting afresh in such circumstances can take a special sort of courage, since putting roots down in new soil must often be a lonely business, and one whose outcome is uncertain.

All this points towards the human importance of particular traditions. Knowledge about the traditions in which you find yourself, or for that matter into which you insert yourself, comes especially through learning history. And historical learning not only takes you out of yourself by locating you within certain traditions, it takes you further out of yourself by locating those traditions within a broader picture that includes traditions (cultures, ways of life and thought, physical environments...) in which you play no part at all. Hume, himself a historian of note, would in this connection speak of the extension of one's natural sympathies to people in distant times and places; which, if 'sympathies' is understood in a sufficiently sophisticated (un-Empiricist) manner, is one way of putting things. History is the biography of the human race, and as a source of personal knowledge and understanding it has the power of which Wharton writes, the 'power of broadening and deepening the individual existence, of attaching it by mysterious links of kinship to all the mighty sum of human striving'.

And there is an even bigger picture, of which the history of the human race is itself an element, i.e. the *natural* history of human beings—also that of the animals around us—and more generally, of life and nature. A perennial topic for thinkers, poets, and artists has been the cycle of nature, as embodied in birth, reproduction, and death, and it is a familiar idea that a kind of immortality can come from having children, from 'continuing the line'. This idea is not tantamount to any thesis. It is rather a picture, and as we have seen earlier in this book, pictures pervade our thinking in ways that certainly allow us to talk of better, or fuller, or truer, pictures. One way with death's sting is to contemplate that picture of human life in which generation follows generation, and in which there is a unity that is perceivable only if you stand back from the picture a suitable distance.

A person who by habit of reflection upon the larger scheme of things finds it natural to do so will, I think, have a sort of armour in the face of imminent death which cannot be vouchsafed by Lucretius' 'symmetry' argument, to the extent that the latter relies on the ordinary self-interested point of view in the way I have alleged it does. Such armour is not invulnerable: it is no doubt easily pierced by animal fear or by an encounter with human evil. And there are other armours available to human beings, such as that worn by those who know they are dying for a just cause. Could it be said that the contemplative armour is more widely available—there for anyone who chooses to reflect adequately on his life? Only up to a point. For those who are still young, it must often be out of reach; and this is *one* of the reasons why terminally ill children and young people deserve our special consideration.

Contemplation of the worlds which you occupy, and of your place in those worlds, can be a source of understanding, the sort of understanding that contributes to human happiness—or so I have been arguing. I have put this in a way that at least allows for the finitude of human life. But of course it would make quite a difference to one's place in the scheme of things if bodily death were not the end of existence, and if the afterlife were as it is depicted, e.g. in the teachings of one or another religion. In that case, although the picture of oneself as embedded in earthly traditions, history, and nature, would be unimpugned, and would still serve as an object of contemplation and a source of understanding, there would be another and vaster picture deserving of contemplation. Someone who felt the truth of this picture to be as certain as that of the other might well regard ignorance of the vaster picture to be almost a misfortune. Hence one very natural motive for proselytization. But it is a moot question whether it is *possible* to be as certain of the truth of any eschatological account of human existence as it is possible to be of the truth of human history, natural history, and the rest. This is a question that lies outside the remit of this book; but it is obvious that any person seeking after an understanding of the significance of their life and of the world they live in will at least want to consider seriously the issue of whether bodily death must be the end of existence, or not.

5

Philosophy

I.

Etymologically speaking, the word *philosophy* means *love of wisdom*. It is derived from the ancient Greek *philosophia*, and for the Greeks the question 'What has philosophy got to do with life?' would be similar to the question 'What has wisdom got to do with life?' Of course, the modern usage of the term 'philosophy' does not allow of a purely etymological explanation. Philosophy, it would usually be said, is a subject, with a certain subject-matter; or if it does not really have a subject-matter, then it can at any rate be characterized by reference to a list, probably open-ended and vague, of issues or questions—which had better include questions that turn out on investigation to be empty or nonsensical. The debate as to the nature of philosophy is, notoriously, a philosophical one. But you do not have to supply a worked-out account of what philosophy is before you can approach the question, 'What has philosophy got to do with life?'

In the mouths of people who think that philosophy is bound to be irrelevant to real life issues, this question is merely rhetorical. But it is uttered in more exasperated tones by those who think that philosophy ought and could be relevant to those issues, but in its present form fails to be. This second form of complaint deserves to be taken seriously, and a number of philosophers have taken it seriously. In recent times, the complaint perhaps hit hardest when philosophers were themselves in the habit of saying that the subject was by its nature unable to yield any guidance, however general, on social or ethical matters. Such philosophers tended to endorse subjectivist or similar theories of 'moral language', according to which moral statements are at bottom expressions of individual preference, unsusceptible of rational criticism or philosophical assessment. Subjectivism has not died out, though the 'hands off' style of meta-ethics has more or less disappeared in English-speaking philosophy departments. And in fact there are many professional philosophers who would now boast of the relevance and practicality of their philosophizing, especially of course if they are ethicists. 'Practical ethics' is a well-worn phrase. But it is a phrase that has to a large extent become associated with utilitarian and consequentialist philosophy, as is witnessed by the fact that *Practical Ethics* is the name of a best-selling book by a world-famous utilitarian, Peter Singer.

It is an interesting fact that critics of modern moral philosophy have often agreed in pointing to the ancient Greeks as a source of forgotten, or alternatively just *available*, enlightenment.[1] Some, though not all, of these philosophers would be regarded as adherents of virtue ethics, so called. And there is no doubt that a fresh examination of such concepts as virtue, vice, character, human nature, and flourishing has done wonders for the moral philosophy of the last half century. But it is not only in connection with this family of concepts that the opportunity exists for getting something from the Greeks. In the last chapter, I made use of a notion of contemplation and of the contemplative attitude that was intended to link up, at the least, with Aristotle's claim that the highest happiness is to be achieved through contemplation (*theōria*). Aristotle's claim can be taken as extolling *philosophia* or the love of wisdom, since the aim of contemplation is wisdom. I have already noted the fact that the modern meaning of 'philosophy' is distinct from that of *philosophia*, and in the last chapter I said that philosophical understanding was just one species of understanding, among many that could be regarded as contributing to human happiness. But despite these facts, there is, I want to argue, a link between the two activities of thinking about your life and of thinking philosophically—and hence, as it might be put, between *philosophia* and philosophy. If there is such a link, a kind of relevance of philosophy to real life can surely be made out. By 'philosophy' I mean 'philosophy properly done': the complaint against philosophy discussed in the previous paragraph may stand, if most philosophy is not properly done.

---

[1] Some of the most obvious examples being Anscombe, Foot, Geach, MacIntyre, and Williams.

What is the link between thinking about life and thinking philosophically? It is this: in both cases, an appreciation of a thing's significance typically and crucially depends upon coming to see how it figures in, or against the background of, a larger and richer setting. I have phrased the point in terms of one's appreciation of a thing's significance. And just as linguistic meaning is not independent of people's grasp of linguistic meaning, so significance, in the sense or senses I have in mind, is not independent of people's appreciation of significance. So the present point could equally be put another way: with both life and philosophy, a thing's significance typically and crucially depends on how it figures in, or against the background of, a larger and richer setting. One consequence of all this is that some of the key virtues of thought required for thinking well about human life are not dissimilar to, are indeed substantially the same as, some of the key virtues of thought required for thinking well philosophically.

I have already sketched how the contemplation of the worlds one occupies, and of the part one plays in them, might bring one closer to the sort of understanding which puts death in its place, and which (in that and other ways) can contribute to human happiness—to being on good terms with the universe. These 'worlds' include family, tradition, history, the human race, the animal kingdom . . . It is in our nature to put Self centre stage, but that tendency is a source both of human evil and of human misery. The more a person looks outwards the more the tendency is tamed, and the less the person is prey to narrowness, magnification of worries, blindness to others, and so on.

These ideas are not novel ones, and have been expounded over the centuries in various ways by dozens of thinkers. More novel, perhaps, is the idea that something analogous can be said about philosophy. But in fact the principle *Look to the bigger picture* has a good claim to being one of philosophy's guiding principles.

A famous example is what has been called the Context Principle, enunciated by Frege in the Introduction to *The Foundations of Arithmetic*, where the author enjoins us 'never to ask for the meaning [*Bedeutung*] of a word in isolation, but only in the context of a proposition'. Wittgenstein echoes Frege at 3.314 of the *Tractatus*: 'An expression has meaning only in a proposition'; and in his later philosophy, he can be seen as invoking various contexts besides that of the proposition, such as that of a language-game, or that of a particular imaginary conversation. For Frege, Wittgenstein, and many other twentieth-century philosophers of language, the tendency to be resisted is that of focusing on a certain expression and trying to gauge its meaning by attending to the expression on its own, or to whatever is found to be 'in the mind' when one says, hears, or in some other way produces the expression. One application of the Context Principle is Russell's Theory of Descriptions: it tells us that an account of the meaning of a definite description like 'the tallest man in Derby' can only be given by showing how to construe whole sentences in which it occurs. There have been many other applications of the principle besides Russell's, and we need not here go into the question of precisely which applications are successful. Many of them evidently are; and the principle has been of enormous value to philosophy.

The tendency to be resisted, I said, was that of focusing on a certain expression and trying to gauge its meaning by attending to the expression on its own, or to whatever is found to be 'in the mind' when one says, hears, or in some other way produces the expression. A tendency that goes hand in hand with this natural tendency is that of thinking that a grammatically well-formed sentence all of whose constituents are meaningful expressions must itself have an unimpeachable sense. The expressions carry their meaning, and their meaningfulness, around with them—so the resultant of these various meanings, where they have been yoked together according to the rules, must surely be meaningful! What the Context Principle reminds us is that a 'meaningful expression' is a sound or shape or similar that *can mean something*, not a sound or shape or similar that somehow glows with meaning, even in the dark; and 'can mean something' points to conditions that must be met in order for the expression to mean something. Those conditions will include not just the rules of syntax, as recorded in grammar books. But what other conditions will there be? To answer *this* question, we have to first step back, and ask, 'What are we doing with words when we use them intelligently, in language?' This of course is the sort of question which Wittgenstein made it his business to tackle.

'Isn't all this just philosophy of language?' No, it is not. Here is an instance of the tendency to think that a grammatically well-formed sentence all of whose constituents are meaningful expressions must itself have an unimpeachable sense: in his 'Proof of an External World', G. E. Moore considers the sentence 'I know I have two hands', and the assumption that it has a clear sense all on its own informs his whole approach. For given this assumption, the question immediately arises as to whether the sentence is in fact true, since if indicative and meaningful, surely a sentence ought to be either true or false? (This principle is itself one of those subjected to scrutiny by post-Fregean philosophy, but let it pass.) But how are we to assess whether 'I know I have two hands' is true or false? In addressing this question Moore very naturally finds himself falling back on his *intuition*, i.e. his gut feelings, since no other avenue appears to present itself. Just staring at his hands again, or waving them around, would hardly establish that Moore knew he had hands in any non-question-begging way—he is after all trying to refute 'The Sceptic'. Moore's intuition, naturally, assures him that he does know he has two hands. There is the proof.

But 'I know I have two hands', said just like that, does not have a clear sense. The concept of knowledge is connected with that of justification, of giving reasons, where giving reasons is something you do in response to such a demand as, 'How do you know?' This demand itself only makes any move at all in the course of an enquiry if there exist background standards for what count as good or bad reasons, and if the actual context of the enquiry allows for those standards to apply. Such standards do not come down from Heaven; they derive from the actual needs and proclivities of human beings interacting with one another. Wittgenstein illustrates the point with one of his pleasingly surreal examples:

Suppose that I were the doctor and a patient came to me, showed me his hand and said: "This thing that looks like a hand isn't just a superb imitation—it really is a hand" and went on to talk about his injury—should I really take this as a piece of information, even though a superfluous one? Shouldn't I be more likely to consider it nonsense, which admittedly did have the form of a piece of information? For, I should say, if this information really were meaningful, how can he be certain of what he says? The background is lacking for it to be information.[2]

These are matters that were discussed in Chapter 1, where the Cartesian notion of a contextless enquiry was criticized.

Is this now philosophy of language or epistemology? It is BOTH. But there are many who will object to that statement. Among them are philosophers who believe in the dichotomy *philosophy of language versus epistemology*, and in similar dichotomies, and who typically object to what they term 'linguistic philosophy', as represented in particular by the later Wittgenstein. For ease of reference I will call such philosophers Ontologists, after the habit, shared by many of them, of granting honorific status to questions or theories that are 'ontological'. A moment ago I mentioned the

---

[2] L. Wittgenstein, *On Certainty*, para. 461.

'context of enquiry', and this will probably lead some to say I am propounding, or trying to propound, a contextualist theory of knowledge. If they are also Ontologists, they may go on to characterize a decent contextualist theory as being about the mental state of knowledge, not about the concept *knowledge*, and still less—God forbid—about the English word 'knowledge'.

There seem to be two ways of putting things, of which Ontologists will prefer the second: (i) Whether 'S knows that p' is true depends upon the context of utterance (or of enquiry); (ii) Whether S enjoys the mental state of knowing that p depends upon the context which S occupies. Two remarks may be made about the suggested preference of (ii) over (i). First, one who says that (i) is about words and not also about knowledge appears to ignore the fact that '"S knows that p" is true' is generally equivalent to 'S knows that p': statements about what possible knowledge-claims are true are generally tantamount to statements about whether people know certain things. Secondly, if the contexts mentioned in (ii) are in fact intended to be contexts of utterance (or of enquiry), then we evidently have a 'linguistic' account after all. Now many philosophers would here invoke such possible contexts as there being many fake barns built in Jones' vicinity (Jones having pointed to an unusually non-fake barn and innocently said, 'There's a barn', thus allegedly failing to express true knowledge)[3]—and surely that is a physical or geographical context, rather than a linguistic one? Maybe so. But how do fake-barn-quotients come to determine the identity of our mental states, to speak for a moment in Ontologese? We could fall back on Moorean intuition here and say, 'They just do'. But we need not do this, since a philosophical account is in fact ready to hand, namely one that addresses the questions (a) how Jones could try to justify his statement, and (b) whether, given the empirical facts, his justification would count as adequate. Given a context of possible *enquiry*, i.e. given a possible enquirer asking 'How do you know it's a barn?', we may indeed have reason to doubt that Jones manages to address the query just by saying 'It looks like a barn'—for one thing, in fake-barn-country, the demand 'How do you know it's a barn?' will rather often involve an unspoken contrast: '...rather than a fake barn?' Whether background empirical facts of the sort used in such examples *do* undermine

---

[3] See A. Goldman, 'Discrimination and Perceptual Knowledge', *Journal of Philosophy* 73 (1976): 771–91.

knowledge-claims is a question I leave undecided; the point is that the route to deciding it will lie partly across linguistic terrain.

Enough of Ontologism, for the moment. The lesson I want to draw from the sort of examples we have been considering, examples having to do with knowledge, is that it is looking to the wider contexts that helps us to address the philosophical issues. And this means: linguistic and other contexts. (Language and life are intertwined.) We must not forget the linguistic contexts, especially because the source of a philosophical problem is often a forgetfulness of linguistic context. One source may indeed be a picture of linguistic meaning as happily context-independent, as I suggested was the case with Moore's assumption that 'I know I have two hands' has a clear sense all on its own, and as Frege and Wittgenstein saw when they argued in their different ways for the Context Principle.

II.

The inclination to focus on a word in order to gauge its meaning is closely related to the inclination to focus on what is going on in one's mind in order to gauge the nature of a mental state. Indeed, the two inclinations are really one in the case where a philosopher focuses, not so much on a word, as on what he finds in his mind when he says or thinks of the word, in order to gauge the word's meaning—the latter, he supposes, being something mental (e.g. a Lockean idea).

We have already encountered the inclination to focus on what is going on in the mind in order to gauge the nature of a mental state. The inclination was discussed in Chapter 1 (pp. 28–32), both in its traditional dualist form and in its more modern physicalist form. The latter phenomenon was illustrated by the sort of investigation into religious belief or into the emotions that makes use of fMRI scanners. I hope that my discussion of the emotions, in particular, went some way to showing the futility of such enterprises, enterprises whose technical glamour tends to be inversely proportional to their intellectual respectability. But the inclination in question is not a recent development; it is both natural and perennial. The cure for it is to look to the bigger picture. And this means: to look to the wider human phenomenon—the person and the life in which emotions have their being—and *also* to look to the wider linguistic phenomenon— the ways the emotion-term is used in real life, its connections with other terms, and so on. Doing the first will typically involve doing the second, and vice versa.

Is this philosophy of psychology or philosophy of language? It is both.

In Chapter 2, a similar case was made as regards *wanting*. 'I want to be a frog' might seem to make perfectly good sense, being after all a grammatically correct sentence whose constituents are meaningful expressions. And if Smith says it one day, won't he therefore say something that *could* be true? (For it doesn't seem to be a contradiction.) Our consideration of the background constraints on the intelligibility of 'I want . . . ' led us to doubt the meaningfulness of any old utterance of 'I want X'. The illusion that Smith could want to be a frog, even if there is nothing he would or could coherently describe as his succeeding in becoming a frog, arises partly from the thought that the sentence 'I want to be a frog' makes good sense, and partly from the thought that wanting to be a frog is an inner state, with an intrinsic character, essentially independent of other things (such as behaviour or the giving of reasons), and authoritatively knowable by the subject. The cure, once again, is to look to the bigger picture. And this means: to look to the wider human phenomenon—the person and the life in which wants have their being—and *also* to look to the wider linguistic phenomenon— the ways 'want', 'desire', etc., are used in real life, their connections with other terms, and so on. Doing the first will typically involve doing the second, and vice versa.

Is this philosophy of psychology or philosophy of language? It is both.

Moving on to Chapter 3, it was pleasure, in particular, whose nature was at issue. I considered the view of pleasure as an inner state, with an intrinsic character, essentially independent of other things, authoritatively knowable by the subject, and produced in the subject by those things she takes pleasure in. And this view was found wanting, though considerably more compelling than the analogous views of emotions and of desires. One main reason for the greater plausibility of such a view of *pleasure* is that 'Why do you want what's pleasant?' has an absurdity to it that is lacking from 'Why are you angry/sad/nervous/etc.?', and from many instances of 'Why do you want X?' Pleasure seems more divorced from reason and reasoning than emotion or wanting—it seems more self-sufficient. But it is not, I argued, divorced from reason and reasoning, in so far as there are, once again, constraints of intelligibility on statements about what you find pleasant; and there is in fact an important class of explanatory answers (which I called rationale-giving answers) to the question 'What's the pleasure of that?' Our cure was to look to the bigger picture. And this meant: to look to the wider human phenomenon—the person and the life in which pleasure has its being—and *also* to look to the wider linguistic phenomenon—the ways 'pleasure', 'fun' etc., are used in real life, their connections with other terms, and so on. Doing the first will typically involve doing the second, and vice versa.

Is this philosophy of psychology or philosophy of language? It is both.

Thus the course of our investigations has itself pointed to the truth of what I am now arguing—that a guiding principle of philosophy is to look to the bigger picture. Moreover, that 'bigger picture' involves our language, or languages. It is in language that human concept-schemes are primarily made manifest. And if philosophers can contribute anything distinctive to our view of the world, it will be because philosophy addresses itself to questions about aspects of the world as they feature in, or are embodied in, our concept-schemes. Does that mean that philosophy is about words, not things? At the risk of being repetitive: philosophy is about BOTH. And it is one of the scandals of recent times that philosophers have themselves turned their backs on this truth, just as it was a scandal of an earlier generation that philosophers turned their backs on ethics, and on the ability of philosophy to address ethical questions. One of the reasons for the latter scandal was that many philosophers believed in the dichotomy *words versus things* and took philosophy to be about words—while the more recent scandal begins from the same false dichotomy, but takes philosophy to be about things. This is the stance I have dubbed Ontologism.

Ordinary language philosophy of the 1950s and 1960s often erred on the 'linguistic' side, and some of its exponents came close to adopting the role of urbane lexicographer. No doubt it was partly in reaction against the excesses of that period that Ontologism began to develop. But Ontologism would not have been a movement at all if it had simply involved criticism of another movement. A positive self-image characterized the new movement, or one major branch of it, and that was the image of philosophy as 'continuous with natural science', or even as 'handmaiden to science'. One feeling often expressed, not only about ordinary language philosophy, but about linguistic philosophy generally, e.g. as represented by Wittgenstein, was the feeling that philosophy would be a pretty poor thing if it were as linguistic philosophers made it out to be. Therapy for conceptual confusion? Showing the fly the way out of the fly bottle? Is that *all*?? By contrast, if philosophy is a sort of cousin (or servant?) of natural science, it might share in the kudos of natural science. It might even attract funding.

The kudos enjoyed by science and by scientists in our society is undeniable, nor of course is it utterly undeserved. If nothing else, the technological, medical, and other advances of the last century or so have led people to feel a compound of gratitude and amazement towards science, or towards certain sciences. Considered as a human phenomenon, Western technology is as much a mixture of good and bad as are human beings themselves, having been responsible for bombs, factory farming, and television, as much as for antibiotics, washing machines, and grand pianos. But there is truth in the thought that such facts are irrelevant to the value of science, for science (from *scientia*, knowledge) aims at knowledge and understanding, just as does philosophy—when each is properly done. To pick up on an earlier thread, such aims are among the aims that a person may have who leads a good life for a human being.

Nevertheless, philosophy is not a part of science, nor is it any more continuous with science than with history, or anthropology, or literature. The differences between philosophy and physics/biology/chemistry/etc., are indeed so obvious that you might wonder how scientism in philosophy could ever have become a prevalent view, and the answer will surely have to be largely sociological. As I said, it can just *feel nice* to think of what you're doing as respectable in the way that science is, doing your bit in some imagined research programme, contributing to Progress. And many will not bother to ask themselves, 'What *am* I actually doing? What *is* the point of this?' A defence mechanism may even evolve: that of calling 'What is philosophy?' an uninteresting question—certainly not a question which a philosopher need worry himself about, except to the extent that he might have to give some sort of rough and ready answer to it for those wondering whether to study the subject.

To see some of the issues at stake here, let us consider the question of different kinds of philosophers' relationships with words. Let us for the sake of argument call any philosopher 'linguistic' who would endorse the Wittgensteinian thought that philosophical problems are often (and in characteristic ways) traceable to aspects of, especially confusions about, our own concepts, as these are expressed in language. It might then be thought that a linguistic philosopher would be more at risk of allowing words to get in his way, or assume fantastic roles, or enslave him altogether, than a philosopher whose eyes are fixed firmly on Reality. But if anything the reverse is true. It is no accident that Wittgenstein, Malcolm, Ryle, Austin, Anscombe, Foot, Diamond, etc., on the whole avoid technicalities and neologisms in their philosophical writings; for although technicalities and neologisms may from time to time be useful, as in any discipline, progress in philosophical thought is in general not achieved by means of them, and that fact will be more obvious to philosophers who see the 'bite' of philosophical problems as connected to their expression in our already-existing language. The appetite for technicalities and neologisms is more a mark of Ontologism than of linguistic philosophy. It stems partly from that desire to imitate science I have already touched on, but that is not its only source. Another is a kind of superstitious reverence for the power of words, of just the sort that Wittgenstein had in mind when he talked of the 'bewitchment of our intelligence by means of language'.[4] We discussed a common or garden variety of such superstitious reverence in Chapter 1 (Section VII), when we looked at the concept of the offensive, and the phenomenon of the euphemism. Philosophers, you might well hope, would by and large be more clear-headed about the power of words; but such clear-headedness is unlikely to come if you make it your policy not to think about words too much.

'But what's wrong with a few technicalities and neologisms? Don't they at least save time?' A piece of jargon only saves time where it is a genuine abbreviation of some agreed formula. And this is almost never the case in philosophy. Ask a group of philosophers for the meanings of the following philosophical terms: realism, subjective, nominalism, naturalistic fallacy, deontology, behaviourism, tenseless, normative, qualia, fact. The diversity of answers which you will get is not a reflection of differing 'substantive views' *about* realism, nominalism, and the rest (assuming the philosophers have understood your question), but is a reflection of vagueness at best, confusion at worst.

Now there is in fact a philosophical reason why '-isms' will tend to be *less* precise than ordinary words, a reason which can of course only be appreciated once one has done a little (a very little) philosophy of language. It is this: the meaning of a word is a matter of how people use it, and the usage of a word like, say, 'knowledge' (i) goes back centuries and

---

[4] *Philosophical Investigations*, para. 109.

(ii) pervades each person's life, cropping up in many and varied situations. The effect of (i) and (ii) is that the word's meaning is honed and polished, and maintained in that condition; for owing to the practical purposes of language-use, disagreements in usage need ironing out and sorting out, the alternative being misinterpretation and confusion. But a word like, say, 'non-cognitivism' has simply not had the *opportunity* to acquire a very precise meaning. It was introduced into philosophical discussion not very long ago, and if it was ever given an explicit definition, either everyone has forgotten it, or competing and variant definitions have come to jostle with the first[5]— and as far as actual usage goes, there has been no process of continual honing of the sort I described in the case of 'knowledge'. This is simply because— generally speaking—not much hangs, of an immediate and practical nature, on the fact that a bunch of philosophers happen to be at cross purposes.

A result of all this is that when philosophers speak of 'intuitions' as guiding some enquiry, they will appear credible if they mean such intuitions as whether so-and-so is a case of knowledge, but will not, if they mean such intuitions as whether so-and-so is a non-cognitivist view. Your intuitions about knowledge are confident to the extent that you are confident how and in what situations to use the words 'knowledge', 'know', etc. It is unsurprising if you find your intuitions getting weaker when asked, 'Was Kant a non-cognitivist?'—or for that matter when asked, 'What is a tenseless fact?', 'Are days of the week Universals?', and so on. Some technical terms, like 'universal', have indeed been around for a long time, but even that doesn't guarantee their having a clear sense.

None of this is to attack the use of '-isms' *per se*. After all, I have used quite a few myself in the course of this book. But it is important to be aware of the limitations, as well as of the advantages, of technical vocabulary. One fence that is sometimes felt by non-philosophers to have been

---

[5] It could be alleged that non-cognitivism is the theory that there is no knowledge in some area; so that e.g. moral non-cognitivism is the theory that there is no moral knowledge, or knowledge of moral truths. But for this definition to be interesting, it had better not restrict itself to theories that use these very words ('There is no moral knowledge', say)—it had better include theories that amount to the claim thus expressed, or that entail that claim. But until a theory or opinion is spelt out, it is just not clear what is meant by 'moral knowledge', or 'moral truths', or indeed (notoriously) 'moral'. A spelt-out theory can endow a certain retrospective sense on the term 'non-cognitivist', but now we don't need the term to characterize the theory, having the theory on the table in front of us; and if we apply 'non-cognitivist' to a different theory, there is little guarantee that we will be using the term univocally.

erected between them and philosophers is this fence of jargon, and large parts of it could in fact be demolished without much loss.

Nor am I inveighing against vagueness of meaning; a lot of vagueness is positively useful. Finally, I am not saying that everyday terms like 'knowledge' are philosophically unproblematic, which would be a very perverse statement. But to know which features of language use are harmless and which are potentially harmful you have to be prepared to think about language.

III.

Although philosophy is neither cousin nor servant of natural science, it shares with science the aims of knowledge and of understanding. This is a very broad statement, but some will see it as sufficiently determinate to provoke a worry, or even a possible objection. The worry would be that there appears to be no real progress in philosophy; the objection would be that, given this lack of progress, it is surely questionable whether philosophy *does* in fact aim at knowledge or understanding.

'Progress' can mean many things. What does it mean when it is said that there is progress in the natural sciences? Does it mean, 'We know progressively more and more in scientific matters'? It does seem to mean something like that, and construed thus, it is surely true. But who, it might be asked, are 'we'? The claim is not, or not usually, intended as meaning that the average amount of scientific knowledge had by an adult citizen progressively rises, something that is a function of educational standards (and quite possibly false in the UK). Nor is the claim even about the average amount of scientific knowledge had by a scientist. There is much division of labour in scientific research, and it is surely a strength of the research community that it is structured so as to allow both specialization and the pooling of results in a common pool (or pools). A result of this is that it may be possible to say, 'We know all about how mammalian endocrine systems work' when no individual person knows all about how mammalian endocrine systems work: what is being talked of is the common pool of knowledge about mammalian endocrine systems, an element of what Karl Popper would have called World Three, the world of shared theories, stories, etc.[6] The same

---

[6] See K. Popper, *Objective Knowledge* (Oxford: Clarendon Press, 1972, 1979).

goes for 'We know progressively more and more in scientific matters'. This means, 'The pool is getting bigger and bigger'.

What is it that makes a scientific theory common property, or that makes a pool of shared results a pool? The answer to this has to do with authority and the nature of expertise. A specialist in astronomy will justifiably accept on trust what a specialist in particle physics says or publishes, and vice versa, not because he has established the good credentials of the other scientist—which would often require him to be an expert in the same field, something only possible in a world without much specialism—but because among the practical requirements of information-sharing is the requirement that there be a rule or custom that within certain contexts one simply *counts* as being justified in taking another's word for something. The same goes for education of the young: education can only work at all if pupils are meant to take their teachers' words for things—if they didn't, their education couldn't even get started. We have already seen in earlier chapters how the criteria for what counts as a good reason for believing or doing something depend upon background empirical conditions, and here we have another case of this. The background empirical conditions relevant to one's reasons for believing some scientific theory include facts about what is needed for information to be passed on and built upon. The information that can be passed on and built upon is the common pool of knowledge— 'our' common pool.

Philosophy is not like this. In philosophy, you are not in general meant to take your teacher's word for things, unless those things are non-philosophical facts, e.g. the approximate dates of Plato's dialogues. Metaphysical and ethical theories *could* be taught as if they were scientific theories; we *could* have a set-up in which a student was simply meant to learn and repeat such theories. But if these theories were taught in this way, how would they have arisen in the first place? And how would they ever change? For them to be recognizably *philosophical* theories, they must exist in a context of rational debate—otherwise, they would be mere doctrines, or world-myths, or similar. (Perhaps some early Greek philosophy, or 'philosophy', had this status.) So in our imaginary set-up, there must at least be some context in which philosophical theories get thrashed out and debated. Maybe the custom is that you are allowed to join in philosophizing when you are old enough—thirty, say. But whatever the details, the subject won't be philosophy at all unless the prime mode of going in for it is by means of rational debate, rather than by repeating things learnt from authorities.

The reason there is no such thing as a common pool of shared philosophical results is not that, in philosophy, everything is subjective, or a 'matter of opinion'. It is rather that in philosophy there are no practical requirements analogous to those that make sense of having a common pool in the case of natural science. For at this level, philosophy and natural science have different aims. The practicalities of the two domains depend on the nature of their aims, and the prime aim of philosophy is *individual understanding*. The reason a person goes in for philosophy is so that he or she can acquire understanding, a certain sort of understanding, roughly delineable by reference to an open-ended list of topics or questions. 'Progress in philosophy' should therefore primarily mean progress in a particular person's philosophical understanding. And such progress is certainly both possible and frequently met with.

We can also speak of the broader philosophical culture, of course; indeed, given that social character of reasons and justification upon which I have been so insistent, individual philosophical understanding cannot be something utterly individualistic, since it only counts as a species of understanding at all against the background of shared or shareable norms of philosophizing. So there is also room for the notion of progress at the level of a philosophical culture. It makes perfectly good sense to speak of the early twentieth-century advances in logic, for example, as constituting a sort of progress in philosophy, progress in the philosophical culture, that is. Such advances will count as progress to the extent that they are taken on board by enough philosophers, where 'taking on board' involves understanding and absorbing things at the personal level. The primacy of the personal remains intact.

Individual understanding is also the primary aim of the activity *thinking about life*. Though you can indeed learn from those more experienced and wiser than yourself, you won't count as learning at all if you can't take on board what you hear from them. Understanding here is not manifest in what sayings you can repeat—in fact it is manifest in what you can *say* only in the sense that your words are among your deeds. There must be some relationship between thinking well about life and living well, and the goal of the first is typically the second.

Here, then, is a parallel between thinking about life and thinking philosophically: the primary aim of each activity is individual understanding. The scientific model, with its notion of a common pool of knowledge, does not apply naturally to these activities. I have already discussed other parallels. There is a sense in which a contemplative attitude is to be aimed at both in thinking about life and thinking philosophically; and a guiding principle of both activities is, or ought to be, to look to the bigger picture. Philosophy and *philosophia* turn out in the end to be related.

IV.

Two philosophers whose ideas have cropped up repeatedly in these pages are Aristotle and Wittgenstein. Aristotle takes a life of contemplation to be the highest form of human flourishing, contemplation having as its aim philosophic wisdom. In the *Nicomachean Ethics* he does not say much about *what* you are meant to contemplate, and one might worry that Aristotle is in danger of having to praise any old learning, however trivial. But of course he means contemplation of higher things, and he has in mind especially the 'bigger picture': the universe, and the relationships that eternally and necessarily bind many things together into a sort of whole.

For Wittgenstein, philosophic wisdom is likewise a matter of gaining an overview of a whole and of the myriad relationships among the things comprising it, though this whole and these relationships enjoy a large measure of contingency (non-necessity), unlike Aristotle's. The 'whole' is our language, or if you like our thought, as it is expressed or is expressible in language. But that doesn't mean that Aristotle recommends thinking about the universe while Wittgenstein recommends thinking about language *instead*. An overview of our language, of the sort Wittgenstein is after, *is* a sort of overview of the universe—more specifically, of those aspects of the universe concerning which philosophical puzzlement arises. The word 'puzzlement' may raise Ontological hackles; but remember that puzzlement is a close relative of wonder. It is not merely an irritating sensation. Wittgenstein talks of philosophy as therapy, and of philosophical problems as having their roots in confusion. But his view of philosophy is not therefore merely negative, for if a philosophical problem has the form: 'I don't know my way about',[7] philosophical enlightenment consists in knowing your way about. And this sort of knowing your way about your

---

[7] *Philosophical Investigations*, para. 123.

own language is not simply that level of linguistic competence that suffices for being counted a speaker of a language. For one thing, that level is set as low as it is for practical reasons, to do with the smooth running of human practices of language use: induction into those practices is generally taken as established in early childhood, and a child is said to *speak English* (or French, or Italian . . .). This does not prevent the child from getting into knots in his talk and thought, in familiar ways. Nor does 'mastery of a language' prevent an adult from getting into knots in his talk and thought, also in familiar ways. If a philosophical mind is more immune to these problems, can philosophical aptitude be a mere negative? Health is but a relative absence of disease and disability, but it would be strange not to think it a positive thing, if we are to talk this way at all.

But there is another point to be made. Knowing your way about language is something that is positively manifest, or manifestable, in your life more generally. For language is embedded in human life in countless ways, and thoughtfulness in speech tends to go hand in hand with thoughtfulness in deed. Similar remarks go, *mutatis mutandis*, for rashness, or dishonesty, or showing off . . . in speech or in deed. These are generalizations, of course. But they are clearly relevant to the question of whether philosophy, conceived of as Wittgenstein conceived of it, is something important in human life.

So far, a parallel of sorts can be drawn between Aristotle and Wittgenstein. But the two thinkers would seem to differ on the question whether philosophy and natural science are distinct, Aristotle saying 'No' to Wittgenstein's 'Yes' (very roughly), as also on the question of what *form* philosophic wisdom takes—specifically, whether it is systematic or non-systematic. Aristotle asserts that a body of knowledge, a science, is a deductive system based upon first principles (*archai*).[8] This is a sufficiently ambitious view of physics or biology; can it possibly apply to philosophy? Wittgenstein is not the only philosopher to have denied that it can, but he is perhaps the one to have gone furthest in the other direction, arguing that philosophy, properly done, is unsystematic, being more about assembling reminders than about constructing theories.[9]

And yet it would be hasty to say that all philosophizing is regarded by Aristotle as a matter of constructing, or wielding, deductive systems

---

[8] See especially his *Posterior Analytics*.

[9] See Wittgenstein, *Philosophical Investigations*, para. 127.

based upon first principles. For the term 'philosophy' includes ethics, and Aristotle takes ethics to be concerned with contingencies, as opposed to necessities, this being connected with the fact that it is practical; and for that reason, Aristotle would say, ethics cannot be based upon first principles, which must be necessary. In addition, he sees ethics and political science as having to do with things that are uncertain, and/or with things that are only generally true, rather than universally true.

> The same exactness must not be expected in all departments of philosophy alike, any more than in all the products of the arts and crafts. The subjects studied by political science are Moral Nobility [*ta kala*] and Justice; but these conceptions involve much difference of opinion and uncertainty . . . We must therefore be content if, in dealing with subjects and starting from premises thus uncertain, we succeed in presenting a broad outline of the truth: when our subjects and our premises are merely generalities, it is enough if we arrive at generally valid conclusions.[10]

So in fact, as regards systematicity, Aristotle's view of ethics and politics is not so different from Wittgenstein's view of philosophy more generally, although Wittgenstein would probably have mentioned context-dependence and irreducible complexity where Aristotle mentions 'difference of opinion and uncertainty'.

Connectedly, Aristotle's characterization of practical wisdom (*phronēsis*) as a capacity to judge matters soundly in a way resistant to encapsulation by rules indicates a conception of ethical knowledge as unsystematic and unsystematizable. And Aristotle's virtue of practical wisdom appears to have a partial analogue in that philosophical 'nose' of which Wittgenstein speaks[11]: the capacity to tell in advance which avenues are likely to be fruitful and which dead ends, to sense the relevance of one topic for another, to see an apparently new theory as essentially the same as an old and familiar one, and so on. Both practical wisdom and a philosophical 'nose' are achieved by practice and experience, they both give a person guidance, and they are both in their nature irreducible to a set of rules.

The question how far similar and how far different two great philosophers are will always be interesting in its own right, and much more could be said about the intellectual relationship between Aristotle and Wittgenstein than

---

[10] Aristotle, *Nicomachean Ethics*, I.iii.1, 4.

[11] E.g. ' . . . if you have a nose at all, you will smell that there is something queer about saying you recognize truth by inspection.' (*Lectures on the Foundations of Mathematics*, (Chicago: University of Chicago Press, 1989), p. 173).

I have said here. My present aim has only been to call them as witnesses. Both philosophers, in their different ways, saw philosophy as relevant to real life, and not as a self-contained subject or hobby. The relevance of philosophy to real life, and to the ancient ethical question 'How should I live?', has more than one aspect; but if the argument of this chapter is at all cogent, one way in which philosophy is relevant to life would seem to be that thinking well about life and thinking well philosophically require similar traits of mind and character. Philosophy is not just something done by professional philosophers: any remotely reflective person philosophizes from time to time. And it is good for a society or a culture if the habit of philosophizing is generally valued.

But we shouldn't imagine that this is the sort of thing that can be brought about in any direct way by government policies. For one thing, current ideas as to the purpose of education are in a state of deep confusion; for another, while public policy may be able to facilitate, or to provide a suitable setting, it cannot produce practical wisdom or individual understanding in citizens. This is simply because of the nature of practical wisdom and individual understanding, neither of which can be understood on the model of a common fund of scientific knowledge.

Scientific knowledge itself is something that *can* be taught as part of the educational package, and in tackling the question 'How should I live?', a person may well benefit from having some—as also from having historical, psychological, anthropological, and literary knowledge. But such a person will also need to know what to do with all this knowledge. That is where philosophy can help.

References

Anscombe, G.E.M.: *Intention* (2nd ed., Oxford: Blackwell, 1963).

—— *From Parmenides to Wittgenstein: Collected Papers Vol I* (Oxford: Blackwell, 1981).

—— *Metaphysics and the Philosophy of Mind: Collected Papers Vol II* (Oxford: Blackwell, 1981).

—— *Ethics, Religion and Politics: Collected Papers Vol III* (Oxford: Blackwell, 1981).

—— *Human Life, Action and Ethics* (ed. M. Geach and L. Gormally, Exeter: Imprint Academic, 2005).

—— 'Modern Moral Philosophy', in *Ethics, Religion and Politics*, 26–42.

—— 'Practical Inference', in *Human Life, Action and Ethics*, 109–47.

—— 'Rules, Rights and Promises', in *Ethics, Religion and Politics*, 97–103.

—— 'The Intentionality of Sensation', in *Metaphysics and the Philosophy of Mind*, 3–20.

—— 'The Question of Linguistic Idealism', in *From Parmenides to Wittgenstein*, 112–133.

—— 'Who is Wronged? Philippa Foot on Double Effect', in *Human Life, Action and Ethics*, 249–251.

Aristotle: *Metaphysics*.

—— *Nicomachean Ethics*.

—— *Posterior Analytics*.

Augustine: *The City of God*.

'Belief and the Brain' (anon.), in *Blueprint*, February 3, 2005, Vol. 5, no. 6 (Oxford: Oxford University Press).

Blake, W.: 'A Poison Tree', from *Songs of Experience* (1793).

Carpendale, J. and Lewis, C.: 'Constructing an understanding of mind: The development of children's understanding of mind within social interaction', in *Behavioral and Brain Sciences* 27, 2004, 79–150.

Carroll, L.: 'What the Tortoise Said to Achilles', in *Mind* 4, 1895, 278–280.

Diamond, C.: 'Eating Meat and Eating People', in *The Realistic Spirit* (Cambridge, Mass.: MIT Press, 1991), 319–334.

—— 'Wittgenstein and Metaphysics', in *The Realistic Spirit*, 13–38.

Foot, P.: *Natural Goodness* (Oxford: Oxford University Press, 2001).

—— 'Virtues and Vices', in *Virtues and Vices* (Oxford: Blackwell, 1978), 1–18.

—— 'Moral Beliefs', in *Virtues and Vices*, 110–31.

Franklin, B.: 'The Speech of Miss Polly Barker', in *Benjamin Franklin: Autobiography and Other Writings* (ed. Seavey, Oxford University Press, 1993), 246–50.

Frege, G. *The Foundations of Arithmetic (Die Grundlagen der Arithmetik* – 1884).

Gaita, R.: 'Goodness beyond Virtue', in *A Common Humanity* (2nd ed., UK: Routledge, 2000), 17–27.

Geach, P.: 'Good and Evil', in *Theories of Ethics* (ed. P. Foot, Oxford: Oxford University Press, 1967), 64–73.

Goldman, A.: 'Discrimination and Perceptual Knowledge', in *Journal of Philosophy* 73, 1976, 771–791.

Grayling, A.: *Against All Gods* (London: Oberon Books, 2007).

Hume, D.: *Enquiry Concerning the Principle of Morals* (1751).

—— 'Of the Standard of Taste' (1757).

Hursthouse, R.: 'Intention', in *Logic, Cause and Action* (ed. R. Teichmann, Cambridge: Cambridge University Press, 2000), 83–105.

—— (ed., with G. Lawrence and W. Quinn): *Virtues and Reasons* (Oxford University Press, 1995).

Kenny, A.: 'Practical Inference', in *Analysis* 26, no. 3 (1966), 65–73.

Korsgaard, C.: *Self-Constitution: Agency, Identity and Integrity* (Oxford: Oxford University Press, 2009).

Lewis, D.: 'Mad Pain and Martian Pain', in *Readings in Philosophy of Psychology, Vol. I* (ed. N. Block, Cambridge, Mass.: Harvard University Press, 1980), 216–222.

Lucretius: *De Rerum Natura.*

McDowell, J.: 'Two Sorts of Naturalism', in Hursthouse, Lawrence, and Quinn (ed.), 149–179.

MacIntyre, A.: *After Virtue* (UK: Duckworth 1981).

Mann, T.: *Doctor Faustus.*

Mencken, H.L.: *Notes on Democracy* (1926).

Mill, J.S.: *A System of Logic Ratiocinative and Inductive* (1843).

—— *On Liberty* (1859).

—— *Utilitarianism* (1863).

Miller, A.: *Timebends* (London: Methuen 1988).

Moore, G.E. 'Proof of an External World' (1939), in *Philosophical Papers*, (London: Allen & Unwin), 127–150.

Müller, A.: 'Has Moral Education a Rational Basis?', in *Moral Truth and Moral Tradition* (ed. L. Gormally, Dublin: Four Courts Press, 1994), 203–225.

Nagel, T.: 'What is it like to be a bat?', in *Mortal Questions* (Cambridge: Cambridge University Press, 1979), 165–180.

Plato: *The Apology.*

Popper, K.: *Objective Knowledge* (Oxford: Clarendon Press, 1972, 1979).

Prior, A.: 'The Runabout Inference Ticket', in *Analysis* 21, 1960, 38–9.

Ryle, G.: 'Pleasure', in *Dilemmas* (Cambridge: Cambridge University Press, 1969), 54–67.

Savulescu, J. and Devolder, K.: 'The Moral Imperative to Conduct Stem Cell and Cloning Research', in *Cambridge Quarterly of Healthcare Ethics* 15 (1), 7–21.

Scholes, P.: *The Oxford Companion to Music* (10th ed., Oxford: Oxford University Press, 1970).

Sellar, W.C. and Yeatman, R.J.: *1066 and All That* (London: Methuen, 1930).

Singer, P.: *Animal Liberation* (New York: Random House, 1975).

—— *A Darwinian Left: Politics, Evolution and Co-operation* (Yale: Yale University Press 1999).

—— 'Ethics and Intuitions', in *Journal of Ethics* (2005) 9, 331–352.

Smart, J. and Williams, B.: *Utilitarianism: For and Against* (Cambridge: Cambridge University Press, 1973).

Stoppard, T.: *Rock 'n' Roll* (2006).

Strawson, P.: *Individuals* (London: Anchor, 1959).

—— 'Freedom and Resentment', in *Freedom and Resentment and Other Essays* (London: Methuen, 1974), 1–25.

Teichmann, R.: *The Philosophy of Elizabeth Anscombe* (Oxford: Oxford University Press, 2008).

—— 'The Functionalist's Inner State', in *Wittgenstein and Contemporary Philosophy of Mind* (ed. S. Schroeder, UK: Palgrave, 2001), 24–35.

Thompson, M.: *Life and Action* (Cambridge, Mass.: Harvard University Press, 2008).

—— 'The Representation of Life', in Hursthouse, Lawrence, and Quinn (ed.), 247–296.

Tolstoy, L.: *War and Peace*.

Watson, J.B.: 'Psychology as the Behaviorist Views it', in *Psychological Review*, 20, 1913, 158–177.

Wharton, E.: *The House of Mirth* (1905).

Williams, B.: 'The Human Prejudice', in *Philosophy as a Humanistic Discipline* (ed. A. Moore, Princeton: Princeton University Press, 2006), 135–152.

Wittgenstein, L.: *Tractatus Logico-Philosophicus* (trans. D. Pears and B. McGuinness, London: Routledge, 1974).

—— *Philosophical Investigations* (ed. and trans. G.E.M. Anscombe, 2nd ed., Oxford: Blackwell, 1967).

—— *On Certainty* (ed. and trans. G.E.M. Anscombe, G. H. von Wright, Oxford: Blackwell, 1969).

—— *Lectures on the Foundations of Mathematics* (ed. C. Diamond, University of Chicago Press, 1989).

Index

addiction 109–10, 113–14
animals 41–7
Anscombe, G.E.M. xiii, viv, xv–xvi, 4 n.
    3, 9, 14 n. 13, 17, 19 n. 19, 27 n. 25, 33
    n. 30, 58–9, 60, 61, 63, 70–1, 72 n. 15,
    74–6, 86–7, 97, 105–6, 115, 121, 150
    n. 17, 167 n. 1
anti-speciesism, *see* speciesism
Aquinas 74, 105
Aristotle ix, x, xv, 7, 34–5, 57, 60, 62,
    66, 74, 76, 81, 95, 105, 107, 119,
    131–3, 137, 139–41, 143, 149, 154,
    158–9, 160, 167, 181–3
art 109, 124–5; *see also* music
Augustine ix n. 1

Barker, Polly 87
Beethoven, L. van 125–6
Bentham, J. 51, 87
bigger picture 139, 162–5, 168, 172–4, 181
Blake, W. 36 n. 33
brainless man 99–101
Bush, G. 89

Candlish, S. 6 n. 5
Carroll, L. 64
Carpendale, J. 42 n. 37
causation 90–2, 121; *see also* reasons vs.
    causes
Christianity 16–17, 36, 136 n. 7, 154–5;
    see also Judaeo-Christian thought
Cloward, R. 135
colour-judgements 19–20, 24–5
consequentialism 86–92
contemplation 81, 132–4, 147–9, 156–8,
    160–1, 163–5, 167–8, 181; *see also*
    philosophy
Context Principle 168–9, 172
Crowley, A. 82–3

Damnjanovic, N. 6 n. 5
Davidson, D. 8
Dawkins, R. 48–9, 51
death 161–5

deduction 64–5, 67
de la Mare, W. 45
democracy 85–6, 144
Descartes, R. 11, 49
desirability characterizations 71–3, 74–6,
    78–9, 97, 102–7, 111, 113–15,
    117–18, 158, 161
desires, *see* wants
Devolder, K. 87, 89, 90
doing vs. resting 140–8, 160
Diamond, C. 45, 47 n. 43, 154

emotions 27, 31, 32–4, 36–40, 127–8,
    172–3
emotivism 38–9, 56–7
ends, ordering of 73, 79–81, 140
enquiry ix, 9–11, 68–9, 79, 170
euphemisms 39–40
Existentialism 110–11

first nature ix–x, xi, 35
flourishing 59–61, 80, 133, 138, 152–3;
    see also happiness
Foot, P. 27, 57, 130–1, 141, 167 n. 1
Frankfurt, H. 110
Franklin, B. 87
Frege, G. 168, 172
fun, *see* pleasure
function (*ergon*) 58–9, 123
functionalism 23, 96, 98–100

Gaita, R. 152–6, 161
Geach, P. 57, 72, 167 n. 1
goodness; the good 56–8, 71–3, 74–6,
    89, 101–2, 117–18
Glover, J. 48
Goldman, A. 171 n. 3
Grayling, A. 136 n. 7
Greenfield, S. 29, 31
Guinness 62–3, 71–2

happiness 82, 130–4, 140–1, 149, 158,
    160, 165; *see also* flourishing
harm principle 82–4